33 DAYS

Touring In A Van. Sleeping On Floors. Chasing A Dream.

Bill See

Published by Lulu

Acknowledgements

My profound thanks to these good folks:

Ian Bader, Russ Bates, Marie Bechtel, Julie Mercer Carroll, George
Edmondson, Jon Edmondson, Marjorie Edmondson, Patty Everhardt
Gillette, Tom Hasse, Conrad Heiney, Mary Susan Herczog, Brad
Holtzman, Ron & Tania Jolly, Joy Knapp, Holly Knapp, Maureen
McElroy, Vitus Mataré, Cindy Maya, Kelly Mayfield, Anthony Mora,
Rajesh K. Makwana, Melody Muraca, Lisa Muraca, Doug Nyland,
Christine Rothman, Mark Sanderson, Dave Silva, Dave Smerdzinski,
Shannon Smerdzinski, Laura Smith, Kimberlie Traceski,
Kenneth Wagner, Clifford Yates, Margaret Yates
Nancy Yates Mekelburg, Susan Harper Yates,

My special thanks to the following. The journey
would have been a lot shorter without you:

Gina Arnold, Jim Carroll, Rosemary Carroll, Felicia Dominguez,
Dennis Duck, Steve Hochman, Craig Lee, Corey Lesh, Gerrie Lim,
Robert Lloyd, Falling James Moreland, Scott Morrow, John Payne,
Doug Schoemer, Russ Tolman, Mike Watt, Neal Weiss, Steve Wynn

Finally, an extra dose of gratitude to these kind
souls for their invaluable counsel and assistance as this
book evolved over the course of 12 years:

Mary Susan Herczog, Cindy Maya, Rajesh K. Makwana, Melody
Muraca, Laura Smith, Kenneth Wagner, Susan Harper Yates.

Published by Lulu
Printed in the U.S.A.
ISBN 978-0-557-75881-4

Front and Back Cover Design by Rajesh K. Makwana
Back Cover Photo by Dan Barnett, Cicero's, St. Louis 8/21/87

CONTENTS

This book is dedicated to
Maeve Yates Mayfield.
Listen to your muse,
chase the joy…shine on.

* * *

This book would not have
been possible without
Rajesh K. Makwana.
Brothers, always.

About 12 years ago, I was rummaging through a bunch of old boxes and came across the journal I kept during, really, the most remarkable time of my life. The 33 days me, Raj, George, Dave and our road manager Ian spent in an old beat-up maroon Ford Econoline van on Divine Weeks' first tour in the summer of 1987.

This is a true story, but it's not a perfect historical account. This is the way it looked, sounded and felt like to me. These are the stories I chose to tell, and I weaved them together like I did to bring to light all the baggage we brought with us as we set out to chase a dream together. If I missed anything or got it wrong, I'm sorry. It wasn't intentional. If anything I quoted or shared in this book was a breach of confidence, I really did try to make sure it was O.K. with you, but for whatever reason, I wasn't able. All I can say is I tried to share these stories with love and respect and great reverence.

This book is for everyone who's stood at their crossroads with a dream screaming inside wondering whether to choose the road that goes off the map or fold up their tent and head back home.

Bill See
Los Angeles, CA
January 19, 2011

From left: Raj, George, Bill, Dave, Divine Weeks publicity shot, April '87.

Divine Weeks – Don't Hassle It Tour '87

7/25/87	Los Angeles, Lhasa Club
7/30/87	Portland, Satyricon
7/31/87	Seattle, Scoundrel's Lair
8/4/87	Vancouver, The Gaslight
8/6/87	Calgary, National Hotel
8/7/87	Calgary, National Hotel
8/8/87	Calgary, National Hotel
8/9/87	Calgary, The Ga-Ga Club
8/10/87	Edmonton, The Piazza
8/11/87	Edmonton, The Piazza
8/12/87	Regina, The Club
8/13/87	Winnipeg, Curtis Hotel
8/14/87	Winnipeg, Curtis Hotel
8/15/87	Winnipeg, Curtis Hotel
8/16/87	Minneapolis, Uptown Bar
8/17/87	Chicago, Gaspar's
8/19/87	Iowa City, Gabe's Oasis
8/20/87	Columbia, Blue Note
8/21/87	St. Louis, Cicero's
8/22/87	Kansas City, Elijio's Cantina
8/24/87	St. Louis, Euclid Records
8/26/87	Tulsa, The Palace
8/27/87	Dallas, Deep Ellum
9/4/87	Los Angeles, Club Lingerie

"All men dream: but not equally. Those who dream by night in the dusty recesses of their minds wake in the day to find that it was vanity; but the dreamers of the day are dangerous men, for they may act their dreams with open eyes, to make it possible."

— T.E. Lawrence.

Day One
7/28/87
7:05 a.m.

The time has come to be brave.

For the first time in my life — all 22 years of it — I wake up today with this crazy-ass belief. If I can just get myself in that van, I might have a chance…to make it possible.

Today the door opens. The culmination of three years of maniacal drive toward a singular goal. To get out of this haunted house and get my band, Divine Weeks, on tour. It's all I've thought about the last three years, daydreaming in class and writing out imaginary tour dates. Toiling at my windowless shit day job, shuffling papers everyday, helping rich men get richer while my dream just sits out there waiting for me to seize it.

Nothing holds me in this house anymore. It's been like this ever since my grandfather died last year. My mom's been hitting the bottle pretty hard, acting more and more erratically. My grandmother's Alzheimer's is getting worse. Then late last year, my girlfriend Mary confessed she'd had an affair. Something snapped right then. I've been spinning ever since.

I used to think all heaven was an ear, but it's like I've been screaming into the void — eulogizing stalled dreams — but I never stopped that one continuous plea. So it went: someone's got to save me. Straightaway, I bought into that whole idea that the gods send down lightning bolts to split us all in half and set us out on a perilous journey to find our other halves and become whole again. I thought Mary was that other half, but maybe I've had that all wrong.

"Inner City Blues" by Marvin Gaye just ended, and I'm putting on "Bad" by U2. I must have listened to "Bad" a hundred times right after my grandfather died. "Let it go…and so to fade away…" That and "Hardly Getting Over It" by Hüsker Dü. I played those two fucking songs to death last summer.

I'm pulling out *Let It Be* by the Replacements to play next. "Unsatisfied" is my favorite song right now. "Look me in the eye, then, tell me that I'm satisfied…"

We've spent the last few days scrambling around. Gathering contact information of bands, promoters and press to call and radio stations to drop in on. To the Price Club to buy peanut butter and jelly, bread and Cheerios in bulk. Down to Venice Beach to buy a bunch of stolen calling cards. Then to Guitar Center with a tall tale about how we're going on a very high-profile tour promising to play exclusively on whatever gear we can scam off them. Worked too. Gave us some drum skins, some cymbals, a mountain of guitar strings, patch cords. The smarmy store manager then groups us all together and takes our picture with one of their moronic sales reps who has on about the goofiest grin you can imagine. Man, Guitar Center. Where else can you find a grown man wearing pink spandex pants, a pompadour and a cheese-eating mustache?

Tom Hasse is going to be here in just a few to pick me up so we can go rent the van. No one will rent to us because none of us have a credit card, and we're all under 25. Then my friend Dave Silva told me his friend Tom would lay down his credit card for us to rent the van. Now, I don't know if ol' Tom's just too stoned to know better than to rent a van for a rock band going on tour for over a month. A band that's not even traveling with the guy who rented the van. A band that's not only taking the van outside of California but clear out of the freaking country.

Our friend Ron Jolly, a courier, turned us on to his mechanic who showed us how to disconnect the van's odometer so we can save on mileage charges. You get something like 500 free miles, so the plan is we'll go to about the 600-mile mark and then disconnect the thing. After the mechanic tells us how to do it, we were all quite pleased with ourselves until he turns to us and says, "But you guys *do* know it's a Federal crime, right?"

* * *
7:30 a.m.

I'm trying to figure out if I've forgotten something, but really, all that's left is the letting go. The time has come to be brave. I keep saying that over and over as I pace around my bedroom listening to as many of my favorite songs as I can before I leave. Just trying to get my fill of this music that's been my one salvation here. Music that staved off the madness surrounding me and kept my heart from closing shut.

I just put on side two of the Meat Puppets' *Up on the Sun.* I wonder what George is listening to right now. Probably the Clash. I've got to remember to ask him later. Fuck, what time is it anyway? 7:30? George probably isn't even up yet.

George is my best friend and Divine Weeks' bassist. The ubiquitous Phast Phreddie, the ultimate scenester himself, says George is the best bass player in L.A. Pretty good considering L.A. is home to Flea of the Red Hot Chili Peppers and Eric Avery of Jane's Addiction.

I started the band with two friends from high school — George and my other best friend Raj, our guitar player. In high school, the three of us were basically losers — either laughed at, dismissed, or never even thought of. Earlier this year, it started getting back to a lot of folks we went to high school with that Divine Weeks was starting to make a dent in the L.A. club scene. We'd see familiar faces come to a show, snicker and leave. Some of it was jealousy, or maybe it was a sense of order being disrupted. Like seeing Radar from *M*A*S*H** play a saloon singer in a movie or something. You just can't accept it. High school's like TV a little. You get typecast. Those first few years after high school are threatening. People keep tabs on you and not so they can cheer you on from the sidelines.

Now let me make something clear. Divine Weeks is not some big arena band on a major label with oodles of cash behind us.

You probably never heard of us unless you're one of the few thousand people who pick up the *L.A. Weekly*, *L.A. Reader* or *BAM* every Thursday to check what's happening around town. We're not part of L.A.'s "in" crowd, and we don't have any hip cache. One of the earliest bits of press we ever got was: "These guys will grab you by the scruff of your collar and demand attention despite the fact that they look like four college Joes waiting for a bus." It's one of those backhanded compliments we've used as inspiration.

Just seven months ago, we were limping along playing late weeknight gigs with no record deal, a drummer that was never going to work out, and virtually no press at all. Just after the first of this year, we got signed to the Dream Syndicate's Steve Wynn's Down There label, found an incredible drummer, got named one of the top local bands by the *L.A. Times*, and we've been getting great reviews for our live shows and for our just-released debut record *Through and Through*.

This is not just our first tour. Aside from our drummer Dave, who's been on his own for a few years now, it's basically our first time out on our own at all.

This is not some big tour by plane or train or bus. We're just throwing two old love seats I found in my garage into the back of a Ford Econoline cargo van, putting them face to face to sleep on, and the rest of our stuff we're storing in back.

Aside from maybe Springsteen, there's no rock stars for role models. They've all let me down. It's like they all lusted after stardom and once there, looked us in the eye and then fled. I've stood there outside after shows and watch them treat fans like an annoyance, get whisked away in their limos and isolate themselves in their extravagance and wealth only to moan about it later. I'm done with it.

That's what drew me to the Do It Yourself (DIY), just-get-in-the-van credo pioneered by bands on SST Records. Although we don't sound much like bands like Black Flag, Minutemen,

Hüsker Dü, Meat Puppets and Sonic Youth, we're inspired by their ethic and aesthetic. Success doesn't come to you. You go to it. Eschew major labels. Put out your own records, book your own tours. You don't stay in hotels, you beg from the stage for a floor to sleep on. Create a community. Call like-minded bands, ask to open for them and promise to help them when they come to your hometown. Drop in on college radio stations and beg people to come down to your shows. No roadies, no high powered promoters. Black Flag pretty much invented it and bands like the Minutemen taught us how to go and do it. Mike Watt (formerly of the Minutemen and now fIREHOSE) calls it "jamming econo."

Musically, we're closer to the Who at Woodstock by way of early R.E.M. But ideologically, more than any other band, the Minutemen are the closest to what Divine Weeks' core is all about. Egalitarian, working-class, politically conscious, smart. Like us, their friendship and loyalty to each other shaped their very essence. The Minutemen were like indie rock teachers. They showed us and a lot of bands that being indie was a righteous cause — fighting the good fight against the bloated, arrogant and self-important hierarchy of major labels and radio programmers that keep good music off the air and relegated to garages.

Every time we climb on stage, write a song, meet a fan, deal with a booker or a radio programmer, we feel the eyes of the bands that showed us how to do it are watching. We can't let them down.

Once I get in that van today, I plan on never going back to school. Raj, same thing, and Dave washed his hands of school a few years ago. But for George, it's more complicated. He's got to make a decision whether or not to commit to grad school next year. He needs us to make as big a splash as possible on this tour so he can justify not returning to school in the fall.

* * *

It's a typically calm morning here in my house, a place we call 940 (said: Nine, Four, Oh). 940 Bienveneda. Spanish for welcome. 940 is part sanctuary, part roadhouse in that old gospel tradition of sinnin' on Saturdays and prayin' on Sundays. Peaceful mornings follow shoot 'em up, throw 'em down nights. Always been a lot of drinking and mental instability around here. I come out of my bedroom peering around corners for wreckage. See if the coast is clear like a long, slow scan of a battlefield in some Civil War movie or something.

This house holds three fiercely proud generations — maddeningly brilliant, Irish Catholic and dysfunctional. When I was 12, my mom and I moved back here for good after her last nervous breakdown. Most of my childhood, it's been me, my mom, her sister — my Aunt Nancy — and their parents under one roof.

I'm not saying there haven't been good times here, because there have, and I do remember a lot of laughter — especially in daylight. But when the days turn dark and cocktail hour begins, it's like a walk through a minefield.

I never felt like a child here. Never knew limits or boundaries. Don't ever remember being sent to my room or being spared from whatever crisis that came down the pike. In some fucked-up way, it's always been me who mediates the chaos. Mary says it's made me addicted to drama and conflict. I don't know. She says it feeds something I'm terrified of losing because I've never known anything else. Whatever.

Around here, everything always seems so fragile and on the verge of blowing up. Someone's always sick or leaving or divorcing. Don't upset what little balance there is or take anything from somebody else. Better to go without. I'm used to it. Mary says all my self-loathing and co-dependency is a by-product of growing up here. Says it's not normal to choke off my own happiness. I don't know. I guess it made sense to because everyone around here always seemed so fucking miserable so I just pushed everything down.

No one here ever belittled the hours I spent pretending I was an astronaut, a fireman, a TV anchorman or baseball player because it posed no threat. Music's something totally different. It hits too close to the nerve endings in a household of folks from the liberal arts. My aunt and grandmother are teachers. My grandfather, an architect. My mother, a writer. They hate that my dreams — or anyone else's — are still alive. It triggers that sadness they've buried over letting their dreams die.

My haven and my refuge is music. When the shouting starts, I close my bedroom door, put on my headphones, and I'm transported. "Listen to the Lion" by Van Morrison, "The Song Is Over" by the Who, "Something in the Night" by Bruce Springsteen, "Levi Stubbs' Tears" by Billy Bragg, "Moonlight Mile" by the Rolling Stones. Townshend, Strummer and Westerberg provided more spiritual solace than any hollow sermon or church hymn.

When it gets really bad, I make up some lie so I can borrow my Aunt Nancy's car and go out driving. I put in some music, roll up the windows and sing at the top of my lungs until tears are streaming down my face. It's like my own private exorcism.

Ever since I've known music, I've felt that my life could be lifted up by it. Music gave me a specific motivation driven by an indispensable oxygen-like need, not just some wayward desire. Singing gave me a tool to summon a part of me I couldn't otherwise reach. Gave me a little light out in the distance. I'd discovered my lifeblood, and the drive was so strong that denying it became unbearable. It wasn't a matter of choice anymore. That's what my mom always told me: "We had no choice, we're artists." That always *sounded* cool, but until music permeated my bloodstream, I was just walking around dodging bullets.

9:15 a.m.

I've always felt a kinship with Raj down to an almost molecular level. Like me, he's still only in college out of fear of disappointing his family. Like me, he hauls around a lot of shame and struggles with self-worth and feeling deserving. We share the same coping skill when things get ugly: shut down, withdraw, turn to escape. Like me, he's a loner and spends big chunks of time living in the fantasy. Like me, music is his one escape. We'd both be curtains without it.

Rajesh K. Makwana. A kind, elegant, gentle being. Slight in stature, a strong wind could literally blow him off course. He's of Indian descent with dark, striking features. He's got these hungry artist's eyes and a gorgeous, jubilant smile. I love his unaffected open-mouth laugh. A truly beautiful dark creature.

Raj was born in England in a tough London neighborhood called Shepherd's Bush. Same as Roger Daltrey of the Who, he'll remind you. He's the youngest of three siblings, an older brother and sister. Back in England, his dad was a postal worker who delivered mail to the Beatles at Savile Row, and even witnessed the rooftop concert. It's funny. His dad was terrified he'd be fired for not getting his mail truck through all the gawkers and traffic piled up. His mom worked long and inequitable hours in a factory.

His family moved to the U.S. in the late '70s and opened a health food store in Santa Monica which they sold a couple years ago. His parents are the most humble, gracious, trusting and giving people. Sometimes to a fault. Raj won't talk about it, but I think they're in some financial trouble now after being swindled by some dubious family members back in India.

Rajesh K. Makwana   Photo by Dan Barnett

Raj doesn't share much about it, but he's intimated that, culturally, Indian households aren't very emotional or physically demonstrative. Love and support is more implied than expressly stated. On the surface, his family tolerates the band, but it's clear he doesn't hear a lot of encouragement. I've asked him if that bothers him, but all he says is "It's O.K., my family's going through a lot right now" and changes the subject.

For Raj, it's a race against time. At some point, his parents will arrange his wedding pursuant to the traditions of his culture. I've asked him what he's gonna do, but he just changes the subject.

Like a lot of kids who move to the U.S., Raj is being pulled in two directions: by the rigid constraints of his culture and by the more relaxed standards of the West. This gets even more complicated in the murky waters of rock and roll. Ought to be interesting to see how that plays out the next 33 days.

Raj was treated like a lot of Indian kids who grew up in England: like third-class citizens. Kids chased him, threw bottles at him and harassed him all the time. He was regularly beat up, hounded and threatened just for being Indian. Actually the dumb fuckers called him a Paki. His clothes would routinely be stolen while he showered after gym class, all the towels were removed, and so he'd have to try and retrieve his clothes completely naked in front of the whole school. He doesn't talk a lot about it, but clearly it's left him pretty gutted.

The racial taunting and belligerence didn't end in England. I remember when the U.S. hostages were being held in Iran, kids in our class would assume he was Iranian because of his dark skin and fuck with him.

Raj and I take these long drives into the hills talking through the night or just listening to music. It feels safe on those drives, safe to share what's really eating us up inside. I try to get Raj to open up about how the racism has affected him. Sometimes he does, but mostly he just pushes it down. It's when we play music together that I really understand.

From the very beginning, racism has been a galvanizing subject for the band. We're not saints or think we have the answers, but it must be said. Raj's history and seeing what he carries around has had a profound effect on our band. We're a very protective and righteous group. When something insults our core beliefs, we're an unruly lot, and we'll stand up and confront it.

I've always been protective of Raj and feel this strong sense of duty to make the world see the parts of him only I know about. Kind of like how it is with me and my mom. It's probably why I have a strong affinity for the underdog and downtrodden. Forms the basis for my steadfast belief that nobody's free until everybody's free.

Raj and I really started connecting early in our sophomore year of high school. When I first met him, rock music to him was The Beatles. Period. I decided something had to be done about this. The Who documentary *The Kids Are Alright* was playing in an afternoon matinee down in the Marina. Of course I had to bribe him into going by telling him *Wings Over America*, the goddamn Paul McCartney movie was playing with it. So after school, we take the #8 Blue Bus and ride down Lincoln Boulevard, assuring him if he just sits there for two hours he'll never be the same again. So the movie starts, and I'm peeking over to see his reaction. And sure enough, with every Pete Townshend windmill and leap, I can actually see the whites of Raj's knuckles as he tightly grips the arm rests.

There's this scene of Townshend at Woodstock repeatedly pounding his guitar into the stage, and then he nonchalantly walks to the edge of the stage and tosses it into the crowd. I think at that moment Raj started to feel differently about the guitar. Instead of revering it as a delicate object that played you, he set aim to conquer it, will it into submission, and use it as a weapon against every motherfucker who ever doubted him.

In the guitar, Raj found a transportational device. A means to escape with a weapon at his side. There's a reason they call the guitar an axe.

Musically, Raj possesses a wonderful independent vision, hell-bent on originality. He relies entirely on instinct and mistrusts any sort of regimented practice schedule. This produces some sublime twists and turns creatively but also causes some fundamental breakdowns. As a result, we can be equally transcendent or abysmal on any given night.

During our last year of high school, I told my then girlfriend Patty that the sounds and visions in my head were getting stronger all the time and that I felt I was meant to make music. She just looked at me like I was a freak. When September 1983 rolled around, I didn't know how to move my feet, so I sighed in resignation and began college like George and Raj and everyone else. It didn't take long before little scribbled lyrics began to appear on the margins of my lecture notes, but the thought of pursuing music seriously and facing my grandfather's disapproval was just too imposing.

* * *

9:45 a.m.

My grandfather was a grand presence. Humble, highly principled. A classic gentleman. He was the only male authority figure I've ever known — the only one I ever called dad.

He loved to putter around town at his own painstaking pace, take a few extra minutes to talk to Mr. Harrington, who ran the camera shop, or shoot the shit with Dennis at Colvey's Men's Clothing shop. Then over to the local café where Miguel would cook him up the same breakfast every Saturday. Sausage and eggs over easy, rye toast heavily buttered. Black coffee.

To him, one's integrity was the sole determining factor of how you were judged. "Stand for something, or you'll fall for anything," he'd say. He was a "you're only as good as your word" kind of guy. I definitely got that old-school value system from him.

My grandfather was a brilliant architect with a very successful practice of his own. "Architecture begins where engineering ends," he'd say. Many of the homes, buildings and churches he designed still stand here in L.A. He suffered a nervous breakdown after his partner screwed him over. He then came back to become a very sought-after art director for several of the big movie studios. Every morning he'd get up at dawn and have breakfast at the Ships restaurant across the street from MGM and read the paper from cover to cover.

My grandfather remained a voracious, lifelong student up until the day he died. Always had six or seven books going at once, all

opened and piled in a semi-circle around his red leather chair —
one on the Peloponnesian War, another one on the history of the
Catholic Church, another about Buckminster Fuller. He said
there's nothing sadder than someone who willingly chose not to
learn. He'd mock them: "I don't want a book. I've got one."

I was just starting to play music for real when he finally retired
because of degenerative hip disease and heart problems.
Retirement was rough on him. And me. I was spending longer
periods of time out of the house, going to gigs and staying out
later, coming home tired and waking up hungover. I got a lot of
his grief. I'd get home from school and he'd drill me for six
things I'd learned that day. I'd get off the bus and walk up the
street sweating, knowing he wanted those six things I learned. I
think he just missed school, missed feeling involved and
connected.

My grandfather was a Depression-era survivor working two jobs
to put himself through college, one at the morgue on the
graveyard shift, and another after school. You just can't reason
with a Depression survivor. Your pain, your frustration, your
troubles are never as bad as what they faced. It's like a Monty
Python skit. One guy says, "When I was growing up we lived in
a little house and the roof leaked, we had no heater and we about
froze to death." And the second guy says incredulously, "You
had a *house*?!" That sort of thing.

He came from a time when you locked people up who had mental
problems or were addicted to drugs or alcohol — it was all about
a will to overcome. He was raised under this John Wayne cloud.
Said his father told him men don't take aspirin for headaches.
Headaches are something women get. I guess when John Wayne
got a headache he just took out his gun and shot it.

After one of my mom's nervous breakdowns, her psychiatrist
suggested my grandfather sit in on a session. He sat there and
patiently listened to the therapist hypothesize about the root of his
daughter's demons. Finally, he gets up and says, "Sir, I see a

great many diplomas on your walls, but with all due respect, this is all a load of horseshit," and he walks out.

To my grandfather, music was a hobby, a luxury, something with which you killed some free time. My obsession with music just mystified him. I'd come out of the shower, put on Led Zeppelin's "When the Levee Breaks" and just lay there on my floor and let the music pummel me. He'd barge in and start howling in mock agony. It's funny once, maybe twice, but this went on and on until soon I felt ashamed at how good music made me feel. It got to the point where every time I heard him approach, I'd quickly turn off the stereo or stop playing my guitar. May as well have drawn a chalk outline of my body.

* * *

10:10 a.m.

When George, Raj and I started college, we kind of went our separate ways. That fall I went to a lot of club shows around town, mostly by myself. I got angrier and angrier. I'd drive home and find myself pounding the steering wheel and screaming, "Man, I could do better than those fuckers! What the fuck am I waiting for?"

By that Thanksgiving, it'd become impossible to hold back any longer. I'll always remember the date. November 24, 1983. It's a typically crazed, uncomfortable holiday dinner at 940. Ten minutes of eating and four hours of waiting around. Lots of false starts and stops and frozen smiles while my Aunt Nancy sets up a photograph. "Now everyone just smile and be happy!" she'd say. Right.

My mom can't sit still and pops up in five-minute intervals to disappear into the kitchen to swig some booze and then return momentarily calmer. My grandmother, the same thing, slipping into the kitchen quickly downing some Cutty Sark and staggering back into the living room chirping, "Everyone happy?!"

As Thanksgiving dinner finally winds down, I just want to get the hell out of there. I call Raj and ask him if he can come pick me up and take a drive. When I see him pull up in his family's old Honda, I grab my pea coat and pull my newsboy hat down low on my head. I mumble a goodbye hoping to get away before somebody makes it out to the driveway and starts screaming something.

I get in and say to Raj, "Hey come on, let's go," looking back to see if I'd been followed.

"Where to?" Raj asks.

"To the top of the world," a spot up on Mulholland Drive where you can see all of L.A., I say.

The alignment on Raj's old Honda is for shit, and we roll along Sunset Boulevard almost like a crab walks — kinda sideways. Traffic is light, and we make our way through Hollywood, past the Strip — first Gazzarri's, then the Rainbow and the Roxy. Then there's Duke's and the Whisky on the left. The next block, you have Tower Records on the left and Book Soup on the right. A little further east, all on the left, is Ben Frank's, then Carney's, Guitar Center, Rock 'n' Roll Ralph's and a little further, Club Lingerie and across the street Cat & Fiddle. But just before then, we hang a left on Highland, go past the Hollywood Bowl and then take a left up Mulholland Drive.

When we get to the top of Mulholland, we pull along the dirt embankment and stop. It's cold and dry and windy so I pull the collar up on my pea coat. We walk to the very edge of the cliff. The sight of a million shimmering lights and all of L.A. is there for the taking.

"So, how's the college life, my friend?" I ask.

"All right, I guess," Raj says looking down and kicking at the dirt.

"So, what do you think we're gonna have to show for it in 20 years?" I say picking up a rock and chucking it as far as I can.

"Don't know," he says shrugging. "Just living our lives, I guess."

"Yeah, well, I don't think that's gonna be good enough," I say, picking up another rock but not throwing it. I go on. "I keep hearing people say when you get to college you're just getting started on the rest of your life, but that's a bunch of bullshit. It's not the beginning. It's the fucking end if you're living someone else's dream. And that's what we're doing. We're living someone else's dream, Raj."

"OK, but what are we supposed to do?" he asks watching me chuck the rock out into the darkness.

"Don't you see, Raj?" I say moving closer. "Something *happens* when you keep denying what's at your core. Something *happens* when you deny the thing that's your very essence."

I watch him stare out into L.A.'s vast expanse.

"Raj," I say quietly to him. "Soon it'll be too late. You'll be married to someone you've never met before, and I'll be as bitter as everyone in my house. If we don't do this now, we'll hate ourselves for the rest of our lives."

He looks back at me and asks, "Do *what*?"

"For fuck's sake, Raj. Music. We're supposed to make music — you and me," I say feeling a rush scaling my windpipe. "I'm telling you, it's meant to be. Raj, look down there," I say taking off my hat and using it to point at all the shimmering lights. "Let's make every one of those motherfuckers down there know our name."

He doesn't say anything for a full minute. He just keeps staring out at all those lights before the words just tumble out: "Bill, I've wanted to call you and say the same thing for the past three months."

"And you know what?" I say, my eyes widening. "We're gonna be the ones who do it right. No groupies, no rock star poses, no ego trips."

I look at him until a smile creeps up that Raj can't hide.

"I'll call George," I say smiling.

The next morning, I phone George who's living in the dorms at UCLA. I hadn't talked to him since the summer.

Ring. "Hello?"

"George...Bill here."

"Que pasa, my friend," he says in his croaking morning voice. "How've you been?"

"Look, if I beat around the bush I might think twice."

"Well, you don't want that," he cracks.

"Listen, I hooked up with Raj last night. We were talking up there on top of the world, you know, up on Mulholland looking down at the whole city and everything. And man, I've been up there a million times, looked down and never saw any space for me. But last night it didn't look so scary and off limits."

"Oh-kay," he says trailing off.

I exhale deeply and fire my shot. "Look, school's become a joke. I'm only going for my grandfather. And, well, Raj and I were talking, and...we want to start a real band. The goddamn greatest band that's ever been."

George laughs nervously for a moment and then says soberly, "I can't believe you're saying this. I was lying on my bed just last night wanting to call you and say the same fucking thing."

The next week, the three of us gather in George's basement and write one song, "Like the City, a droning but jangly little lark. We record it onto a shitty little ghetto blaster. I still have the tape. I ask George's mom to take a picture of us together so the moment can be captured, certain this will be an important piece of rock history.

After that first rehearsal, we all walk up the steps of George's basement, and it's like we knew we'd just crossed over. We'd played a few parties together in high school but no one dared say it was for real back then. This was different and we could all feel it. Everything up to this day was someone else's, and now everything was in our own hands. When I get home, I write out ten targets I've set for the band with a little tagline under it: "Thanks be to music — the deepest mother, a lover, a soul mate, like no other...a gift from God, a spirit to haunt, an expressway to the soul — toll-free...for wounded hearts tired of lamenting."

* * *
10:25 a.m.

Tom Hasse is still not here. I'm staring at my records trying to decide between Springsteen's *Darkness on the Edge of Town* and the Velvet Underground's first record. I hate when there's no music on. There should be a gizmo that kicks in and plays something while you're trying to decide on the next tune. Maybe "Baby Elephant Walk" from the old *Wonderama* show. I finally settle on R.E.M.'s *Murmur,* basically the band's blueprint our first year.

The last gig we did in town was a few days ago at the Lhasa Club opening for fIREHOSE who recently started up out of the ashes of the Minutemen after D. Boon tragically died a little over a year ago.

Just a few months ago before a show I'd pace back and forth in front of Club Lingerie or the Anti-Club or Raji's, thinking if I fretted long enough out in the cold more people would magically appear. Of course they don't, and I head back inside, and we play our hearts out in front of eight or ten people at most.

Because the Lhasa is so intimate and we're so loud, we always bring great heartache to the soundman there, an uppity little Frenchman like the Lhasa's owner, Jean Pierre. During soundcheck, the soundman tells George he's too loud so George says, "O.K., but if I turn down any more I won't be audible." Guy marches toward George and spits out in his heavy French accent while striking a bass player's pose, "We're not going to lose our license because some silly little bass player wants to go boom, boom, boom." George just stands there dumbfounded while the little fellow pivots on his boot heel and storms back to the soundboard. So, we do what we always do. Turn down at soundcheck and crank it when the show starts.

Before we go on, these two girls, Kimberlie and Jennifer, who've been coming to our shows the last six months, give me a Divine Weeks shirt they had made. It's crazy. They tell me we're their favorite band and want to know if they can get backstage passes when we play the Forum one day. I try to tell them we're no rock stars, but Kimberlie says we're already rock stars to them. It's like an out-of-body experience hearing stuff like that. I put the shirt on for our encore, and I hear them both squeal.

I think Kimberlie, the shy one, likes Raj. She seems sweet. Raj blushes when she comes around. Over the last few months as we've started to gain some notoriety, it's been amazing watching Raj onstage gaining more confidence. Instead of hiding behind his guitar, he now holds it like a weapon, like he's fighting all those fuckers from his past that treated him like shit. Offstage, he's still shy and very much the self-effacing guy I met in 9th grade with the Beatles T-shirt on every day.

The first ten minutes of our shows are like this massive release. We come out and do three songs balls-out. A full-frontal offensive and assault to the senses. Reaching, craning, insinuating ourselves. Then for that fourth song, we jam on the coaster breaks and draw people in. Usually we do "Bitterness," a song about generational bigotry sung by a child who stops the cycle and triumphs. That's where we show the whole arsenal. George, moving the song perpetually forward with that soulful swinging dance-hall groove. Dave, letting the song swing dangerously loose like a rope whipping in the breeze before seizing back control of it and driving it majestically to the finish. Raj, ringing chimes as he climbs the neck of his Les Paul and imbuing crucial moments with colors not yet named. And me, the orator and conductor, the filter through which all this comes through, measuring the mood of the crowd, gauging its elasticity to see how far I can push the envelope. By the time we finish "Bitterness," people love us or hate us. Nothing in between.

Ever since Dave joined the band in March, something's different, and you can feel the crowds moving closer and wanting more. It's not like it was early on where you could feel the sense of obligation from people we'd drag to the shows. You knew they were doing you a favor coming down. Something's definitely changed — especially the last month or so.

For our encore I ask what everyone wants to hear. It's a rock star thing to say but who can resist the opportunity to hear "Free Bird!" shouted back at you? Never fucking fails. Finally, someone yells what I'm waiting for. I want to do "Dry September." It's my favorite song to perform. The one that lends itself most to improvisation. Musically, it's kind of a hybrid of Neil Young's "Needle and the Damage Done," R.E.M's "Pilgrimage," and "Mother" by John Lennon. Lyrically, it's a William Faulkner-inspired tale about a black man coveting a white woman in the Deep South and the ensuing lynching. After Dave joined the band, the song got real theatrical. He added these dynamic accents like he's playing tympanis.

Raj has adopted "Dry September" as his own personal catharsis of the racial taunts he absorbed growing up Indian in England. Every time we play it, it's like we're all fighting the power of his past together. The middle section of the song is like an exorcism. As the band pounds out a strident staccato marching beat, I wail my guts out. Every night we play a different version. It just keeps evolving. Live, this is the true essence of Divine Weeks. The one song I'd offer up if we had only one left to play.

Me in my pea coat, Lhasa Club. Photo by Casey Riddle

Before fIREHOSE takes the stage, Raj offers to move Mike Watt's skyscraper-like SVT amp onstage and poor waif-like Raj can't handle it and about gets crushed to death. Right before the amp topples on him, Watt's massive hand reaches down and pulls it up just in time. Watt just smiles and says "I got this one, Raj." Like he's done with countless up-and-coming bands, Watt's sort of taken Raj under his wing, and it's really had a profound effect on Raj who's now totally bought into the whole DIY approach.

During their set, Watt, in his inimitable style, pays us the ultimate tribute when he says "This is dedicated to Divine Weeks," and he hits a big booming D note, lets it sustain and points at Raj. Few get it, but it was fucking high praise.

After the gig, I grab a bite to eat with my friends Corey, Ellen, Joy and Melody. We all squeeze into a booth at the Denny's on Sunset where it crosses the 101. I tell Corey that even though we'll be eating peanut butter and jelly sandwiches for the next month and don't know how we'll pay for gas to get us to the next town, as far as I'm concerned, my life is finally just starting. At the end of the night we're saying goodbye, and Corey pulls me aside and says, "You guys are the first from our little community that's becoming something." Then he hands me $50 and says, "Bill, take this. We've all seen Divine Weeks become something from nothing. You guys are making a lot of us believe we can go chase our dreams too. Good luck to you guys."

* * *
10:45 a.m.

I didn't get the mom from the Norman Rockwell painting, the one with the perpetual smile and calm reply to my latest trouble. More like equal parts Sylvia Plath and Jack Nicholson from *One Flew Over The Cuckoo's Nest*. A brilliant mind and truly original writer and observer, she's a bona fide eccentric artist — just born in the wrong the time. Not a shred of discipline for her craft, and so she remains tragically unknown. Anyone who knows me understands no one's broken my heart more or influenced me more. She's the sole reason I write, sing and climb on a stage. Our relationship is complicated. Codependent. Toxic. Sublime.

I spent a lot of mornings trying to wake her up so I could get to school on time. Strewn beside her bed I'd find tiny little brown glass bottles with white chalky residue inside. I'd chuck them one by one like grenades over the third-story balcony of our old apartment and watch them explode on the ground.

One time I had to bail her out of jail. She stole a stupid carton of cigarettes and got nabbed. I went down to Sybil Brand women's detention center with $1,000 stuffed in my sock to post bail. After getting jacked around for hours I finally get her out, and as I drive her home, I realize I've become the mother and she's become the child.

Mom.   Photo by Bill See

She's always been called the black sheep of the family, a favorite target of my grandmother who never lets my mom forget she was never good enough or the equal to her younger sister Nancy, the good daughter. My mom's damaged goods. Studies her shoes, keeps her best parts bottled inside. I've always felt a duty to protect her and bring out the side only I know about. Like I said, kind of like me and Raj.

When I was 13, my mom split. Couldn't take the abuse anymore. It was an unusually warm April night. The night I found out I had a sister named Lyric and a brother named Danny. I'm in my room and hear yelling and door-slamming. Nothing terribly unusual, but the screaming sounds more insidious than usual so I get curious and venture out. My Aunt Nancy and my grandmother are giving it to my mom who's just learned an old friend died and is distraught. My mom shouts out how could they be so callous on her firstborn's birthday just as I appear.

My mom runs out the front door and everyone retreats to their own quarters leaving me there to try and process it all. A minute or so later, I walk slowly down the front driveway toward my mom who's sitting on the curb in front of the house smoking a cigarette. She glances up at me then quickly looks down again. I sit down beside her on the curb.

"No matter how old I get, when someone yells at me I'm four again," she says.

She drags hard on her cigarette and stares out. "Are you ashamed of me?" she asks.

"No," I say quietly.

She looks up at me and then quickly back down at the asphalt again.

"Mom, why do you always feel so alone?"

"How do you know I do?"

"Don't you know?" I ask. "*I'm you* and *you're me*. And no matter what anyone in that house says, it's always been just the two of us, and that's never gonna change."

She bursts into tears. Just heaving uncontrollable tears. It scares me. Like it always does with her when I feel her start to spin. I hold her until she pulls away, and she starts talking in that strangely calm voice she gets when she's actually really losing it.

"I have to go away, B," she says. "I can't stay here anymore. Those people in there are going to destroy me."

"Where are you going?" I ask strangely calm.

"Just away — with some people I know," she says taking another drag. "Come with me, B."

I think about all the people she calls friends, the fuck-up boyfriends and people she's let in our lives who've ripped us off. Finally I say: "I'm gonna stay here, Mom. I'm…sorry." I know that hurt, but as fucked-up as it is here, if there's one thing I know it's survival, and I know how to make it here.

She tells me that somewhere out there is my older sister Lyric, and my younger brother Danny.

Lyric was born the year before me. My brother Danny, the year after me. We all have different fathers. Lyric's father is supposedly a longtime family friend who never knew about her. My grandparents feigned Catholic shame over their pregnant teenage daughter and sent her away while she was pregnant with Lyric. My mom says she never considered having an abortion. Said she felt beautiful carrying a baby. When Lyric was born my mom refused to give her up, and the two shared a little apartment in Hollywood but couldn't make ends meet. My grandmother then sent my grandfather to her apartment with orders that she either give up Lyric or she wouldn't be welcomed home again. I'm pretty sure being forced to give Lyric up is the single most painful demon that haunts her.

I never knew my father, John Van Cott. My grandparents let my mom keep me because John married my mom for about five minutes. He split right after I was born.

My father was apparently a real winner. A druggie and a philanderer. Right after I was born, money was pretty tight so my mom tells him he should try to get a job. After all, peace signs and good vibes can only go so far. He says, "Listen, jobs aren't what's happening now" and within a week he split.

My mom once told me I met him at a party when I was about two years old long after he'd split. I'm in my mom's arms resting on her hip. He comes up to say hello, and she deadpans, "Hello John…you remember Billy, don't you?"

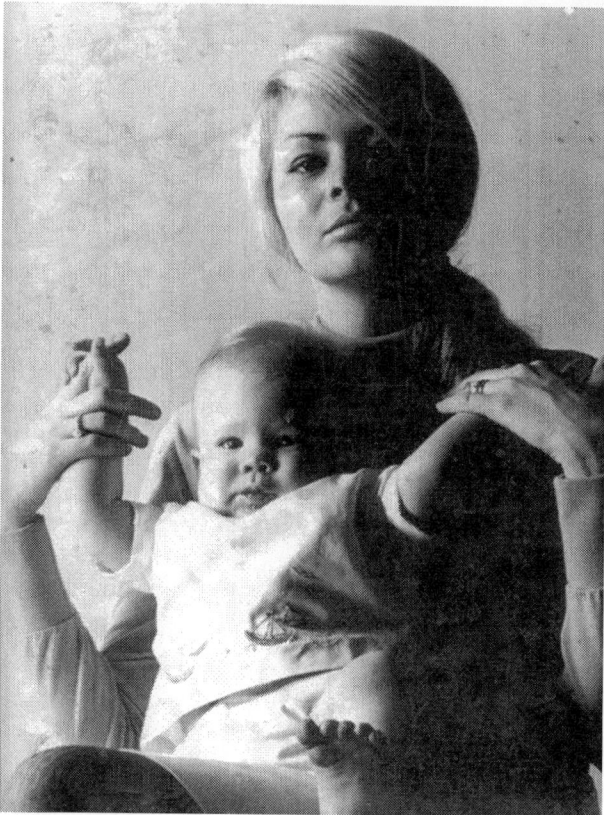

Me and my mom, late 1965. Photo by H.J. Brown

His grandfather used to call me apologizing for what my dad did until I finally told the poor old bastard to stop calling and work out his guilt elsewhere.

Danny was born about a year or so after me. It was apparently some scandalous affair, and he was given up for adoption. Our family is close to the local Catholic parish and one of the young brothers apparently was in doubt about carrying on in the seminary. This was the '60s and one member of the Catholic hierarchy had the brilliant idea that counsel with a young member of the parish, someone "hip," might help this poor brother through his period of doubt.

All my mom ever told me about it was that while she was *counseling* him, the Stones' "Let's Spend the Night Together" came on the stereo, and the rest as they say is Danny, er, history.

As for my father, it's just too much of a cliché. Cowboy walks into the sunset. Roll the closing credits. I've never heard from him. Whatever.

Mary says I'm walking around with mom-and dad-shaped holes inside; that I make whoever I think can fill those holes into gods, only to hold them up to such high standards God himself couldn't live up to them. Whatever.

While my mom was away that summer, everyone else here felt entitled to parenting me. That summer, my mom and I write each other these long letters. I tell her it's madness here and to do what she needs to do. My grandmother rages on through the summer about how my mom is a disgrace. My mom calls collect from the road begging for money to be wired to her. My Aunt Nancy gets on the line and implores her to return and raise me. I feel like bait. Then they put me on the phone, and I can tell she's just spinning wildly out of control. I hang up the phone and think to myself, why would anyone want to come back here?

* * *
10:55 a.m.

I just called Tom, but he's not there. Must be on his way.

I put on "History Lesson Part 2" by the Minutemen — "Mr. Narrator, this is Bob Dylan to me, my story could be his songs, I'm his soldier child."

It's my grandmother's birthday today. She hasn't been doing too great in the year since my grandfather died. I never knew a time when my grandmother wasn't ailing in some capacity. Angina, emphysema, high blood pressure, strokes, or from her latest drunken fall. Still, she's always seemed indestructible to me. Lately though, she's so fragile — like a gentle summer wind could snap a limb of hers right off.

My grandmother's the family matriarch. Irish Catholic. Fiercely proud, keeper of the faith, a mercurial, brave, feisty lady. The shepherd with a heart of gold. A kook. Mag the bowlegged hag, she calls herself.

I owe my fierce loyalty to her. If there's a family trademark — its strength and its weakness — it's our undying loyalty. After everyone's let go, we're the ones who keep holding on.

I learned to be a martyr from my grandmother. We all have. And see, martyrs get more bitter and vengeful when someone dares to soar. This plays out most when you're trying to leave the house. Like when my mom or Aunt Nancy leaves on a date or when I'm trying to get to a gig. It's such an absurdist drama. You stand there paralyzed at the foot of her bed waiting for her to say anything positive so you can leave and not feel like shit. She puffs away on her cigarette, the TV flickering images against the walls. Of course she knows she *has* you. Finally, she takes another puff, exhales and says, "You go out and have your fun, and I'll stay here feeling as sick and forgotten as I do."

My grandmother's the type of person who needs lots of people around her, people who make her feel necessary. But the truth is I don't think anyone can give her the amount of love she needs because she places her expectation level just high enough so that disappointment is always ensured. I've probably got that too.

When I got my first guitar, a shitty old nylon-string acoustic, I'd bang away at it and make the most horrible sounds. I was barely functional on the damn thing, but that moment when I struck the sweet spot of a D chord off a G chord, I'd be transported to the safest place I'd ever known — a place that felt so good it hardly seemed possible it existed in the same world.

Seemed like every *fucking* time I began to ascend, my grandmother would start sweeping leaves right outside my window and intentionally bang the broom against the wall of my bedroom. With each thrust, the windows of my room would violently shake, and I quickly fall back to earth. She looks through the window with her hair flying in every direction, barefoot and in that fucking tattered old light blue nightie and through those gritted yellow teeth she'd hiss, "Havin' fun in there?" I apologize profusely, toss the guitar away like she caught me mainlining and quickly start sweeping the leaves for her. I look back now and think…*apologize*!? What was I fucking apologizing for? See, something *happens* to you when you keep apologizing for things that make you feel alive. It's fucking crazy.

* * *
11:25 a.m.

I can't stand waiting inside anymore so I take all my stuff and pile it out front and wait for Tom out there. My mom brings me some orange spice tea and sits with me on the old wicker chairs out front. While she chain-smokes cigarettes, we reminisce about when she was married for a short time to my stepdad Larry See, and we lived in his big fucking house. I was almost five when they married. Larry was a See's Candy family heir, so we didn't want for much, but that didn't mean I was going to call him dad.

What I remember most about that time was the stultifying boredom as I was dragged from department stores to antique shops to fancy restaurants. It's the type of crashing boredom that literally pulls a child down to the floor into mini bouts of madness. I must say, though, that it was in the depths of those impossibly long hours, while I was curled up on a dressing room floor at Bullock's department store or waiting in the car staring into nothingness, that marvelous sounds and visions first began to come to me. This writer named Donna Tartt wrote, "These negative spaces are precisely where the aesthetic sense is formed, where the bored little mind turns in on itself, and presto! Spaceships, talking daffodils, entertainment!"

That whole world with Larry See and his bratty rich friends seems like a dream now. Hard to believe I was ever part of it. No wonder I have problems with people with money. Type of people I've grown up despising. Rich kids playing with expensive toys. People who've never worked a day in their life, never had to absorb the consequences of their actions because a safety net was always underneath them. Any problem comes up, just throw money at it.

Larry's wandering eye finally shook things down and he took off. He started seeing some blonde and took very little care hiding her from us. One night right before he split for good, he pulls up in his blue pickup truck right in front of our house and leaves the interior light on. Inside his blonde girlfriend is staring up at me unashamed. I stand at the front door with all the attitude I can muster from my nine years. Larry passes without looking at me and disappears inside the master bedroom. I hear my mom screaming at him, and I walk toward the bedroom. Before I can get there, the door flies open, and he passes without a glance, climbs back into his truck and speeds off.

A week or so later, Larry splits for good and moves up north. He promptly sends down word that he wants us out of the house so he can sell it. I tell my mom we don't need his fucking money. She takes me quite literally, too, and lets herself get good and fucked in the divorce settlement. I don't know what the final tally was, but we lived dirt-poor after the divorce. Sometimes I wonder how that was possible considering what Larry supposedly had. My mom tried to go back a few years later to renegotiate for more child support but was shot down. Sometimes I get pretty pissed off about that. I don't give a shit about the money. I just hate when people with money use it to fuck people, and I hate people who stomp over others just because they can.

Larry quickly marries the blonde and has me up once to his place in Sonoma for a part of the summer. I have an O.K. time, but then next summer he sends down word that he and the blond are expecting their own child, and I'm no longer welcome because they don't want to have to explain me. Haven't heard from him since. Mary says I'm pushing down my feelings about him. Whatever.

* * *

11:35 a.m.

My mom puts out one cigarette and lights another just as Tom finally pulls up in his white convertible. "Well, here goes," I say getting up. "I guess it's time to step out on the highway."

I can tell she's doing her best to show me it's no big deal I'm leaving her behind in this madhouse. She's really tried not to lay my grandmother's gut-wrenching guilt trips on me. Instead, she goes completely to the other extreme, abandoning herself in totality, never letting anyone know how alone she feels.

"Well, it's your time now, B. I'll hold the fort," she finally says.

"Be happy for me, Mom," I tell her. "Please?"

"You know I am, B. Now listen. Remember, what I've always told you: you and me, we had no choice. We're artists. We're wounded birds. Descending, ascending. But always chasing the muse. Now get outta here. You're boring me."

I shake my head and smile, throw my duffel bag and sleeping bag over each shoulder and head down the driveway. What I'm wearing and all that fits in my bag will have to make do. Three pairs of pants, two pairs of shorts, four shirts, my lucky serape, my favorite old newsboy hat, a white and blue bandana and a red and white bandana, a black vest, four pairs of socks, my oxblood Doc Martens, my beat-up old Pumas; my books: *Cane* by Jan Toomer, Jim Carroll's *Forced Entries*, *The Ballad of Reading Gaol* by Oscar Wilde, a Marvin Gaye biography called *Divided Soul*; my journals, a box of cassettes and my Walkman. And the entire contents of my bank account: a whopping $107.

I throw my stuff in Tom's trunk and plop myself down hard in the passenger seat. As we pull from the curb, I look back one last time, and there's my mom standing on the top of the driveway staring hard at me trying to smile. Looks like that scene from *M*A*S*H** where Radar is saluting Colonel Blake as he gets shipped home. I better not think of that. Fucking Colonel Blake ended up getting shot down. Whatever. I can't let myself get pulled back again. I gotta shake this goddamn albatross of mine that nobody's free until everybody's free.

Tom turns left onto Sunset Boulevard and floors it as "Back in Black" booms over the stereo. The wind feels good blowing into his convertible. He shouts over the music, "So, is this the first time you've been away from home?"

"Yeah, basically," I say trying to stay cool as Tom weaves recklessly through traffic.

"Is your family freaked out about you splitting for over a month?" he asks.

"Freaked?" I chuckle. "I don't think anything could freak my family out...any more than it already is."

I've learned to be careful about giving out too many details when people ask me about my family. I used to reel off insane bits and pieces of memories like someone making wisecracks while flipping through a stack of Polaroids stored in an old shoe box. I look up and see these blank expressions and realize we had secrets to keep. Like any kid, you just figure your family is like any other. Your world is so insular, and I took to the madness around here like the calamitous manner in which a child can assimilate to anything. Whatever. After today, I just don't care.

Straight up, God gave me music to comfort me. I'll never understand why I was belittled for turning to it. All I wanted was a chance to feel free to be what I'm meant to be. To be delivered from this insane asylum to somewhere you don't find grandmothers passed out drunk and bleeding on kitchen floors, where mothers don't split for summer vacations, or OD on percodans, get arrested or have nervous breakdowns every few years.

* * *

12:15 p.m.

We pull into Raj's driveway and honk. Raj comes out and tells me to drop my shit with the big pile of stuff accumulating on the driveway.

"Well," Raj says in his Ronald Reagan voice and shaking his head with a big smile on his face. We both stand there in front of each other and start breaking up. "Amazing," he finally says. "We're really going. You gonna get me back in one piece?"

"Ah Raj, we'll be fine, but I really feel sorry for those poor bastards out there. Fuckers won't know what hit 'em," I say. "Come on, get in. Ian's waiting for us."

Ian's our road manager. Ian Bader. Ian basically dropped out of the sky. A godsend really. In the weeks leading up to the tour, I was panicking about taking care of business out on the road and knew we had to score a road manager. We put a few feelers out there within our trusted circle, but no one was either willing or able. Can't bring Mary. You can't throw a relationship into the back of a tiny van. Plus, she's more valuable coordinating things at home base.

See, Mary is not only my girlfriend, she's also Divine Weeks' manager.

Ian's our friend Russ Bates' roommate. Russ told us Ian's a gamer and would give us a hand for the adventure and a chance to travel the country.

Russ is the one who did our video for "In the Country (For Jim Carroll)." Like George, our friends Laura Smith, Conrad Heiney and Mary and her best friend Julie Mercer, Russ is a DJ at the UCLA radio station, KLA. Russ is in film school with Mary, and said he could utilize the editing facility on campus. Last month, he filmed our show at Club Lingerie and then interspersed some footage from down in the reservoirs near Long Beach. Turned out great. Did it all for $95.

MTV just told us they're debuting it on *120 Minutes* this Sunday while we're in Seattle and plan to run it for the next four weeks. This is kind of a big deal.

Ian's about the easiest guy in the world to get along with. A sweet, considerate *gentle*-man. Ian's from San Francisco, from a stable home with two available parents. Striking looks, medium build with curly, sandy-colored hair that falls just above his shoulders. A dead ringer for Kevin Kline in *The Big Chill*. A good listener and patient. Cerebral but without pretension. He's an English Lit major at UCLA — like George. Ian possesses an inherent caretaker side which makes him about as perfect fit for the job as possible.

Other than very casually, we didn't really know Ian well. So last week, we were scheduled to play a benefit at Al's Bar and asked him to come down as a test run to see if we'd all click. The bands' pay was free beer. After the show, we all got pretty lit, and in that great Irish tradition where — after the proper amount of lubrication — the stranger on the next barstool becomes your best friend, Ian was let in to our little circle.

Ian tells us he's drawn to the tour by the limitless possibilities. "Let's not forget," Ian says by now pretty toasted, "we don't know shit. And that's a virtue. So why fear what's out there? Something life-changing for us all could be just waiting for us. So let's make this tour our own *On the Road*."

"Right on, brother," goes the chorus of us.

"Then don't hassle it," Ian says proudly looking around at us all. And with that, we christened our journey the "Don't Hassle It" tour.

Ian.   Photo by Dave Smerdzinski

* * *
1:10 p.m.

After we pick up Ian from Boys Town, we head back down Santa Monica Boulevard. Tom asks if we want to smoke some pot. Ian and I raise an eye at each other then beg off deciding we'll need too much ambition today to burn out so early. Undeterred, Tom turns to Raj and asks, "Well, Raj, would you mind packing a bowl for me?"

Now asking Raj to pack a bowl is kind of like asking Scooby Doo to fly the space shuttle. Raj, the drug novice of all drug novices, sort of holds the pipe looking around nervously until Ian does the deed and helps Raj off the hook.

Everything goes smooth at the rental company. After we promise Tom we'll get it back in one piece, we all climb into the big maroon Ford Econoline cargo van we'll call home for the next month. I take first turn at the wheel, and as we head back Santa Monica Boulevard toward Dave's place, I feel more free than I've ever felt in my life. I feel like I'm a third person looking down on it all. It's unreal. We're really going.

I hang a left on Tamarind and pull into Dave's driveway. His stuff is already piled up out front. His duffel bag, sleeping bag, first aid kit, a toolbox and a lantern. I shake my head. Dumb fuck that I am, I'm packing books to read and tapes to listen to, and Dave's packing toolboxes and emergency flares. Thank God we're bringing him along, or we might all end up curled up whimpering in the fetal position staring at our first flat tire in the bowels of Oklahoma.

Dave Smerdzinski. Born and raised in Falls Church, Virginia, just outside of Washington D.C., big family, both parents still together. Kind of short and stocky but built like a tank with newly dyed black hair that he wears to his shoulders. Dave's a survivor. A life lover. Likes to party a little bit. Dave's played in oodles of bands whereas none of us have known anything but Divine Weeks.

Dave is a couple years older and has more street smarts than the rest of us combined. Dave's done it all, lived on his own, and survived on nothing while the rest of us lived our sheltered little lives. Even lived out of his car for a while. Dave's resilient, pragmatic, takes it all with a shrug and moves forward. He just lost his job and his unemployment is running out. Unfazed, he just asked Mary to keep sending in his unemployment status reports while we're gone. No biggie, he says. "It'll work out.

Always does." Add unemployment benefit fraud to our growing rap sheet.

Dave.   Photo by Dan Barnett

Dave is the band's legs, its power, its engine. Without him, we'd just be a bunch of good ideas echoing off some high wall.

Everybody dug Dave right away. Not only because he's such a good drummer, but because he's such a solid person. No hang-ups, secure with himself. The guy is real. Not a phony bone in his body. Dave's the only drummer who can take his shirt off onstage without a shred of pretension. It's not some rock-star statement. You know, he just got too fucking hot to play with the damn thing on. He's got no patience for scenesters or hipsters and doesn't really give a fuck about appearing cool or connected. He keeps me and, particularly, George grounded.

Before Dave joined the band, I think we all secretly had a fear of success. Not that anyone dared speak of it. Instead, it manifested itself in a sort of self-deprecating humor we used to keep the stakes just low enough. It was like a safety net to cope with the disappointments. Like our first bio said, "If rock 'n' roll is a big party then we're throwing up in the bathroom." We figured even if our flyers wound up trampled on the ground, at least they were being trampled on at the most happening shows. When Dave came on board all that kind of talk ended, and we dispensed with that "just happy to be here" mentality.

I first really bonded with Dave a couple months ago, right before *Through and Through* came out. Mary threw a record release party at her house, and a whole load of folks who've followed us from the beginning, and some we met along the way, came by and crammed into her living room to hear the record.

After the party, I offer Dave a ride home. He climbs into my car above Mary's driveway and asks if I want to share a joint. While Dave rolls one, he pops in a Hendrix tape with a song I'd never heard before called "Peace in Mississippi." As the song starts to soar, it feels like we're levitating. We laugh for a bit and then turn quiet. "You know Dave," I say. "I feel like I've been just barely living my whole life. And...there's just *got* to be something more than survival."

"Me too," he says exhaling. "I came out to L.A. with like *nothing*. All I wanted was to play my drums and connect with people who really *cared* about music. Until I met you guys, I've just been...*waiting*."

"You know," I say, "I've been having these visions ever since you joined the band. I don't know what it is just yet, but I feel like something extraordinary is about to happen to us. I just know this tour is going to be life-altering — if we just let ourselves, you know? Especially Raj."

"Totally," he says, taking another hit. "I just can't believe I hooked up with you guys and this band. I mean, you guys as *people*. I've been in lots of bands, bands that had really talented people, but I never played music with people that really *believed* every *moment* you play is like *life and death*."

* * *

2:15 p.m.

Last stop is to pick up George. George Edmondson. He lives on 16th Street right across from Santa Monica College. Must be one of only five houses west of the Mississippi with a basement.

The Edmondson house is our headquarters. After rehearsals, we go up to George's bedroom and take turns putting on records exhorting the others that "*this* is what we should sound like." George puts on the Clash or the Ramones or maybe something funky from Stax/Volt. I counter with the Replacements, Echo and the Bunnymen or maybe something soulful like Marvin Gaye or Van Morrison.

Afterwards, we walk over to the Burger King at 20th and Pico — a King session, we call it — and talk endlessly. We must have talked ten times as much as we played that first year together. Made sense too. We couldn't play worth a lick, but we sure could yak at each other. George and I wave our arms wildly about, trying to put to words the latest far-out-of-reach sound we're absolutely certain is our answer. Raj sits there with those faraway eyes unconsciously dipping his French fries in his strawberry shake.

George, ever the frustrated guitarist, is a little pushier with Raj. It's George's personal mission to turn Raj into the Guitar God he envisions. For the most part, Raj tolerates it, but I know it gets on his nerves.

George's little brother Jon greets us at the door. Jon's a great artist and designed the cover for *Through and Through*.

"OK, how long ago did he get in the shower?" Raj asks.

"See for yourself," Jon says smiling.

George — who usually only goes at his own painstaking pace — is all packed and ready to go.

"Well, what do you fuckin' know about that," I say dumbfounded.

"Hey," George says wearing a *Never Mind The Bollocks* shirt and an old misshapen tan cowboy hat, "I'm ready. Time to get outta town, man. The world awaits."

As I help George load his stuff in the van, I remember to ask him what he was listening to this morning.

"Oh, the first Clash record," he says. "Why?"

"Don't let 'em say I don't know you, brother," I say, very proud of myself.

George is tall, perpetually thin with long bony limbs with sharp angles. Round wire rim John Lennon glasses adorn his face. He wears his straight, light brown hair long like mine. He's got a wonderful life-loving smile. When George is happy everyone gets on a high. In turn, when he's on a down, everyone gets pulled down with him.

I met George in 5th grade. He always had on this Hawaiian T-shirt that said Primo on the front. I'd see him around, but I was sort of a loner and he hung out with a different crowd. It wasn't until about 10th grade that we finally started to click. He was going out with my girlfriend Patty's best friend Niki, and the four of us were pretty inseparable through high school.

When I first met George, his dad was a very successful attorney, and they lived in a big house in Santa Monica north of Montana. Then his dad got caught up in some trouble, was disbarred and had to do some jail time. So among many things, George and I share some absent parent and abandonment issues.

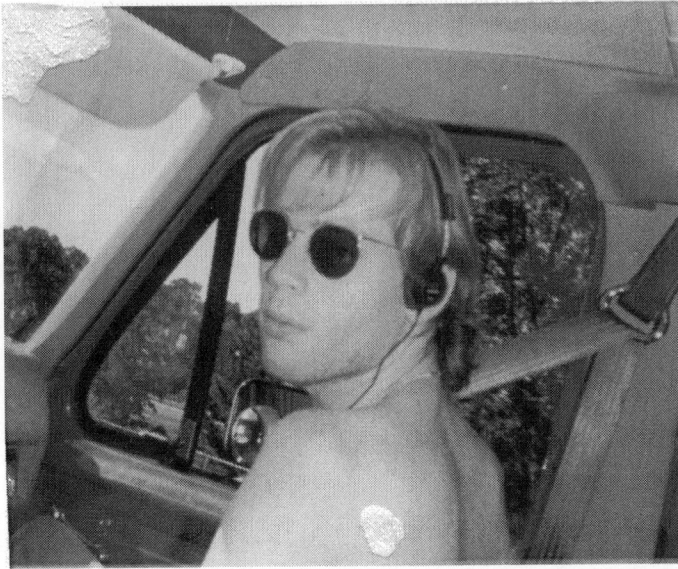

George.

George turned 16 before the rest of us, so he got his driver's license first. That first year he could drive, he took us to all sorts of shows around town. Big ones like Springsteen, Pretenders, the Clash and the Who and club shows like X, the Go-Go's, George Thorogood, the Blasters and the Dead Kennedys.

I've always looked up to George. It's his self-assuredness and air of confidence he projects that I envy. I've never felt comfortable in my own skin. I've always envied that ease with which he carries himself, that seemingly effortless grace and composure.

Same with him and his girlfriend Deborah. No drama, no tug of war, no push and pull. They don't seem needy, desperate or panicked. Man, I don't know what that's like. I have a hard time believing things will last. I always end up strangling things to death and then looking back wondering what the hell just happened. That's basically Mary's and my relationship.

You kind of have to know George to love him. He's always late and doesn't really care that you're waiting on him. His self-assuredness comes off arrogant to some people, but he's also the smartest, funniest and most charismatic person I know. Totally indispensable member of the band. A lot can go by George without him raising an eyebrow, and he can be a bit of a back seat driver. But when something insults his sensibilities he's the first to call it out. George is the band's conscience.

Me, I'm all passion and heart on my sleeve. Music is like rapture, my religion. George is more pragmatic, guarded, a little jaded. He worries a lot about appearing uncool and can let a random comment from a stranger completely change the way he feels about a gig. I know my impulsiveness and idealism worries George and cringe at times. In turn, he knows his visions of grandeur embarrass the rest of us every now and then.

Along the way, he and I have suffered some growing pains working out that dynamic that inherently exists between two headstrong personalities. See, George and I don't entirely agree on the band's goals — at least short-term. I've bought into that whole DIY touring ideology, sleeping on floors, the nobility of taking it to the hinterlands and winning people over one by one. George, who was into punk before the rest of us, naturally appreciates the ground war approach, but it's no secret he wants to be as huge as Zeppelin and sooner the better. I mean, we *all* want to *make* it, but while the rest of us accept we've got to pay our dues, George kind of already sees himself as a rock god, and he's sort of just waiting for the rest of the world to catch on. I mean, he's honest about it, and his sense of entitlement is, for the most part, endearing. It's Deborah, a staunch indie devotee, who tempers him on balancing his sold-out arena ambitions with the required indie principles. Big as Zeppelin but dressed like the Ramones is kind of the message. But Deborah can be overbearing. She's in George's head about how we should be bigger and further along, and this does cause some conflict.

* * *

3:45 p.m.

When we get back to Raj's place to finish packing, George starts spray-painting Divine Weeks on all our gear. I figure it'd make a good shot and as I stare through the viewfinder, I pause. There's George with this big defiant knowing grin that says: "No motherfucker's gonna get in our way ever again."

Raj has been in a good mood all day. I was getting the feeling he just might let himself be taken as far as this trip could take him. Unfortunately, right before we leave, his mood turns dark. While the rest of us are waiting in the van, all loaded up ready to go, Raj disappears inside for a real long time. We don't know if he's subjected to some sort of 11th hour guilt trip, but when he returns all he says is he wants to drive the first leg, so I take the front passenger seat. Then as Raj starts to back the van out of his driveway, there's his mom standing at the front window looking hard at him. I look over, and Raj is paralyzed staring back at her, torn in two frightful directions. He finally snaps out of it but doesn't say anything as we make our way out of town.

We're all bummed our gig in San Francisco fell through, but we'll try and hit it on the way back. We're staying at Ian's folks' place in Frisco tonight and tomorrow, and then head off early Friday morning for our first gig in Portland Friday night.

Driving through the San Joaquin Valley, we share our first meal. PB&J sandwiches with Wheat Thins and EZ Cheez. In back, after Dave, Ian and George pummel each other with wadded-up pages of a *Spin* magazine, the laughter dies down, and you can feel that initial rush of getting out of town has passed. It's like, "Now what?"

Here up front, Raj still isn't talking. I rest my head against the side window. I can't stop thinking about what happened when I went in to say goodbye to my grandmother. Blew me away.

* * *

I sit down on the corner of my grandmother's bed, the room unlit but for her burning cigarette and the flicker of the TV. She tells stories about growing up in Benton Harbor, Michigan. I'm astounded as she recounts with pinpoint accuracy every minute detail. Because of the Alzheimer's, I don't think she can tell me a thing she did yesterday, but her memory of her childhood is impeccable. I ask her to tell me more. Her back straightens and her eyes come alive.

She confesses — for the first time to me — that it was her dream to be a musician. A concert violinist. For years, I saw a violin case that sat collecting dust in a far corner. The only time I ever saw her take it out of the case, she was so drunk she could barely hold it. I ask her why she didn't pursue it, and she turns quiet.

She takes a deep sigh and squints at a far wall as if to get a read on some old lover approaching. "When I was at college at St. Mary's," she begins, "I was a music major. My sophomore year, a small group of us took a train to Chicago to see a recital by the great Jascha Heifetz. I even took my violin with me just in case I got to meet him so I could show it to him. He was my absolute hero. I got my hands on every piece of his music I could.

"So, the concert was remarkable. Transcendent. Heifetz played the Stradivarius with such fluidity. I sat frozen clutching my violin case soaking it all in. I was just fascinated with what made him tick. What lifted him to that place so few had gone? How was it that he made that divine sound? I just *had* to know. Do you know what I mean, Bill?"

I bow my head and nod, thinking about all those hours I stared into Bob Dylan's eyes on the cover of *Highway 61 Revisited* imagining "nowhere's great rainbow."

"So afterwards, we talked our way into the reception," she continues. "Very upscale affair. You should have seen me, the only one carrying around a violin case. A long line of well-wishers waited for a chance to speak with Heifetz. When I finally got up to him, I told him what an inspiration it was to hear him play in person. I took my violin out and handed it to him excitedly telling him I practiced my fifths religiously."

She pauses and turns silent. "And?" I ask hesitantly.

"Bill," she begins before catching herself. "He took my violin in his hands, looked at it a moment and sniffed, 'Well, it might make do for kindling' and he waved me off."

"What did you do?" I ask.

"Well, it would have felt better had he kicked me in the teeth," she says quietly and looking off into the distance again, then adding: "Something just died right then."

I'm floored. We sit in silence until I finally tell her I have to go. I lean over to hug her, and she keeps holding on so I just let her. "Do you really have to go?" she asks.

"If I don't go now," I say, "something's gonna die in me too."

She just looks at me. I'm not sure if she understands where I'm going today, but I can tell something's been awakened, something that was abandoned and forgotten. For years, I heard her rave on in drunken fits about how she could've had a different life, that she gave up everything and settled for less with my grandfather. God, I hated her for saying that. All I heard was the anger and bitterness. Today I heard the regret behind it. Man, I'm never gonna fucking let that happen to me.

* * *

As we work our way up I-5, Raj and I look back and see everyone's dozed off. He looks over at me and finally opens up.

"Bill, I...I almost came out to tell you guys I couldn't go," he says quietly.

"What?" I ask, kind of shocked, kind of not.

"In the Indian culture," he begins, "when someone leaves on a journey, you say a little prayer, eat some blessed sweets and get the bindi, you know the red dot on the forehead, as a blessing."

"O.K.," I say, "that's cool, but what else happened in there?"

"You have to understand the culture," he sighs. "Family unity is what holds everything together. I don't think I ever told you, but before my big sister and brother were born, my family lost their firstborn. No one talks about it. But you combine that and all the bigotry we faced in England, and it's made my family close ranks. We just don't really know how to be apart. They're scared we might crash out here and lose me. They laid into me pretty hard and even asked why can't I just go for a few days."

"A few days?" I ask incredulously. "But Raj, they *do* know how far the band's come the last six months don't they?"

Raj blinks a couple times, pauses, and then says, "Maybe I just don't make that very clear."

"But *why*, Raj?" I ask. "Aren't you proud of what we've done? And proud of yourself?"

"I am, I...I am," he says trailing off. "I just don't want them to think I've abandoned them. I just wish there was a way to be there for them and have *this*."

"Raj, there is," I say resting my hand on his shoulder. "You'll come back safe. I'll make sure of that. We'll *all* make sure of it. You never have to think you're facing anything alone again. And Raj, you *can* have this."

After we stop for gas near a little town called Tracy, Dave takes the wheel. Raj and I climb in back with Ian. George takes the navigator seat up front and pops in a Hendrix tape and proceeds to lecture Raj on how he should sound. George, bassist and perpetually frustrated guitarist. I'm face to face with Raj and we smile at each other — Oh, George, here we go again.

We're still about an hour outside of San Francisco, near Altamont. It's sunset, and I'm looking at the sun rays shoot past all the wind turbines on the hills we're passing. I think about last night when I dropped by Mary's to say goodbye.

Altamont Pass   Photo by Bill See

Mary and I have been going out almost three years. It's been a steady cycle the last six months: she runs, I follow. I run, she follows. One of us pulls back. The other becomes obsessed with the chase. When we first got together, we were totally devoted to each other. We lured from the darkness a part of the other that for too long had been forgotten. Somewhere along the line, we lost sight of that because it's too subtle for people like us to appreciate, because we've got too many holes inside. Now that the band's starting to take off, it's feeding the biggest and hungriest of the holes, our insatiable need for outside approval.

Mary.

Last night, as I watched her put together lists of critics to call, radio stations to drop in on, promoters to bug, I think about the last time we fought. She said I'd asked too much from her, more than anyone could have possibly given. I wanted to tell her I leaned so hard because she was the only one who made me feel safe, but the words got stuck. It's the eve of what we've all worked toward for three years. The only thing we've got now is this great thing we all dreamed up and put all our energy into.

It scares the shit out of me to leave town facing disintegration with Mary, unattached, free to roam. We tell each other all the things you're supposed to say: "It's just a month," "we'll talk on the phone." But all I can think about are the things we don't say, and it feels like the last chance just slipped through our fingers.

* * *

Day Two
7/29/87

When we pulled in to Ian's folks' place last night, we're all so sky high, we don't come down for hours. It's basically the first night Raj and I have spent out in the world alone. Raj looked a little lost and stayed close to me as we all tried to settle in.

It took a crane to lift George this morning. George is not a morning person, and his voice stays in this very low register until the early afternoon.

Frisco is Ian's hometown, so he's playing tour guide today. Not that that's easy. To get five people anywhere, it's a little like a field trip with a grammar school class. You know: come on everybody, don't fall behind. Who's hungry? Does anybody need to hit the head before we get back in the van? Real rock star stuff here.

First stop, Haight-Ashbury where we're reminded, quite often, that it's the 20th anniversary of the "Summer of Love." George commemorates it by buying some love beads and a headband to go with his black leather jacket and motorcycle boots.

As George emerges, Raj takes a long look at him. "Why George, you look like a totally different person from the guy we left with."

Ian tries to come to George's defense. "So, he looks a little like a pseudointellectual Hell's Angel. That's the man's inalienable right. And George, I'll defend to the death your right to look like a damn fool."

"Thank you, Ian," George says smiling. "That really means a lot to me."

As we walk down the Haight, Dave regales us with a few verses of "We Built This City on Rock and Roll," Jefferson fucking

Starship's godawful hit that you can't go anywhere without hearing.

George is nothing short of exultant. He's practically gliding with an extra swagger to his gait. Not a care in the world and exuding this supreme confidence. He says this is our time now, and he's not wasting one minute out here. It's intoxicating, and I feel like I'm gliding just above the sidewalk walking with him.

It's a real struggle for George balancing his scholastic aspirations with his rock and roll dreams. Unlike Dave, Raj and myself, George loves school. He's born to be an English Lit professor. He and I had this deep conversation while we were tripping on mushrooms a little while after the band first started. We're walking through the Botanical Gardens at UCLA late at night, and he keeps going on about how Sting is able to be scholarly *and* a rock star, like he's trying to reconcile these two extremes for himself.

For the rest of us, the band's all we've got right now. Call it blind faith or just plain stupidity, but we've put school aside for now. For George, he has another calling. Between professor and rock star, believe me, he'd prefer the band to make it, but he hasn't reconciled any of this. He's got this looming decision on grad school hanging over him, and he's counting on this tour giving him enough tangible evidence that we're on our way so he can justify devoting himself entirely to the band. I get that, but it's a Catch-22. There's no fast track to success when you're DIY. I mean, it's not like we have other offers or options. When you're on an indie label, this is just what you do. Get in the van and take it to the people.

Late in the day, while we're walking through North Beach, George pulls me aside and tells me, "I'm telling you Bill, we've *got* to make it happen right *now*. We've got to make some serious inroads on this tour, we just have to. If we don't, I'm not sure what."

"I know what you're saying George, but it's going to be a process. Little by little, day by day, one great show begets another. It's word of mouth. A slow steady climb. You know that."

"Well, I think we're better than that," he says dismissively, shaking me off. "This is *our* moment now. *Our* time, and I know all we need is to just be put in the right place at the right time and it'll happen for us. Nothing back home matters now."

I'm doing O.K. Well, except for late in the day I have a flashback to my mom standing on the driveway yesterday when we said goodbye. Steve Winwood's latest hit "Finer Things" came on the radio. My mom's been playing that song all summer, singing it at the top of her lungs. I don't even fucking like that song, but I could hear her voice singing along to it, all hoarse and breaking. I hate when that happens, you know? A song you fucking hate, but for some innocuous reason it completely throttles you and you just go dead. Then just as I'm coming out of it, we pass this movie revival house playing *Harold and Maude,* one of my mom's absolute favorites. If you know anything about that movie and the Maude character you've got a good idea of my mom's wandering spirit. Thinking about all that kinda pulled me back home for a minute.

As the day winds down, I notice Raj falling behind the rest of us. So we ditch the guys for a little while, and he confesses he's feeling awful guilt about abandoning his family. He says he called home this morning and his mom's arthritis is bad and they want him to try and score some cheap medicine for her when we get to Canada. He says he's terribly conflicted and isn't sure if he's supposed to stay the quiet, "shy little Indian boy" his parents raised in the light of his sacred culture or can he chase that crucial part of himself that comes alive when a guitar's in his hands? He keeps repeating that phrase, "shy little Indian boy," and I notice as he's talking, he keeps rubbing a bracelet he's wearing. I ask him about it, and he says his family gave it to him for good luck.

Clearly we're all going to have to be each other's support group. From time to time, one of us is going to be on a down, and somebody will have to be there to listen and help pick the other back up. We're going to have to learn how necessary it is to turn to each other because that's all we've got out here. I don't know how bands that aren't really friends survive out here.

At sunset, we stop in a bar just around the corner from City Lights Bookstore for a last round. We order up and then toast the great unknown, for it all begins tomorrow.

* * *

Day Three
7/30/87

Ian blows reveille at 5:00 this morning. A 12-hour drive awaits. We're out the door by 6 a.m. Not that that was easy. We had to practically dress George ourselves and carry him to the van. George has always done things his own way at his own pace. After a gig you get soundmen, especially the fat one at Club Lingerie with his pants sagging below butt level reprising Dan Aykroyd's refrigerator repairman role, who scream at you to move your shit off the stage for the next band. At moments like these, George has this special knack for getting into deep conversations leaving Raj and me to hustle his gear offstage.

We stop at a rest area near Redding to pee. Right before I left, I dyed my hair fiery red, and it's down to my shoulders. So I'm at the urinal doing my thing and this trucker pulls up next to me and looks me over. He sucks some air through his teeth then says, "Guess no one told you this here's the men's room." When we get back in the van, I write postcards to Steve Hochman of the *L.A. Times* and our friend Conrad, who's just taken over as music editor of the *Reader*, and share that story.

I put on George's cowboy hat that's on the dashboard and take the wheel. As we near the Oregon border, I pop in a Marvin Gaye compilation tape. I'm really into him now. I'm reading his biography, and there's this quote where he's talking about how he writes lyrics. He tells the band to groove on something repetitive, and he just begins mumbling over it until his mumbles turn into words. That's how he positions himself to receive God's gifts. I want to try that.

As we make our way through Oregon's wide-open spaces, Marvin Gaye gives way to Van Morrison on the tape deck. As Van sings "she kiss-a-my-eyes," my mind drifts back again — to almost three years ago to the day, the night I first met Mary.

* * *

The band had only played one gig. We were all going to see R.E.M. at the Greek Theatre and had an extra ticket so George offered it to another DJ at KLA. He didn't say much about her except that her name was Mary and that she was cool.

I drove that night, and after picking everyone else up, George tells me Mary lives in Brentwood up Kenter Drive on a quiet little street called Greencraig. While George gets out to fetch her, the rest of us stay in the car debating the greatest debut record of all time. Mary's driveway disappeared below street level leading to a nice two-story house hidden by heavy foliage. As votes are cast for the Pretenders, the Clash and the Velvet Underground, everything stops as this head with long straight blonde hair and big orbit-blue eyes slowly rises up the driveway into view like a sunrise riding an escalator.

"Hi, I'm Mary," she says, her eyes darting about the interior of the car. She speaks fast and loud. Sounds a little nervous. I would too, climbing in a small car with four guys. I can't stop looking into her eyes, big blue ocean-light eyes with tiny pupils that make her look like she's seen visions.

We gravitate toward each other most of the evening. I make sure of that. She walks with a sort of stride all her own. I like that. As we walk along the steep grassy hill leading up to the Greek Theatre, I feel myself sort of fit at her side like a wayward boat that shores into a snug harbor. Sometime during the evening, she says she's about to go away to school — to England no less — in just a week. I try not to get that worked up about her, but over the next few days my mind keeps flashing on her walking toward me and her heavy-lidded eyes that close halfway when she says something to draw you nearer.

* * *

We're running a little late so we stop by the side of the road and Ian calls Lisa, the booker in Portland. When Ian comes back to the van he looks like he's eaten the last cookie.

"What's with you?" George asks.

"Nothin' " he says, now smirking.

"She sounded hot, didn't she?" George pushes.

"She didn't sound ugly," Ian assures.

"I don't get it. How does a girl sound hot?" Raj asks weakly.

"Raj," Dave says, donning his paternal duds, "let's hope by the end of this trip, we can get you caught up a little bit, O.K.?"

Ian says we can stay at Lisa's place tonight after the show, and as we close in on Portland, a hearty debate ensues over whether it's best if this Lisa girl is pretty or not.

We're all stoked to be playing at the Satyricon, pretty much *the* place to play in Portland. We bring our gear inside and look up at the swirling day-glo paint designs behind a very high stage.

The Satyricon bathroom is a trip. The Trough, the soundman says it's called. Stickers and posters cover the walls and ceiling — a who's who of the indie world. I add a Divine Weeks pin in between a Dead Milkmen and a Leaving Trains sticker.

The Satyricon is run by a very cool fellow named George Touhouliotis. Very accommodating, down-to-earth guy. Buys us a round of drinks and gives us a tip on a cool record store to check out down the street after soundcheck.

As we nurse our drinks, we watch a local band get uppity over monitor levels while they soundcheck. After they finish up, we try to convince them to switch slots with us so we can play second instead of first and maybe play in front of more people. The singer says O.K., but the heavy-on-attitude guitarist says nay. Oh well. We were looking for something to dislike to take our minds off first-show jitters.

After our soundcheck, the soundman gets busted for possession. It's not going to matter much. This place is so ambient the sound's going to bounce all over the place. Plus, we're so full of pent-up aggression from being stuck in a van for 12 hours, "12 fucking hours" that is, that we're just going to go out there to seek and destroy as hard and furious as possible.

Shortly after 9 p.m., we climb onstage and look out at probably no more than 15 people in the audience. I flash on Raj and me standing outside the Blue Lagoon Saloon in Marina Del Rey, our third gig. A Tuesday night, midnight. The soundman's dog takes a shit on stage. Four people are there for our set. You haven't lived until you've played your guts out only to hear the sound of two hands clapping.

Opening night in Portland.   Photo by Ian Bader

I'm still wearing George's cowboy hat as I step to the microphone and tell the crowd they can tell their grandkids they were there for the opening night of Divine Weeks' first national tour. Dead silence. Perfect. I was counting on the indifference to kick us in the ass, and it does. As predicted, the sound is for shit, but we're on fire and by about our third song, we hit a nice pocket and start to connect. Like always, we play like the place is packed, and as we near the end of our set, the club starts to fill up. All through the set, I'm watching people arrive and whisper to other people who've been watching us. Then they start pointing up at us. I figure that's a good sign. I know that feeling coming into a club and hearing something compelling and wanting answers.

Tonight we realize how much easier it's going to be playing for out-of-town crowds. It's like a rebirth. We can leave behind our history and growing pains and just be whatever we become out here.

We try to stretch out our set but start getting cross looks from the owner George. Still, he knows we're going over well, so he lets us come back for an encore. We pound home a maniacal version of "Look Book," and when it's over we get a huge cheer from the now nearly filled club. We can't help but feel a little bummed over how many people are pouring into the club just as we finish, but we do all we can to make as big a ruckus as we can in the time we have — not just onstage, but after too. As we're moving our stuff offstage Dave, Ian and I keep working the crowd. Everybody we talk to says they're sorry they got there late and want to know when we'll be back. We take down names and addresses, and say we'll let them know when our fall dates get set.

Even as Dave and I are loading the last of our equipment in the van, we spot two guys who we'd seen by the stage near the end of our set walking through the parking lot toward their car. Dave calls out, "Hey, remember Divine Weeks, O.K.? We'll be back in the fall."

"Yeaaah," one of them calls out. We close the sliding door of the van and hear the two of them busting up laughing at us. Oh well. If we don't make the most of our time out here, we'll hate ourselves for it. Whatever, we're not going to wait around for people to notice how special we are. Success doesn't come to you. You go to it.

A band called the Dharma Bums closes the show. Local band. Not the most original sound, but they have some good songs, and their singer looks like he's possessed. He actually reminds me a lot of myself, and the band sounds a lot like early R.E.M. Like we used to. I talk to him after the show. Says his name is Jeremy. He gives me their demo, and I tell him when they come down to L.A., I'll try to give them a hand and help create a community like we learned from Black Flag and the Minutemen. Jeremy raves to me about a guy who just started a band from up north in Aberdeen, Washington. Says the band's led by an extremely shy guy named Kurt Cobain.

* * *

Day Four
7/31/87

We crashed hard last night drained from 12 hours stuck in the van and the rush of the first show. I awake to the sound of rain absolutely pouring down. As I come to, I have this feeling like something's different. Maybe this is what it *really* feels like to be reborn, not that hollow religious rebirth shit. I know it doesn't sound like much considering I'm stuffed inside a sleeping bag on a hardwood floor, packed in a tiny room with four other guys in sleeping bags, but for the first time in my life it feels like I'm exactly where I'm supposed to be and in total control of my destiny.

This is how we heard it'd be from all those bands that showed us how to do it, that went out to chase down their dream in rented cargo vans. We were told we'd be blown away by people out here who'd lend a floor and some hospitality. Being from L.A., we don't know hospitality. We know bars over windows and guarded glances. I'm ready for this to be the first of many floors we'll collapse onto. No way am I going back to school next month.

While we all sit eating Cheerios at Lisa's kitchen table, we count up our grand total of $50 earned from last night. And we had to haggle to get that much.

Lisa, who by the way is pretty cute, gives me the "Fight Racism" sticker I was admiring on her refrigerator, which I promptly stick on my guitar case. She wishes us luck in Seattle, and we set off in the pouring rain.

As we make our way out of Portland, we experience the completely alien concept of doing exactly what we want to do while the rest of the world carries on with their dull and dismal Saturday morning errands. Back in L.A., you play a gig then face the tremendous letdown of returning to your shit day job, school, mid-city traffic, whatever. For us, it's back on the highway to follow the breadcrumbs left by our heroes in this sort of parallel universe.

Dave's driving, and I'm up front playing navigator sort of unconsciously watching people in cars drive by. I look down at this one guy in a beat-up old Ford Escort like mine, windows up, and he's singing like the world is about to come to an end. His face is all red, eyebrows arched outward like two hands reaching to the heavens and tears are streaming down his face. He feels my eyes on him and looks up completely mortified. I give him a peace sign and a look to let him know it's cool. I get it.

As we continue north across the Columbia River into Washington with the Replacements' new record *Pleased to Meet Me* on the stereo, the rain softens and the gentle rhythm of drops on the roof sends my thoughts tumbling back again.

* * *

A week or so after we all go to the R.E.M. show, I call George under the guise of band business knowing full well he'd invited Mary over. I ask what he's up to. "Oh, remember Mary from the other night? She's over here taping all my Velvet Underground albums for her trip to England," he says.

"Hey, you want some extra company?" I ask as nonchalantly as I can.

It's a hot, muggy, late summer night and even hotter inside the Edmondson house where George moved back for his second year at UCLA because money was so tight with his dad being disbarred and facing jail time. George is changing records from *White Light/White Heat* to the Velvets' third record when I get there. Mary is sitting on George's bed with her head buried in a book. She senses me approaching and looks up at me and smiles. "Hi Bill," she says patting a spot next to her on George's bed which is strewn with clothing. "Here, there's room for one more."

"I don't want to sit on the laundry that George has so nicely stacked," I crack.

George is fiddling with the tape player, looks up and says, "Hey, I've got a very precise system going here. I know where every last thing is in this room."

Mary looks back at me and smiles. I finally ask her, "So, how's it coming?"

"Well, George is having quite a problem with the cassette deck."

"I'm doing just fine with this goddamn thing, thank you very much," George shoots back in his best Jack Nicholson voice. "I just can't seem to find the goddamn screwdriver to tighten the goddamn jack. I *just* had it."

"But I thought you said you knew where everything was?" Mary says smiling at me.

"The fewer cracks from the peanut gallery the better," he scowls.

We all talk for a while doing the best we can to ignore the large white elephant parked in the middle of the tiny bedroom. As George puts on *Loaded*, Mary gets up and says she needs to go outside to get some air. No point sitting there hiding my cool, so I sheepishly follow her out to the courtyard.

We talk for a long time against a dull green stucco wall until I can practically see those guys at the airport with their flashers signaling it's clear for landing. We kiss as the humidity finally gives way to big rain droplets landing all around us and that familiar smell of rain when it first falls on warm asphalt fills the air.

She pulls away and bows her head. I put my hand on her chin and gently lift it until her eyes look up at me. "Hey, what's wrong?" I ask.

"Oh, I've felt close to boys before," she starts. "We kiss and then they don't call again. I give my heart and then the sweetness sours."

I want to say something but don't just then. She continues, "They'd be great and nice and then leave no trace."

She looks off somewhere. "Hey, look in my eyes," I tell her.

She looks back at me and says, "I'm sorry." She smiles again, sweet this time. I know she's further out on the tree limb than she expected to go but so am I.

"Listen, don't believe a word I say. At least not now. Watch and see. I'll wait for you and be here when you come back."

The band was playing a gig the next night, so I ask her if she'll be there. She says if she finishes packing for her trip she'll come by, but she wasn't sure because she's leaving the next morning.

One last kiss, and she climbs in her car. She pulls away from the curb leaving me standing in the middle of the street where I stay until her taillights disappear. Now what, I wonder.

*   *   *

The rain finally ceases as the tip of the Space Needle appears up ahead. We're running a little late, so we head straight for our radio interview at the University of Washington. I tell Dave to bring along his bongos and tambourine and for Raj to grab his acoustic guitar so we can do a song live on the air. We're going to try to make our appearances at radio stations something more than just another part of the grind. We figure it's a chance to charm people into our little version of the world, and plus our essence is live performance.

I've done my share of hanging out at college radio stations —
sitting in on Mary's or George's or Conrad's radio shows at KLA
— hanging out and watching everybody march through the lobby
on the look for what to do, where to go and who to listen to. I
soaked it all in and did what I could to insinuate the band on
anyone that got close enough.

The lobby at KLA is a sort of town square where a lot of us meet,
make plans and then pile into someone's car and head off to Club
Lingerie with the Replacements blaring on the stereo. We line up
along the wall that faces Sunset Boulevard with our fake I.D.s
and pass out our crummy flyers and watch people react like they
were just served with a subpoena. We vow to sell out the
Lingerie and have people queue up around the block for us too.
Selling out Club Lingerie — it's like *the* wildest idea of success.

"So what made you guys start a band?" Faith, the DJ, asks us.

"Our story's not uncommon," I begin. "We're losers. Nobodies
in school. Music's the only thing that gives us a voice.
Individually, we're just self-loathing wannabe, never-will-be's.
Together, we believe we're capable of great things."

I look up through the glass of the DJ booth and Faith is just
sitting there with that "Yeah, right" look on her face.

See, its dodgy being openly idealistic like we are in world of
indie rock. You can't assume just because you're on an indie
label that college radio or fanzine hipsters are your unconditional
allies. A lot of them like nothing more than to point out the
slightest misstep of anyone who passionately holds *any* set of
beliefs. I call them the great levelers — those that stand for
absolutely *nothing* at all. We come across a lot of people who act
like they don't give a shit about anything and call you a sellout if
you actually admit you have ambitions and openly believe in the
healing powers of music. It's bullshit and cowardly, as far as
I'm concerned.

From day one, we vowed to break down the barrier between band and audience by any means necessary, and if we have to pull people onstage and hand over our instruments to whoever doubts that to prove it, we will. Most people sense that, appreciate it. Some resent it. Some just roll their eyes when they catch us on a bad night where all that reaching only looks like a train wreck.

See, Divine Weeks' earnestness, if you will, is looked upon with some suspicion. Onstage, we're passionate and come down on the anthemic side, which is decidedly *not* cool in the indie world. A lot of that is my doing. That worries George, who's definitely the most self-conscious of the band and who frets about what others think and say. That said, I'm glad he's there to rein me in sometimes. I need that.

After we do the shuffling "Idiot Child" live, we hold a quiz for tickets to tonight's show. Then Faith asks us about the state of the L.A. club scene.

Our peers are bands like fIREHOSE, the Dancing Hoods, House of Freaks, the Hangmen, Downy Mildew, Pop Art, Thelonious Monster, Balancing Act and Leaving Trains. We're all sort of indie post-punk rock, heavy folk-influenced. On the other side of the spectrum is your hard rock/glam scene with bands like Guns 'n' Roses, L.A. Guns, Poison and Warrant who are starting to make some noise. Those bands play the Sunset Strip clubs like Gazzarri's, the Whisky and the Troubadour. That scene exists separate and apart from ours, and there's a good amount of disdain from both sides. We think they're posers and shallow, and they think we're dishonest because we won't admit we want to be just as big as they do.

What blew everything up in town and crystallized the two extremes was the arrival of Jane's Addiction last summer. Jane's defies classification. Punks, metal heads, college geeks and rock-critic types all flocked to their shows. And soon, the major labels came calling and a tremendous bidding war began.

Jane's Addiction was dreamt up by a skinny, bug-eyed provocateur named Perry Farrell who used to front an arty band called Psi Com. He and bassist Eric Avery started playing, just the two of them, around town to little notice, but when they hooked up with a couple young guys who played in speed metal bands named Dave Navarro and Steve Perkins, they began to stomp on all the competition. They literally sent bands scurrying off questioning their own approach.

Jane's is a hard rocking band, but are neither hard rock nor metal. Their sound is huge and Zeppelin-esque. But Led Zeppelin would have killed to have the fluidity and soaring funk grace of Jane's. More important, they carry themselves with the same post-punk aesthetic as the crowd we run with. It's so funny. All those guys who lied about burning their Zeppelin records when they were moshing at X shows could rejoice again.

It's George who feels most threatened by Jane's arrival on the scene. That's Deborah's influence. She's been in his ear about them from day one. Jane's is amazing, but they're an anomaly bridging together all those disparate scenes. You can't just make a carbon copy template from them and expect to go anywhere. Probably never going to see something like them again.

Faith spins about half of *Through and Through*, and she lets us play some of our favorites like Jesus & Mary Chain, the Replacements, Hüsker Dü, the Ramones, Billy Bragg and Violent Femmes. Then she asks us what our most embarrassing gig was. We all look at each other knowing the answer.

Every time bands we thought weren't as good as us got signed, we'd be told to stop whining and generate our own hype, earn our own crowd. Don't give people the option of overlooking us, we'd be told. Hüsker Dü, Dream Syndicate and Black Flag put out their own records, so we set out to put out our own record.

We'd been recording demos at Ethan James' studio in Venice and had enough material for a record, but after pooling all our resources, including a loan from our friend Ron Jolly, we were still about $500 short to get our own record pressed.

That's when Mary's dad, a high-ranking executive at the L.A. Zoo, offered us a spot to play a thing at the Zoo called Zoobilee. It was a $500 flat fee — more than we'd ever made before. Three days, two sets a day. One problem. A rock band at the zoo is about as close to *Spinal Tap* playing Six Flags as you can get.

Get this: We shared the bill with a bug exhibit, a puppet show, and a folk singer named Dan Ferguson who closed each of his sets with the plaintive and nauseating "American Pie."

On the first day, we haven't even finished one song when one of the zoo officials races over waving his arms. He's a small, officious fellow with a short-sleeve suit and a pencil protector in his left breast pocket. He tightly holds a clipboard in one hand and a walkie-talkie in the other. When he reaches the stage, he has a pained look. "I am *so* sorry, I mean you guys are all just terrific, but...you see, it's...the elephants."

George moves to the lip of the stage and leans over and asks, "I'm sorry?"

"We just got word," he says. "One of the elephants is troubled by the noise."

We don't know what to say. "I tell you what," he goes on. "Mr. guitar player, yes, um, will you just play gently for a moment and you [pointing at me], turn his thing, his...you know [pointing at Raj's amplifier], yes, that down, and I'll signal when it's at a good level for Louise."

"Louise?" George asked quizzically.

"Our beloved matriarch elephant, Louise," he says.

"Of course, Louise," George says flatly.

As Raj strums his guitar, I slowly turn down his amp looking for any sign of approval. With each turn of the knob, his face looks more pained. He continues to motion with his thumb pointed decidedly down until finally the only sound coming from Raj's guitar was that of his guitar pick hitting the strings with no amplification whatsoever.

"There, there, stop. That's perfect! That's great fellas, that should do the trick," he says quickly turning to go. "You guys are great, thanks a million." And off he goes leaving us standing onstage utterly dumbfounded.

Although rock tradition likely mandated a Sex Pistols-like retort, we just can't do it to Mary and her dad. I finally say to George, "Just keep telling yourself as soon as this is over, we'll have enough money to get our record pressed."

"I know, I know," he says. "Thank Christ, no one's here. Hopefully no one finds out about it."

Just then I see our friend Laura Smith and her friend Monica heading toward us.

"Oh shit," I gasp. "It looks like we'll have to earmark some of our pay toward paying Laura off."

Zoobilee did get us enough money to get our record made which we title *Obviously Four Believers*, taken from the old Dylan song minus one. We christen our own label 221B Records, Sherlock Holmes' address and the number someone put over the door to George's basement. George and I then drive around L.A. hitting all the independent record stores begging them to take our record on consignment. Bebop Records, Poobah, Moby Disc, Rhino. I write these long heartfelt letters to critics and fanzines like *Flipside*, *Maximumrockndroll* and *Forced Exposure*. We even hand-deliver a copy to Rodney Bingenheimer at KROQ. He comes out and chats with us until he realizes we don't have a girl in the band he can fuck.

Tonight's show is at a club called the Scoundrel's Lair. After soundcheck, George leaves to go call Deborah, and I have another long talk with Raj. He's been distant toward me all day, and I know he wants whatever's bugging him pried out.

I've still got on George's cowboy hat, and I take a seat next to Raj just outside the club on a railing. "All right, Raj," I say, "Tell me what's up. You've shut down."

He thinks for a minute. "It's just that last night, I didn't feel we were all together," he says looking away.

"God," I interject, "I thought it sounded just like a band would after being stuck in a van for 12 hours and then playing their first show of their first tour."

"I know," he says looking down. "It's just, I need that sense that we're all one. That's all I play for. You know me. I don't care about stardom or selling records or any of that. Playing onstage is my only escape, the only time I feel any real sense of myself. I need that connection with you guys. Without it, I just can't dig deep enough and find myself. It's like I'm in this cocoon all the time, but when we're all one, I feel like I can leave one side open and drag people in as they pass by."

I smile. I know what he means, and it's true. We're not a great band in any classic sense. When we're not firing on all cylinders, we're a dumpster fire, but when we're on, we have a certain symmetry that none of us can ever hope to achieve without the other three.

Still, there's more to it. We've all been losers together, four college Joes waiting for a bus that wasn't coming. It was nice and miserable there, comfortable and safe. For three years now, going on tour was this completely outrageous idea, the ultimate chance to make it possible. And I understand. It's shocking to wake up one day and realize the only thing keeping you from seizing your dreams is yourself.

I finally say: "Raj, I've heard it said: 'Many of us crucify ourselves between two thieves — regret for the past and fear of the future.' Don't you see? The brave don't live forever but the cautious don't live at all. The only thing that's truly terrifying is the unlived life."

I look over and his head is in his hands. "Raj, listen to me." I move closer to him. "Remember what we promised ourselves when we were up on Mulholland on top of the world? We vowed to do it like no one else. Raj, it's finally *our* time. It's time to draw on some faith, my friend. And you can borrow mine until you have your own."

"I do have faith Bill." He finally looks up. "It may be *all* I have. It's just…you don't understand what it's like to have hundreds of years of culture and expectations thrown into your face every time you dare to dream your own dream. It's just…I can't freaking let go, and I really don't know if I can, Bill."

"Raj," I say quietly, "you *know* I understand. I'm carrying the same fucking weight on my back. But there comes a point where you gotta say, 'it's either them or me, and for once, I'm choosing me. And goddamn it, Raj, I'm not gonna let you piss away your shot either."

"Don't you think I want to be like you guys and just leave the baggage behind?" he says, uncharacteristically forceful. "Listen, I want to tell you something," he says lowering his voice again. "My family is broke. My mom's in bad health too. We're really going through a desperate time right now. Plus, you have to understand the culture. You just *don't* leave family. It's just the way we're bred. No one's ever left family to do something like this before. I know you guys think all you've got to do is just say screw it and that's that, but…there's so much more to it," he trails off. I move closer to him and put my arm around him.

"Come on Raj," I say. "Tell me. I want to understand."

"Paul Fields was a fella I went to school with," he begins. "Almost everyday he would wait for me on Old Oak Road and steal my case, toss my books and slug me in the guts. For awhile I'd try different routes or times but Old Oak was the shortest way home. One time I was walking home, and I got jumped by this guy Paul and a bunch of others. One tied a noose around my neck while two other dudes spit, beat and kicked me. This went on all the time. I'd run home and sometimes I'd tell my family I was harassed, but more often than not, I was too embarrassed and ashamed to say anything. I just withdrew and buried it. This was before I found music, before I had really any escape at all. Back then, I was just trying to disappear.

"Another time, we were playing football and this guy Mark May jumped me, and he and another guy beat and kicked me. Mark held my nose and put his hands over my mouth and said, 'I'm going to kill you right now, you fucking Paki.' A teacher finally intervened, but as we were separated he spit at me and said he meant every word. From that day on, I was terrified I was literally going to be killed. Bill, you have to understand. No one *ever* stood up for me. I was all alone. I'd get beat up all the time, and all I had was my family — literally the only love I knew. So, it's a little more complicated than just rebelling against them."

Raj has shared with me a little about growing up in England, but he's never vividly explained it to me like that before. As I sit there with my arm around him, my propensity to want to protect and absorb pain for those I love creeps up on me. Only the terrifying will of someone bent on demeaning another spurs the equally terrifying rage of the protector. Like that summer when I was 13 and endlessly defended my mom while she was gone. Wild thoughts of violent retaliation overcome me, and suddenly I'm envisioning grabbing a plane right then and hunting down those motherfuckers Paul Fields and Mark May.

Raj and I sit together in silence for a long while on that railing just watching twilight turn to that shade of night-blue that you can't find in the crayon box. Nothing more needed to be said. I think Raj just needed this new world to slow down for a little bit so he can hear a familiar voice chase the snakes out of his head.

I'm wearing my serape over a white long-sleeved shirt, bolo tie, and George's cowboy hat as I step to the mic and say, "Hey, we're Divine Weeks and we're from L.A., but don't hold that against us."

Seattle.   Photo by Ian Bader

Raj is in a long-sleeved black shirt. Like R.E.M.'s Peter Buck, he's got only the sleeve of his strumming arm rolled up. His long mane is tied in a small ponytail by Mary's scarf he's borrowed. I make sure there's more interaction between him and me tonight. We keep our eyes locked on each other throughout the set. He, reading my punctuation and phrasing. Me, playing off his accents. Dual conductors communicating telepathically.

Tables are filled throughout the floor up front, but slowly the place fills up and people just crowd in front of the tables right up to the lip of the stage. I ask if anyone heard us on the radio today and a whole slew shout out that they had.

It's hard to describe, but something comes off a crowd that really *wants* it. You can actually sense its hunger. Tonight was like that, and everybody in the room is with us for long and wondrous stretches. I feel the eyes on us from that first ring of Raj's Les Paul, Dave's first snare crack, and the sound of George's bass rumbling in my chest. We have the room. It's ours.

We're a collective force tonight. More playful. More ourselves. Last night was pent-up aggression and over-the-top release. Tonight, we strike the right balance between light and heavy. Right before we do "Goddamn Real to Me," the song that kicks off *Through and Through*, George, a big fan of Cheap Trick's *Live at Budokan* cracks, "This is the first song on our new album, it's called 'Surrender.'" Then while George tunes up, Raj and Dave, who's wearing my white and blue bandana, play B-I-N-G-O for kicks.

The setlist is coming together too. A new song called "Copper Wire" has settled in as the set opener, then "Goddamn Real to Me" into "In The Country" and then "When I Go." This leads into the anthemic "Bitterness" and then the acoustic and swinging change of pace of "Idiot Child." The emotional centerpiece of the set is the theatrical exorcism of "Dry September" where everything reaches a zenith. Then we segue into our anti-jingoistic "On a Soapbox" before the glorious stretch drive to the finish with "Look Book."

Ian says his cousin Mindy and her husband Sandy live in the suburbs about half an hour outside of Seattle and offered to let us stay while we're in town through the weekend. The catch is they don't want to wait up for us to stumble in during the middle of the night, so Ian promises we'll be there no later than midnight. That means packing up our gear in record time and splitting right after the show. This is a drag because we killed tonight, and you want to reap what you sow on nights like tonight. It also means leaving before the door money is fully tallied, and having to retrieve money from a booker at any time other than the night you play is always a risky proposition.

Plus, for the first time this trip, Raj is in great spirits. Not only because he got wondrously lost in the music, but after the show a very pretty and exotic-looking brunette started chatting him up. Alas, we had to pry him away.

On our way to Ian's cousins' we commiserate over the gap until our next show which is not until Tuesday in Vancouver, four days from now. We didn't have much choice because our Canadian work visas don't become valid until Tuesday morning so we're stuck here until then.

When we pull up, Mindy and Sandy come out and cautiously greet us in their matching jammies with their names monogrammed on the left breast pocket. After some idle chit-chat in the entry hall, they herd us into a little room with just enough space to lay out our sleeping bags. Before we can throw down our stuff, they abruptly announce they're zonked, close the door and shut out the light like we're nine-year olds at a sleepover.

It's only 12:30, and we're all still flying sky high from the gig. I feel like we're packed away in some meat locker, but I don't care. It was such a good night. Feels like Raj is finally with us now. We reached out and connected with strangers tonight. I settle into my sleeping bag with my eyes wide open playing over scenes from the show. Wild flashes of Raj's arms hammering down on his guitar, Dave's cymbal crashes accentuating crucial moments. I can still feel the thundering bottom of George's bass throughout my torso. My ears are ringing with sheets of white noise coming and going like it's filtered through some fantastic tremolo pedal.

* * *

Day Five
8/1/87

When we emerge this morning, we quickly realize what a huge house and surrounding property Mindy and Sandy own. The place is an impeccably clean split-level house in a deathly quiet suburban neighborhood about a half-hour outside of Seattle. Matching Beemers in the driveway. Perfectly manicured garden in front and a backyard lawn a football team could practice on. Inside, — sculptures, paintings, expensive rugs, immaculate furniture and a home theatre with a massive big-screen TV. It's like a museum — pretty to look at, but you're afraid to touch anything.

Ian sets up headquarters at the kitchen table and makes calls all morning as the rest of us eat Cheerios and nurse cups of coffee. Ian says Mary plugged in shows in Chicago and Dallas and is still trying to fill the remaining holes so we have as few days off as possible. Like Mike Watt says, "If you ain't playin' you're payin.'"

As I chomp away at my cereal, I open the front page of the *Seattle Times* to the sight of the biggest goddamn tornado that just hit Edmonton. Twenty-seven killed, hundreds injured. Guess where we'll be in a week?

Mindy and Sandy are your basic '80s yuppies straight out of central casting. They're both in Izod Lacoste shirts, Sandy in light blue, Mindy in pink. Collars turned up. Sperry topsiders. No socks. Even their dog is a yuppie. They named it Roderick, for Chrissake! It doesn't take long to discover we're living on a completely different planet.

"So, you guys are in a *rock* band, huh?" Sandy asks, pouring himself a cup of coffee. "What is this, like a summer project or something?"

We all look at each other not sure what to say. Ian, embarrassed for us, jumps in, "They're on tour promoting their record. It's what you do when you put out a record. You should see. They're getting great reviews. And last night, they packed the place and had it rocking."

"Gosh, that's *so* great," Mindy jumps in. "We have some nice places here in Seattle. Sandy, where was it we saw REO Speedwagon? That was so fantastic! A little loud, but the laser show was a-*MAZING*!"

"We're kind of on a different grid," I say. "We're basically slugging it out in the clubs."

"Oh, we went to a club once," Mindy says. "Remember Sandy? Your boss' son played that, what do they call it? A jig? We had to leave early. Too smoky."

"A *gig*," Ian says looking like he's decomposing right in front of us.

"Ooops," Mindy starts laughing way too hard. "A jig. Well, there *was* dancing!"

It's like talking to aliens. To these two, rock and roll is played in big hockey arenas by big untouchable myth-like caricatures that live like Dionysus off in Fantasyland.

We've got to get out of this place. It's giving us the creeps. Plus, we have to shake down the rest of our guarantee from last night. We were supposed to get $140 but the booker, Jonathan, who's a DJ at the radio station, hadn't tallied up the door and could only give us $120. He told us to swing by the station this afternoon, and he'd give us the other $20.

First we check out the triple-level marketplace downtown by the water called Pike Place. You follow an old brick road that runs right into it. Very European flea market-feel to the place. Stalls everywhere selling food or various knick-knacks. We splurge and buy lunch for ourselves, abstaining from our usual peanut butter and jelly repast. After lunch, we walk around the place checking out all the buskers and toy with the idea of busking ourselves, but shy away.

When we get to the radio station, Faith is there hanging out and acting like we're strangers. She gives us the bum-rush and says this Jonathan guy is nowhere to be found. Tells us to try on Monday afternoon because that's when his radio show is. We know it's just 20 measly bucks, but we need every last cent, and we vowed to stand firm on money issues or we'll set a dangerous precedent for ourselves.

When we get back to Mindy's and Sandy's, a big barbecue is starting. A bunch of their yuppie friends are all holding Coronas with lime wedges. The guys all around the barbecue, their wives all at a table. Mindy and Sandy are dressed alike again. We've started calling them Chip and Buffy. Sandy is bragging about his state-of-the-art barbecue to everyone, "Everything tastes just a little bit better on this bad boy."

We're like a freak show to these people. While we all chow down, we field a bunch of questions. How much money are we making? Do we have binding contracts with every venue? Do we have a powerhouse legal team?

I try to explain the DIY credo when suddenly Sandy erupts like he's just had an epiphany: "I get it! You're *salesmen*! You have the product, the, the, you know, the music, and you guys are the face on the product. And, and, you go out into the field and put that shoulder to the wind and *sell, sell, sell*. Just like us guys!" he says looking at the rest of the clones who are all just standing there nodding with dumb-ass smiles on their faces. I wish you could have seen the expression on Dave's face.

"It's not quite like that," I say trying to let it roll off my back.

George whispers to me, "Fuck it. Don't embarrass Ian. Just let these dicks give us their pat on the head. They know deep down they're living a lie, and they fucking hate us for it."

"So," Sandy says squeezing some lime into his Corona, "What happens if you don't make it?"

"To be honest," I say, "We're more concerned with what happens if we don't try."

"But what's your back-up plan?" Sandy asks, a little condescendingly.

"What's *yours*?" George fires back, now getting a little pissed off and not hiding it very well.

"Don't need one, bud," Sandy says, surprised at the question. "Look around. See those cars in the driveway? I'll be retired before I'm 50."

"Well, *Chip*," George says sarcastically, "that's quite a legacy, but we don't live in your world. It's not Morning Again in America for us."

I can see the pained expression on Ian's face, but I'm getting tired of making nice. "If that's what floats your boat," I say. "But we want to do something more than help rich men get richer."

"You make it sound like we're slaves," Sandy says pointedly. "We're being rewarded for the hard work we do. Everybody wins. You'll see."

"No, *you'll* see," I say. "Every day you carry out someone else's marching orders, you're selling yourself on the cheap. Little by little, day by day, you become less and less until you don't even remember what your dreams were."

"Don't worry about me, bud," Sandy says, reaching into the ice chest for another Corona. "I'm doing *juuuu-st* fine."

"Tell me something," I say soberly. "Wasn't there that one dream you had? You know, the one that gnaws at you? Didn't you ever stand at the crossroads knowing the decision you make was going to impact the rest of your life? That's where we're at right now, and I can't think of anything more horrifying than sitting up in the middle of my life and knowing I was meant to do something else, but I folded up my tent and didn't fire my shot."

It's going to get ugly if we keep going, so I back off. But man, Sandy and his crew can't be more than a few years older than us. Here we are out here feeling like we're reborn, and they can't wait to retire.

One of the jugheads then starts probing us for groupie fodder. As Ian explains we're aiming a little higher, George washes his hands of it and splits to call Deborah, and Raj and I take a walk.

Raj and I pick up the thread from last night. He opens some more veins: the feelings of dislocation, the guilt over leaving his family behind, the divisiveness he feels between his family's demands and the pull of our mission out there. God, the immense amount of shame he's holding onto. He calls himself a "shy little Indian boy" several times again and says he's having more flashbacks to England. "You get shoved, beat up and rejected enough, you finally reject yourself," he says.

"But Raj," I say, "what about the gig last night? I thought that finally got you on board."

"It's just, when there's no gig, and there's downtime, I get pulled back home again," he says looking out. "Being onstage is the only thing that keeps me moving forward."

"But Raj," I say. "Didn't you hear those dicks tonight? If that doesn't justify why we're out here, I don't know what will."

* * *

Day Six
8/2/87

It's a lazy Sunday, and Ian suggests a trip out to Snoqualmie Falls, this huge waterfall about a half-hour away measuring some 270 feet high. Sandy says it's actually higher than Niagara Falls, like he owns the fucking thing or something.

Clockwise from top left: Ian, Raj, Dave, George, me at Snoqualmie Falls.

As we draw closer to the falls, Ian and Dave are on the far side of the river and George and Raj and I are on the near side, and we're throwing a football to each other. Dave throws one a little short of George. George, not the most athletically inclined, lets the football feebly bounce at his feet and then stands and watches it roll slowly off the bank into the rushing river without moving a limb. Raj dives in fully clothed to stop the football from disappearing forever, but it gets caught by a current. I jump in and pull Raj out. He gets out dripping and shivering and walks up to George and says, "George, couldn't you have just taken one step forward and reached down for it?"

"But Raj," George says weakly. "The river is so...how do I say...wet."

Ian takes some pictures of us all together, some more in front of the falls and inside this cool cave — not to mention some nude sunbathers too. Ian's been great making sure this trip is captured.

We stay at the falls until dark, and then head back to watch our video debut on MTV's *120 Minutes*. Chip and Buffy are in all their splendor sporting matching Ralph Lauren Polo tees, chinos and penny loafers with the penny wedged in the front opening.

We don't know what to expect as we all gather in front of the huge big-screen TV. Finally the VJ Kevin Seal says Divine Weeks is coming up in the next segment. We all sit nervously trying to don an air of cool and hopelessly failing.

During the commercial break, Sandy brags over the fact that he bought the biggest big-screen TV available on the market when an ad comes on introducing a new even bigger big-screen TV. Sandy is appalled and pitches a fit right in front of us. We all look at each other and shake our heads. I overhear George whisper to Ian, "This guy can't possibly be serious can he?"

"Sandy married into the family, George. I take no responsibility."

Finally after the commercial break, the VJ comes back on and quotes part of our bio and then debuts our video. Our eyes all widen and we sit frozen in disbelief. While it plays, I feel like I'm watching us all from a far corner of the room. It's just completely otherworldly. The VJ then comes back and announces upcoming tour dates like we're some huge band. Man, it's just so unreal. All of us are standing and pointing at the screen yelling, "Did you fucking see that?"

As soon as it's over we call Mary's house. She invited over a bunch of people to watch it. I get on the phone and ask her how many people are there, and she says excitedly, "Guess!" and holds out the phone and shouts, "Hey, say hello to Divine Weeks in Seattle!" I swear it sounds like the whole fucking world is hollering through the phone. Mary then passes the phone around to everyone telling us how cool it was. It was pretty special.

Deborah then gets on the line with George, and I linger listening to them gush at each other. It's interesting. That first day in Frisco, George sounded like he left it all behind without a care in the world, but the last couple days, he's really been missing Deb. In truth, George is a real romantic, but he projects such a carefree attitude that unless you really know him you'd be surprised to see his heartstrings being pulled like this.

Maybe it's just the distance talking, or maybe I'm over-romanticizing it, but listening to George long for Deborah has me thinking about Mary and me a little.

See, in the beginning, it wasn't hard to separate Mary's and my relationship from band business because the band's gains were so modest. But when the band started to gain some traction, it got tougher to get back to that little hiding place we'd made for each other, and the band started taking on a life of its own.

Like last month when we opened for the Young Fresh Fellows at the Lingerie, I wake up with the worst case of food poisoning I've ever had. It's one of those gut-wrenching, unable to get up and do anything except throw up deals. I didn't see how I was going to rally and do the show that night.

Mary just takes over. Gets a prescription for me to ease the pain, brings me cold compresses and tries to find something I can keep down. I feel a real tenderness toward her like I hadn't felt the last six months. Late in the afternoon when I start to come around, I try to thank her for all she'd done. She smiles and says, "Hey, the show must go on, right?" Part of me wants her to just let down the manager mask, be impulsive and tell me she wishes there's no show so we can drive up the coast. I don't know, maybe she wishes I said it. I only know it didn't get said, and the ever growing machine called Divine Weeks rolled on.

Sandy keeps pouting about not having the biggest big-screen in the fucking world so I join Dave and Raj who are out front sitting on the lawn in the dark talking. Dave starts to tell some very involved story about Tyrant, this hard rock band he played in back in D.C., and my thoughts trail back again.

* * *

Mary ended up getting her packing done for England and showed up at our gig, a stupid battle of the bands — our second gig ever. We end up losing to a very polished pop band and afterwards the losing bands were given all the judge's comments so they can work on their "craft." We find this all terribly amusing.

Mary offers to give George a ride home. George is the front seat of Mary's silver Toyota Tercel, and I'm behind her in the back seat reading the judge's words of wisdom. "Here's a good one. Listen up," I say chuckling. "Singer doesn't make equal eye contact with the left side of the audience as the right side."

"Bill, that's the first order of business next rehearsal," George decrees.

We're on 17th Street approaching Colorado, about a minute from George's house. It's very late and the traffic signals have switched to flashing yellows. We're all laughing. Life is good. I'm sky high because Mary said she dug the show and invited me back to her place for her last night in town.

Suddenly I hear George shout, "Oh shit," and literally out of nowhere it feels like we're hit by the force of an angry god. Before I can look up, a car broadsides us and we go careening across the intersection.

When we come to rest, I hear muffled voices like we've all been pulled underwater. Then, as if we're pawing to the surface, I start to make out the other driver's voice saying over and over, "Oh God, fuck, shit..." I climb out the passenger window and lean into the driver's side window. I freeze at the sight of Mary's bleeding face. I try to help her from the car, but she says she can't walk. The smell of gas leaking spooks us so George and I help carry Mary to the curb and sit her down. I take off my shirt and rip long, thin pieces from it and hold it against her bleeding cheek, eye and arms. She asks me how bad it is, and I don't want to tell her.

As Mary is loaded into the ambulance, I overhear a cop say the other driver was drunk. We ride with her in the ambulance to the ER at Santa Monica Hospital. She's in shock and keeps apologizing in a monotonous voice. As the paramedics start to wheel her into the ER, she tells me to try to get hold of her sister or brother because her folks are out of town.

We find out George broke his index finger, and after it's splinted and the laceration on his chin is stitched up, his dad comes and picks him up leaving me alone there waiting for Mary's family to show up.

Mary's brother and sister finally arrive, and what a sight I am. I'm a mess from the show, and all I've got on is my long leather jacket with no shirt. I'm white as a ghost, in shock and nauseated.

We finally get word Mary broke her right pelvis and left shoulder and she's got sizable lacerations on her right cheek, eye and left elbow. Once she goes into surgery, I start to feel a lot of pain in my ribs. A nurse asks me if anyone is coming for me. I lie and say I don't know anyone in town. After the nurse convinces me I should be checked over, they find some cracked ribs and blood in my urine. They want to hold me for observation but when no one's looking I grab my jacket and split.

I walk up 16th Street to Wilshire and spot a bus stop. The sun's just starting to come up. I sit down on the bench and stare off trancelike. When the bus finally comes, I plop down in the back. I feel like I've fallen into the black-and-white of a dream.

* * *

I snap out of my dreamscape and half hear, "Can you fucking believe it? Our video on MTV?" Dave says incredulously. "Bill?"

"I'm sorry Dave," I mutter. "Yeah. Unreal isn't it? Weren't we just four college Joes waiting for a bus just last week?"

"Hey maybe not anymore my friend," he says. "Not anymore."

"Yeah, another bull's-eye hit," I say.

"What do you mean?" Raj asks as Dave finishes off his beer and opens another.

"Oh a long time ago, right after our very first rehearsal I went home and wrote out this list of ten targets for the band. Not that MTV is the be-all end-all, but getting our sorry asses on MTV was on that list."

"You know," Raj says. "You should look for that list. That would be a trip to look at."

"Not yet," I say. "I vowed not to look at it unless one day we reached them all."

* * *

Day Seven
8/3/87

It's Monday, a workday for Sandy and Mindy and the rest of the world. Last night we offer to be gone by like seven this morning, thinking they'd say not to worry and hang out until nine or ten. We all stand with toothless, frozen smiles as Sandy tells us, "Oh, you don't have to leave that early. Take it easy on yourselves. Make it 7:15." Great.

Just before we leave, I hear Sandy dictating an angry letter into a microcassette recorder: "Speed memo to Alvey's Electronics. Sarah, address it to the president of the company. Dear Mr. whoever it is, I am enraged at the misrepresentation by your sales staff. I was assured that the television set I purchased a week ago was the biggest big-screen available on the market. Ah, new paragraph. Imagine my shock when last night, while entertaining guests, I was made to look a fool when..." and on he goes as we jump back in the van and split.

"Fuck, I'm sorry, guys," Ian says as he pulls onto the highway back toward Seattle. "I know that was like a trip down the rabbit's hole."

"Don't hassle it, Ian," George assures him. "It's a microcosm of Reagan's America. A fucking chasm dividing us."

"Not your fault, Ian," I pipe in. "Plus, we should thank them. It completely justifies our motives and affirms the goal."

"Yeah," Dave says. "Anything but ending up like *that*."

We have some time to kill before heading back to the radio station to take one last stab at the $20 ol' Jonathan promised us from Friday night. I know, I know, 20 lousy bucks, but we need it. Plus, our work visas don't permit us to enter Canada until tomorrow, so we've gotta spend one more night in the U.S. Ian says he knows of a great campsite just short of the border where we can stay.

Dave and I are pretty hungover so we stop at a 7-11 to get some coffee and a box of Pop Tarts. When we get back to the van, I hand George the bag of everything and start the engine. George pulls out the box of Pop Tarts and gasps. "Oh...my...fucking...God," he says slowly and sounding legitimately concerned. "We can't eat these Pop Tarts. *I mean it!* You guys are gonna freak when you hear what the serial number is on this box. 666," he says firmly, his eyes darting about for a reaction.

Dave, hungover and in no mood snatches the box from George and barks "Just give me the motherfucking box of Pop Tarts, George. I'll eat Satan's fucking breakfast if you won't." Poor George is left there with his two empty outstretched hands locked in the same position as when he was holding the dreaded carton.

When we get to the radio station, some guy in a Let's Active T-shirt gives us another phony story about Jonathan's whereabouts. "I don't like being lied to, and I don't like fucking Let's Active," Dave growls.

"Temper, temper," the little dweeb says. "Try again in a couple hours. Jonathan will be in about then."

Dave is fed up driving around so he spots a park and pulls over so we can just relax and try and shake the hangover before the indignation of begging for the lousy 20 dollars one last time. Jovial Uncle Dave has mutated into his alter ego, Roscoe P. Coltrane — with a hangover. Thing is, when Dave gets mad he's hilarious, and no matter how frustrated he gets, you can't help laughing. This, of course, enrages him more. After a long tirade about parks never having enough swings, Dave says matter of factly, "I hate people. And you never know when I might kill somebody."

"I'm curious," Ian deadpans, "did you guys ever do a background check on your drummer? He seems like he might be ready to snap at any moment."

"Didn't we ever tell you about the night Dave auditioned for us?" I ask.

"No," Ian sighs, "but unfortunately, we have a lot of time to kill so fire away."

We fired our drummer Brad around the first of this year. Poor Brad. Guy was just too uptight. Played that way too. God knows, we tried to make it work with Brad. Shit, George and I even took mushrooms with the guy to see if that would free his mind, but it only drove a wedge deeper between us.

From the beginning, we promised ourselves not to be a typical L.A. band, not to be mercenaries and cutthroats. We always frowned at bands that carried on like unfeeling dictatorships wielding about swords with wet blood still dripping, coldly firing band members and managers for a short cut to stardom. It was Vitus Mataré, who ended up producing *Through and Through*, who told us we were never going anywhere with Brad as our drummer.

We crossed the line the day we fired Brad. Broke from that first vow that we'd all make it together, something I'm still trying to reconcile. When George and I went to Brad's off-campus apartment to kick him out, we fully knew that we'd be destroying him and our quaint little band would never be the same.

The Dream Syndicate's drummer Dennis Duck was nice enough to fill in while we looked for a new drummer, but he was about to go back on the road so we had to find someone fast. So, in early March we put an ad in the *Recycler*, and after suffering through the tedious process of fielding calls from would-be L.A. musicians, we invite the best of the lot down and George invites another that our friend Matt McDowell recommended.

George's mom banned us from practicing in her basement anymore because all the noise and vibrations gave her dad a stroke. So, we started rehearsing at Bluebird studios way down

La Brea almost to Pico, run by this great guy named Bobby Hurley. At Bluebird, you have to schlep your gear up this long, thin, claustrophobic stairway. You get an idea what motivates someone to play music when they have to haul their shit up a steep   flight   of   stairs.

So the first guy comes in, the one who answered our Recycler ad. Guy looks like someone from the third incarnation of Molly Hatchet. The whole time he plays he's staring at himself in the mirror. I hate that. Guy wasn't bad, but you always know if you can share intimacy with someone within a few minutes, and we couldn't wait to get this guy out of there as fast as possible.

Then a little before nine o'clock, this stocky guy with a low center of gravity and thick solid arms and legs like tree trunks comes through the door. "Hey, I'm Dave, how's it going?"

He's got a simple drum set. No fucking gongs, or roto-toms, chimes or shit like that. He mentions John Bonham and Charlie Watts as favorites. Doesn't use flashy drummer jargon, and doesn't try to sound like some prog rock or jazzy show-off. Another good sign.

George had given Dave a tape of some of our stuff, and after he gets all his drums in place, he sets down next to his drum stool several pieces of yellow paper with little cue notes on them. Crib notes, if you like. Interesting. Another good sign.

Raj asks Dave, "You wanna do 'Look Book'? You know that one?" Dave looks perplexed.

"Hum how it starts," he says. So Raj obliges, and after a few seconds, Dave's blank expression disappears. "Oh yeah, sure let's do it," admitting later he was lying and had no clue which song that was.

Raj counts the song off 1, 2, riffs over 3, 4, and Dave quickly locks in driving the song harder than it's ever been played. Within just a few bars everyone's shot with adrenaline. We get through the second chorus and move into the break where the song's always begged for controlled chaos, but we never had the horsepower to pull it off.

Raj and George start smiling, and I know what they're thinking. Dave is everything we've been praying for. Raj then looks at me, and we both start laughing and can't stop. I look back at Dave, and he's starting to scowl but keeps driving the song forward. As the song nearly jumps the guardrail, I glance back at Raj again. We're now both busting up barely keeping the song together. It's pure joy. And relief. Everyone's here now. I'm seeing sold-out shows and us on magazine covers when Dave suddenly stops playing and throws down his drumsticks.

"What the fuck's going on here?" he snaps. "If you don't dig what I'm doing why don't you fuckers just tell me? Jesus fucking Christ." He starts packing up his gear swearing under his breath.

"Dave, hold up. We're sorry," Raj finally says. "It's just that…it's so obvious. We're finally all together."

Dave has this quizzical look. Poor guy doesn't know what to think of us. "Who *are* these guys?" must have read the caption. We're ready to give him our testimonial, and he's just trying to figure out if he can trust us.

"Unreal," Ian says laughing. "Beautiful."

I decide to get away for a bit and take a little stroll around the park. The sound of kids playing makes for a nice background. The cobwebs are starting to clear out of my attic, and I think about the last few months since Dave joined the band.

With Dave, the band's able to both rock harder and relax. I remember my friend Melody told me after Dave's first gig, "Before Dave, you guys were all head and heart. Now you're a band that leads with its gut and groin."

Classically, the drummer and bass player lock into a groove and the guitar player glides over it. Once Dave joined the band, the rhythm dynamic of Divine Weeks changed. Dave and Raj look to and play off each other. As a result, George became more of a lyrical and melodious bass player rather than the typical thumping and plodding sound thickener. It's that distinction that makes us stand out. Dave lets us swing a little more loosely leaving more space for me to stretch out my phrasing and improvise. A lot of bands don't realize how important it is to leave space in their music. They're always so insecure and think they have to make everything so dense.

Dave broadened our sights, and when you can see more, you aim higher. So we did.

* * *

When I get back, Dave's laying on a slide still flattened by his hangover. As I massage Dave's neck to get some blood back to his brain again, I realize my wallet's missing. "Oh, wonderful," I sigh. "How in all fuck am I going to get into Canada with no goddamn I.D.?"

"Looks like we're a power trio, my friend," George says finishing one of the dreaded Pop Tarts.

"Thanks a lot," I say becoming sincerely worried.

When we finally track down ol' Jonathan back at the radio station, he gives us a sob story about how the club is going into the shitter, and he just "hated to do it," because we were "such nice guys," but he doesn't have our crappy 20 bucks.

We're not the most imposing group, and we figured one of Raj's vicious Chinese wrist burns isn't going to scare ol' Jonathan much so we wash our hands of it and split.

"Shit, the only reason we hung out this long in fucking Seattle was to collect that godforsaken 20 bucks," George moans as we climb back in the van. "This really sucks. I'm sure the Replacements or Hüsker Dü don't have to fuck about in a goddamn kiddy park all day waiting to beg for 20 lousy bucks. Why do we have to do this kind of shit?"

It's been a long day of screwing around in the city waiting for the money that never came, the hangovers, the cursed Pop Tart box and being all pent up over not playing a gig for three days while staying with the yuppies, so we head out to the campsite Ian suggests.

We're all quiet as we head back north and Neil Young's "Like a Hurricane" fills the van. Man, this *has* been a strange beginning to the tour. With only two shows in the first seven days, it's been more about being forced to know one another — warts and all — and share a certain intimacy we've never known before. Can't hide out here. No safety valves, no escape routes.

I can tell Raj is sinking again. Like he said, playing gigs keeps his mind off home and strengthens his belief in why we left in the first place, but when there's downtime, and he's left with his thoughts, we start to lose him. I ask him what's up, and he says he's bummed the bracelet his family gave him for protection broke off, and he can't find it.

This liberating feeling out here has taken hold of my senses on such a pure and primal level, and all I want to do is just let go and be taken as far out as possible. But I feel so damn responsible for Raj. It's always been that way with us. Me, the protector, the court jester, keeper of the faith. I understand why he's so torn, but it's just so frustrating not being able to lead him to the light. It's like the revolution is going on and while the rest of us are running free Raj is like those old fuckers who refuse to leave the bastilles.

No one's said anything for the last half-hour then Dave makes a thunderous announcement to help us turn the corner. "Boys, we've been dealt a tough blow, but you know what I always say? No show tonight, so let's get wasted."

We all crack up. Except for Raj. He looks up at me, then goes back to rubbing at his wrist where his bracelet was. I know the boozing and drugging the rest of us are doing is alienating, but he's starting to get a little sanctimonious about it, and George, for one, is getting fed up.

Raj makes a snotty comment after Dave says we need to stop and get more beer before hitting the campsite, and George just hits the roof. "Now listen Raj. I'm a grown man. A consenting adult. We all are. If anyone here wants to have one beer or ten beers they're damn well entitled to do it!" Ian and Dave quickly defuse the situation but Raj falls silent for the rest of the evening. Which is a real shame because tonight was truly one of the most bizarre, touching, and liberating nights the band's ever spent.

This campsite is basically at the very last upper edges of the continental U.S. — at Birch Bay just past Bellingham. Ian says we should head down to the lagoon to watch the sunset so we grab some beers and the tape player and set off. We try to get Raj to come along, but no go. We follow a narrow dirt trail that snakes through a dense patch of towering trees. Ian and Dave walk ahead while George and I hang back a few steps. While Neil Young's "Heart of Gold" plays, George opens up about how much he misses Deborah, and how ill prepared he is for spending this amount of time away from her.

"You know," I stop and say. "Maybe it's the distance talking, but hearing you go on about missing Deborah is very touching George. Who was it who said, 'Gravity cannot be held responsible for people falling in love?'"

"Einstein, actually," he says half smiling.

"I was listening to you talk to Deb on the phone last night," I say. "It was like hearing myself last year when things were good with Mary, and I had my head on straight."

We stop and let the others go on. "Let me ask you. Do you still love Mary?" he asks like he's trying to tell me what the answer should be.

"I think we may have gotten better at hurting each other than healing each other," I say ducking the question.

"Maybe both those scenarios are equally lethal," George counters.

I think about that for a minute and then go on. "I always thought she was the one who was gonna save me. But I have to admit, there's always been a desperate fleeting feeling that underscored our relationship."

"You know," he says, pausing to pick up an old branch that would make for a good walking stick. "The one thing a lot of people have sort of said for a while now is, 'are Bill and Mary even still going out? They seem to just fight all the time.'"

"That really saddens me, George," I say looking up at the canopy of trees sheltering us. "But I guess I shouldn't be surprised. I mean, it's been so long since we've shown the rest of the world we care for each other. We never stopped to think what damage was being done keeping our relationship on the down low for the sake of the band. And you know, a relationship needs a brave showing from time to time so..." I trail off.

"So people who care about you can bear witness to it," he says finishing my thought.

"Exactly," I say. I glance up at him knowingly, our thoughts aligned as is so often the case when we talk. It's like I can't get to a part of myself otherwise, and I think it's the same for him.

"See, Mary and I always held on because there was nothing else that filled the holes inside like we could for each other — until the band started to succeed. It's like the more the band took off,

33 Days   **100**

the worse it got for us," I say picking up a rock and throwing it deep into the trees.

"I never really realized that was happening," he says arching his eyebrows and stamping the ground with the walking stick.

I look ahead at Ian who's stopped and looking back at us. I wave him on and continue, "But tell me, George. Did we ever seem in love?"

His face scrunches up. Looks like he's trying to decide how honest an answer he wants to give me, and I stand there not sure what I want to hear. Finally he offers, "Well, there's always been a certain electricity between you two — to a sometimes toxic degree, I might add. So...I don't know if I can answer the question 'in love?' or not. Maybe 'in lust.' But listen, you need to ask yourself if you're in love with someone in the here and now, or in love with an idea stuck in another time. If there's something to save, then leave nothing undone trying to save it," he says placing his hand on my shoulder. "But it just sounds like you're stuck between two selves right now. The one you've been, and the one you could be."

As I chew on that, my mind goes places again.

* * *

The auto accident took away any chance Mary had to go to England. As she lay in bed recovering for the next month, I couldn't help but feel haunted and somehow responsible. I'd quietly wished she'd stay with me and not go to England. For all I knew, all she wanted was to share a laugh until she stepped on that plane to begin her new life abroad.

After the accident, I was pretty shy around her. I knew if I wasn't careful, I'd find myself overmatched. She was whip smart, charismatic, beautiful. I was convinced she was the angel who survived death so she could save me. I was sure that she, alone, could rewrite a childhood for me — one without toxins.

By the time she was on her feet again, Mary had volunteered to manage the band. Soon we were inseparable. Her parents went out of town, and she invited me to stay while they were gone. By then, I'd told her I loved her. I arrived at her door with a knapsack and my guitar like some traveling hobo. After I settle in, she takes me by the hand and leads me upstairs where we finally make love through the afternoon.

She tells me when she was about 13 her mom packed her, her sister and brother up and left because her dad's drinking had gotten so bad. She says her dad then quit drinking and her mom took him back, but he then essentially became a dry drunk, white-knuckling it, not drinking but still exhibiting all the signs of an alcoholic. In order to cope with all this, her mom started going to something called Al-Anon. I tell Mary a little about what it's like at 940, and I guess she tells her mom about it because a short time after that her mom suggests that I should try Al-Anon too. Whatever.

With Mary, I was sure I'd been joined with my missing half. We drew each other's fears out of the far reaches of our souls. And why? Because we knew they didn't belong there. We both knew we possessed precious gifts that hadn't been nurtured so we stood over each other with our mending tools. She said when we were born we had magnets placed between our bosoms that drew us toward each other and that I was meant to fit inside her. For wild, wonderful stretches, we existed in a separate, lovely dimension, but there's always a desperate feeling with us, like it might all go up in smoke at any moment.

* * *

"Hey, you've got to see this," Ian shouts out to us.

George and I join the rest who are taking in the most gorgeous sunset. We all stare out at the ocean after the last of the sun vanishes over the horizon. A fiery red-orange glow still resonates. As we all stand together, you can't help but feel euphoric and defiant. Everything feels possible.

"What a perfect place for a statement of purpose," George finally says breaking the silence. We all look at him. "Guys," he says, "you *do* realize we're gonna make it, don't you? We're going to be kings."

I don't need to look around to know everyone has little Mona Lisa smiles on.

Raj stayed behind. Said he was going to catch up on some sleep, but I know it's because he feels so estranged from us. This is really scaring me now. I mean, I can't make him see what's there for the taking. Only he can. And only if he wants it. I keep wanting to scream at him "What's the fucking alternative? Go home knowing you abandoned the one chance you had to be free?" I've always taken it upon myself to make sure he was taken care of, but I can feel myself letting him separate from us now. I'm really at a loss right now.

We're crossing the border tomorrow, so we thought best to smoke the last of what's been christened Ian's Groove Weed. We light a campfire and sit there for hours just talking and getting increasingly wasted. We move to the sleeping bags and lay there on the dirt staring into the vast expanse of the sky. Crowds of stars seem to be shining no more than an arm's length away. The evening has slowed down and quieted to little more than whispers. I start seeing these old scenes from my childhood and try to describe it for everyone.

"I remember driving up my street the morning after a fire swept through our neighborhood. I must have been about 12, I guess. The night before, two firemen came to our door and told us we had to evacuate. I grab my journals, a stack of my favorite records and a picture of me and my grandfather at the zoo when I was three. The next morning, I ask my grandfather if 940 made it. He says he doesn't know and we slowly drive past house after house reduced to skeleton frames. People are out front just staring with gut-wrenching looks on their faces. We round the last turn before 940, and then we see it. It made it. By four houses. We drive further up the street and there's St. Matthew's Church, all that's left of it. We both get out and walk toward the remains. The dying embers give off an ominous stench. I ask my grandfather how could God let a church burn down? His back is to me and he doesn't answer. I walk around his big frame and see tears are running down his face. That was the only time I saw him cry."

We call over to Raj and ask him to join us again, but he says he's tired and just wants to sleep. I know that's not it. The sliding door to the van is open, and I see him thrashing about.

Meanwhile, these strange and wonderful images flash before me…George's dad coming home from jail and his family going up to Kernville where they always vacationed…then trying to convince everyone that the state of Michigan is shaped like an oven mitt. All sorts of crazy shit.

Then something I forgot comes to me. I sit up, cross my legs and look down into my lap and begin.

"When I was nine, I sat with my mom on her bed just after Larry See split and he gave us notice to vacate the premises. It's late morning and the curtains are drawn, the lights all off. She's speaking in that eerie calm voice she has. The one that means she's really losing it inside, and as she speaks, her body rocks slowly back and forth. She says things are so bad that our lives aren't worth living anymore. She says she's going to take Larry's pistol that's in the psychedelic-designed cardboard box under the bed and first kill me and then herself. I ask her why doesn't she believe in us and tell her we can make it. She looks away for a long, long time just puffing on her cigarette. And I remember this feeling like…this exceeds my capacity to understand, and I have this awareness like I'm working harder than ever to make sense of it. Then all of a sudden, she shifts gears and tells me things will work out and to go outside and play. I scowl, knowing she's lying, but so badly wanting to just be nine and hear things are going to be fine. So I go outside and make a fantasy championship basketball game appear. After a few minutes, I stop and stand still, and wonder if I'll hear a gunshot in the next minute. I guess I'm still waiting for it."

I look up and say: "I've never told that story to anyone before."

I lay there just staring into that huge diamond sky thinking, at last, that third dimension, that world of folly and fantasy I've always sought refuge in, was now gone. Everything I ever ran from isn't here anymore. It's back *there*. What's here now are the possibilities. All within our reach. We are now dreaming by day with open eyes, finally with a chance…to make it possible.

*   *   *

Day Eight
8/4/87

Everything worked out crossing the border. Raj found my missing wallet this morning so we're still a quartet.

We've been gone a week today, and other than the 12-hour drive to Portland, the show there, and then scurrying off to Seattle, the pace has been leisurely. Too leisurely for my taste. It's all about to change. It's Vancouver tonight, then we leave right after because it's a 17-hour drive to Calgary where we begin a three-night stand, two shows a night.

We're already dangerously low on funds. Gas is a lot more expensive in Canada, and we haven't been paid for four days.

We roll into Vancouver to this funky area called Gastown with a cool European feel to it. We're playing this club called the Gaslight that sits over a cobblestone square with a steam clock. Except for all the cars, it looks like it's the late 1800s or something.

We about rupture our backs hauling our gear up the long, thin, spindly stairway leading up to the club. Cool feel inside. Tall ceiling held up by three massive pillars that kind of divide the club up into sections. The stage faces out a big window overlooking Gastown Square.

We throw down our stuff and introduce ourselves to the headliner, Short Dogs Grow. We thought we had tour stories. These guys have been out on the road for three months just wildly criss-crossing the country. On the trek, they've had two members quit, found replacements on the fly, had their equipment ripped off, and their van has broken down three times.

George leaves to call Deborah while the rest of us have a drink with Short Dogs Grow. I take out my journal and write down a Hunter S. Thompson quote their singer shares with us: "The music business is a cruel and shallow money trench. A long plastic hallway where thieves and pimps run free and good men die like dogs. There's also a negative side." Classic.

As we're about to leave for dinner, Raj emerges from the van completely shaven and dressed about as nicely as one can living out of a van. All he says is he has to meet some friends of the family for dinner and he'll see us in time for the show.

When George gets back, he seems preoccupied. As we head down the street to look for something cheap to eat, he pulls me aside. "Listen," he says out of earshot of the rest of the guys, "I know what I said back in Frisco, but that already feels like another lifetime."

"What do you mean?" I ask.

The rest of the guys duck into a little café, and George and I stop before heading in. "I just...I miss Deb. And honestly, I didn't expect her to miss *me* so much. I don't know. I just wish we were bigger. I just wish we had enough money to stay in hotels so she could join us..." He sighs, trails off. I give him a puzzled look but don't say anything. "Come on," he says. "Let's go eat, I'm starving. We can talk about it at dinner."

Not sure what he's getting at but our dinner conversation ends up gravitating toward Raj. While we wait for our food, Ian catches us off guard by asking how many of us think Raj will be with us for the fall tour. We all steal glances at each other. I know it's been a roller coaster ride with Raj so far, but I'm pretty surprised when no one but me raises their hand.

I tell everyone not to count him out yet, but I admit, he *has* seemed pretty manic. Sky high one minute only to nosedive into the depths the next.

"I talked to Raj for a long time last night at the campsite," Dave says taking a huge bite of his burger. "He's dealing with a lot of shit. His family's going through some tough times, and I guess in his culture, you just don't do something like this. You just don't leave your family behind. I told him this was his time now, and that he's meant to play guitar for Divine Weeks and that's that, but he just can't let it go."

"I know, he told me. But listen, at some point," I reason, "he'll be forced to accept he has literally nothing to show for all those years he denied himself what makes him feel alive. And I, for one, want to be around to see it."

"I know, but Christ almighty," George pipes in, "he's become a real drag, and I'm getting pretty tired of him getting sanctimonious about the rest of us taking this whole experience in."

"Well, wait. None of us can understand what he's going through," Ian interjects. "None of us were raised with the cultural constraints or anything remotely similar hanging over our heads. Plus, did he tell you? That dinner tonight he's going to? It's with some family friend from the same Indian village his dad grew up in. Very traditional guy apparently. That's why Raj got all shaved and was trying to look all presentable. He's really worried what this guy's going to report back to his folks."

"Hmmmm, interesting," I say finishing the last of the tuna melt I'm sharing with Ian.

Toward the end of dinner, George catches us completely off guard when he says he and Deb were talking and wondered, since Ian couldn't commit to the fall tour, what we all think about her coming in his place. Everyone falls silent. I know George is lovesick and all, but four guys in a little van is enough of a soap opera. Throw in a relationship, and it's certain disaster. That's the very reason Mary is at home, and we took Ian. I try to divert things by pointing out that right before a show is no time to get into this and promise George we'll talk about it later. He's quiet on the walk back to the club. I admit, I'm shocked he even asked if she can come next tour.

We haven't showered since we were at the yuppies', and my hair is all over the place. I put it up in my white and blue bandana I stole back from Dave. I've got a black vest over my long-sleeve white shirt. Raj is looking mean in George's leather jacket over a white v-neck shirt. Dave walks on stage shirtless and shoeless in a pair of Guatemalan patterned shorts he bought at Pike Place. George is wearing his *Never Mind The Bollocks* shirt, jeans and motorcycle boots.

We're all jacked up playing live again, and the first half of tonight's show is great with a core group up front really into us. Then George breaks a string and for some reason he insists on changing it onstage instead of switching to his backup bass. Totally kills the momentum and kind of pisses the rest of us off. We try to get our mojo back, but we can't quite wind it back up again. Some people in back sit like statues and no matter what we do they are, quite literally, unmoved. Naturally, we become obsessed with winning them over, and the show probably suffers a little bit for it. Very frustrating gig.

While Dave, Ian and I sit at the bar commiserating over it, Ian throws in our faces our own words, a vow we made the night we toasted the tour with Ian. To wit: never punish those who are giving something back because a few are not.

As for Raj, he seemed lost as the gig wore on. Afterwards I ask Ian if he noticed, and he agrees. "Totally disconnected," he says shaking his head. "I'm officially worried."

As we watch Short Dogs Grow's set, we become fascinated over the mood in the club. It's festive. Everyone seems to be celebrating something. Seems like everyone in the whole club is just trashed too.

Dave orders another round and asks the bartender, "Hey, what's going on tonight? Did a war end or something? What's up?"

"Oh, today the welfare checks were issued," he says comping our drinks. "A big percentage of Vancouverites are on welfare, and act like drunken sailors on leave. Checks come in, everyone cashes them, goes out and gets sloshed, and then lives on next to nothing until the next check comes."

"I guess we lucked out playing tonight," Dave says throwing back a shot.

"Yeah," he says pouring Dave another shot. "If you played here last night, you would've been pretty lonely."

It's getting late and while we wait for the owner to tally up the money, something happens that's still got my head humming.

Dave and I are just sitting at the bar when this lady who looks like 40 miles of old dirt road slides over next to me and says, "You know, you look a lot like my son. He's a good kid. 'Least the last time I saw him. Haven't seen him for about 15 years."

I look her over, and I know I shouldn't ask, but I do: "How come?"

"Because I'm a drunk," she says, tossing back the rest of her drink. "Eventually everyone gives up on a drunk. You talked to your mother lately?"

I squint at her and don't say anything. I just nod yes.

"She bad off like me?"

"I don't know you enough to…"

"*Come on son. Look at me,*" she says pounding her glass down on the bar. "Is she bad off like *me*?"

She moves over close enough so I can smell her. I don't know why I say it, but I do: "O.K., she drinks."

"You pour out her liquor? It's a waste, you know? We can always find ways to get more. Ya clean up her messes? Bail her out of jail?

I look out through the window that looks out over Gastown Square.

"Listen, you gotta know something," she says, ordering another drink. "For years, I told my son, if you attack me, it only confirms the shit opinion I already have of myself. Ya see, we hate ourselves enough already. I told him not to let his love for me make him do what I ought to do for myself. But he never listened. Told him not to accept my promises either. Hell, we'll promise anything to get off the hook. You can't believe what we tell you. It's probably a lie. We go on the way we do so long as we know we've got fools who're willin' to hold us up."

She throws back the rest of her drink and stands up. "I told my son all this, and he just kept trying to save me. I told him he'd end up hating me, but he wouldn't believe me. 'Course he finally did. You hearin' any of this?"

We stare at each other until she finally sniffs and lurches away. I look back at Dave and stare until he blinks and turns away.

It's time to check on the money. I walk toward the owner's office and grab Raj for courage. I stand at the doorway and the owner holds up his hand at me and continues on with his phone call. I still feel a little disjointed as I straddle the doorway. The owner then hangs up and motions for us to come in and sit down.

The guy starts in about how tough times are and my stomach starts to tighten. It's not like back in L.A. where we can just trudge back home with a shrug and an "Oh well." We need every last penny. I look over at Raj, and I have an epiphany of sorts. Those days of feeling like we're just lucky to be there are now just a pair of taillights on the horizon. I know I can't sit on my feelings and let us get taken. Meekly accepting some bullshit story is only going to leave us stranded in the Canadian Rockies.

When he finishes I say, "Listen, we don't fucking have gas money. This isn't some story to pad our huge earnings here. I don't think we're going to fucking make it to Calgary unless you pay us what you *agreed* to pay us. Forget eating. I'm talking gas money just to get there. We delivered what we promised; now it's your turn."

I hold my breath as he stares holes back at me through tiny eye slits. Then a remarkable thing happens. He sighs and reaches into his back pocket and pulls out our guarantee plus an extra 20 dollars Canadian. "All right," he says. "You guys put out tonight. And to boot, you've got some balls. I like that. Good luck to you."

* * *

Day Nine
8/5/87

We leave straight from the club and hit the road for Calgary. Seventeen hours we're told. The rest of us are trashed so Raj takes the first shift driving, and I join him in the front passenger seat while everyone else sleeps in back.

Ian in the back of the van. Photo by Dave Smerdzinski

Up front, one drives and the so-called navigator's job is to make sure the driver doesn't nod off and kill us all.

Unless you're completely zonked and just want to sleep, there's a little competition for who gets to be up front because the three in back are packed in like sardines laying in opposite directions so you've got someone's feet in your face all the time. There's no windows back there so we've taped to the ceiling posters, postcards, assorted one-liners, inside jokes, and other odds and ends. Any diversion from having to stare at each other endlessly. Plus, it's like a sauna in back, no ventilation and, frankly, it stinks. Talk about getting to know each other intimately. We don't even bother trying to lie and deny it — everyone knows each other's farts.

Where no one wants to get stuck is the spot closest to all the gear which is stacked high up to the roof of the van. It's pretty harrowing when we hit a bump or a big turn and whoever is stuck in the unenviable spot under the teetering pile just stares up praying an anvil case doesn't come crashing down on him.

Deep into the Canadian Rockies just before dawn I about have a fucking heart attack as I wake up to Raj shouting over and over: "Oh…my…God!"

I look over and Raj looks like he's just been hit by something, madly looking around in every direction. "I remember getting gas a while ago," he says slowly, "but I don't remember...the last 20 minutes...*at all.*"

Scary. It's a miracle more bands who tour like this aren't killed. The all-night drives, the drinking, the comedown from the high of the show. D. Boon of the Minutemen died that way — asleep in the back of a van that went off the road.

We finally pull into Calgary at about 6:30 p.m. Well, it wasn't 17 hours. Only 16.

The Winter Olympics are coming here next summer, and it's obvious that the city is trying to clean up all the sleaze and riff-raff to a small two-block area around a dump called the National Hotel. The Nash. Where the red light shines brightly. Naturally, that's where we're staying the next four nights.

Simply put, the Nash is a hot pillow joint. A brothel. They rent rooms by the hour. The owner is a distasteful little troll named

Caesar. He shows us to our rooms and tells us very matter-of-factly to be careful sleeping under the sheets. "We have a nasty case of crabs going around so be careful, boys." As we walk down the long corridors, it smells equal parts smoke and piss. Doesn't seem like anyone is actually staying here — any more than an hour that is.

Our van parked in front of The Nash, Calgary. Photo by Ian Bader

Caesar tells us he's unilaterally moved back our three-night run of shows here until tomorrow night. We're pretty gutted from the all-night, all-day drive, so we don't mind much. We go downstairs to check out the band playing. The banner behind them reads U.I.C. From Toronto. Pretty rockin' band. After they finish a song that sounds a lot like "I Wanna Be Your Dog," I lean over to George and say, "Big Stooges fans, eh?" While George thoughtfully rubs his chin, they begin the familiar intro to, yes Virginia, "I Wanna Be Your Dog."

Good guys though. After their set, they invite us back to their table where they give us the scoop on touring Canada. They say you get booked to play these hotels for several nights. You play two sets a night, the hotels put you up for free and pay decently — better than the clubs actually. Then they give us their take on the Canadian welfare system. They just cruised through Vancouver, picked up $150 Canadian worth of food stamps and are now headed back to Toronto. The guitarist says it's not socialism, it's taking care of your own.

"We'll drop that sentiment in Mr. Reagan's suggestion box," Ian says.

"Yeah," George cracks, "it can keep company with all the other social reform programs gathering dust in there."

They tell us Calgary is an old cowboy stop that still hosts the Calgary Stampede every year. Like a time warp, real cowboys still roam these parts. Makes for an interesting population mix. A hip, arty, intellectual college crowd mixes uneasily with old high plains drifters — or as the locals call them, dirtheads.

We talk well past closing, hopelessly trying to keep pace with Canadian drinking habits. We practically have to crawl back to our rooms. Heeding Caesar's warning about the crabs, we put our sleeping bags on top of our beds. These mattresses have big sinkholes in their midsections. You lay down, and it's kind of like having your ass get sucked down some imaginary drain.

"I reckon these mattresses weren't done in by kids playing trampoline on them," Ian offers.

Just then we hear through the paper-thin walls grunts and groans mixed with the squeaking sounds of bedsprings being over-worked.

Eeee-eh, eee-eh.

"Oh baby, yeah…"

Eeee-eh, eee-eh.

"Oh Jesus, yes, yes…"

"No, I imagine not," George concedes before face-planting onto his bed.

* * *

Day Ten
8/6/87

This morning we get our money exchanged into Canadian at a mini-mart just down the street. Later in the day, we realize we got royally screwed. The guy told us the exchange rate was $1.15 Canadian per U.S. dollar, but after we run a few errands and mail some postcards home, we learn it's really $1.31 per dollar. The price of an education is getting steeper and money is getting tight. We haven't been paid since the gig in Seattle a week ago, and Ian tells us that until we get paid at the end of our three-night stand at the Nash we've got to be careful.

On travel days, we can usually hold out until midday and can get away with just eating a PB&J and then hopefully scam some free food off the club or someone we meet and we're good. But bunkered down here for four days at the Nash where we won't get shit from that tight-ass Caesar, we'll have to space our meals out carefully. That's why sleeping in past lunchtime has its benefits. A couple less meals to worry about each day.

Dave and George shopping for hats.   Photo by Ian Bader

The best thing about our run at the Nash is we get to keep our equipment set up and rehearse anytime we want. During the drive yesterday we were listening to the Who's *Live at Leeds* and got the idea to piece together a Who medley out of the *Tommy* bits found on side two. This afternoon, Raj and I worked out an arrangement. The plan is we'll start with part of the "Overture," then go into "Sparks" and finish off with "See Me, Feel Me." George and Dave weave together a nice rumbling roller coaster ride rhythmically. We're calling it "The Who Thing."

We have some time to kill before the show so we go back upstairs and have our daily PB&Js. While I catch up on my journal, the rest of the guys all gather around Dave's bed where he's holding court. He opens a few beers and passes them around, then regales us with what he claims is a tape of his old band, Tyrant, from his club days in Washington D.C., playing Hendrix's "Purple Haze." As I write all this down, I'm amazed. They sound big and professional as all hell.

George says incredulously, "Shit Dave, you guys were *rockin'*." At the end of the song, the crowd noise is huge and deafening. It sounds like they're playing in front of thousands.

"Jesus Dave, where in all fuck was this?" Ian asks having just returned from doing laundry downstairs. "Christ, how many people were there?"

"I've been telling you guys things are different back East," Dave says now getting a little more animated and knowing we've bought it. "Yeah buddy, Tyrant worked up a nice little following." Silence falls over the room for a minute as that sinks in.

Finally Dave can't take it anymore and starts howling, confessing that we're listening to fucking Randy Hansen at some Woodstock revisited live gig he taped off the goddamn TV in the '70s. Dave rolls on his bed holding his side laughing. "George, you should've seen the look on your face."

"George's gullibility is one of his more endearing qualities," I stop journaling to announce.

"Oh yeah?" he protests. "Name one instance."

"Oh George," I say getting up to grab a beer and join the others. "Don't make me tell everybody about the time I called you right after your 18th birthday and convinced you the U.S. government had changed the rules of the draft and classified you as part of the first group to be called."

George's eyes widen. "That's *right,* you fucker. I still haven't gotten over that!" he screams.

"Bill, how *could* you?" Ian scowls.

"Hey, what about that old VW bug you had, Bill?" Raj asks.

"That wasn't my fucking fault!" George cries out.

"Are we going to talk about sparks, George?" I ask.

"You're goddamn right we're gonna talk about sparks!" he shouts.

"Sparks?" Ian asks.

My shitty old Bug had a terrible electrical problem and sparks would inexplicably go off under the dash. George would be riding shotgun and a spark would go off and he'd shout, "Did you see that?" pointing frantically. Naturally I'd deny seeing it.

It was especially exciting in the rain. It's a fucking wonder I didn't blow up or get shot in that old thing. Only the high beams would work so I'd come up behind someone and they'd suddenly become enraged, flipping me off and pointing menacingly.

"Admit it!" George demanded wildly waving his arms. "Sparks flew out of that fucking dashboard! *Admit it!*"

We're now all laughing. Except for George. The man wants redemption. Thing is, like Dave, when poor George gets mad he's terribly funny.

"All right, George," I say very quietly to him. "There were sparks. I saw them every time too."

"At last!" he screams. "I hope everyone heard that! Did everyone hear that? Everyone?"

"I'm sorry, George, I missed it," Ian says dryly. "What was that?"

"Bill, would you say it again please. Ian missed it."

"Say what, George?" I ask innocently.

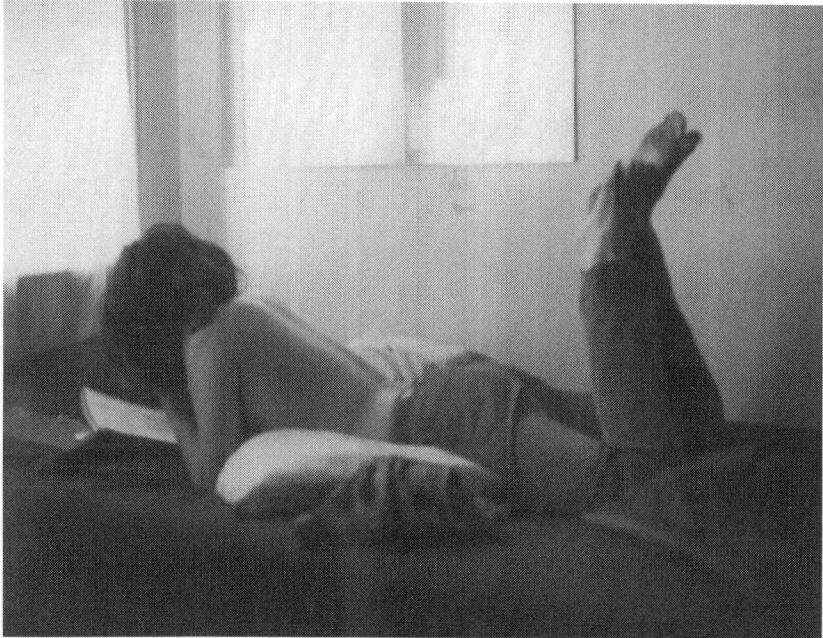

Me catching up on my journal, the Nash, Calgary. Photo by Ian Bader

"The part about the sparks. You know, that I wasn't crazy, and they were going off and, you know…the sparks…that were…sparking…"

I stare at him blankly. "Sparks George? What sparks?"

"*Ahhhhhhhhh*!!!"

When we walk downstairs, the crowd consists of three people sitting at three separate tables. Two dirtheads and a frightening-looking exotic dancer who wasted little time telling us her name was Mickey Saturn (not clear if that was her destination or place of origin), and she's looking for company.

Mickey is pretty scary. Ian tells me later she goes up to him while we're onstage and explains that her old man is a trucker who's been away too long, and she has to fuck somebody. Ian says she asked him what her chances were getting me in the sack. God bless him, he says, "Well, two, I guess: slim and none. And slim just split."

"Then how 'bout that brown one," she says pointing at Raj.

"You know," Ian tries to explain, "I'm sure there's some charming fellows back there in the pool hall who won't give you much resistance."

After we do a quick soundcheck, we sit and have a drink before the show. Dave is in the middle of a story about tripping at a Dead show earlier this summer when we notice George wander up onstage and start adjusting the knobs on Raj's Marshall. Kind of like cooking with someone who adds more pepper to the soup when you're not looking.

"George, we just soundchecked," Raj says trying to be patient. "What's the story?"

"Just refining your sound, my man," he says unapologetically.

Dave, never concerned with sounding impatient, or pissed off, for that matter, gets up and barks, "George, leave it the fuck alone, or I'll start refining your ass."

"Sor-ree," George shoots back, now exasperated. "Just trying to help Raj sound big and burly."

"How about this, George," Dave says, now very animated, "during the set, if I don't like the way you sound, I'll just reach over with my drumstick and *refine* your sound, fair enough?"

The soundman said the place would slowly fill up so we do a bunch of throwaway covers for a good half-hour before getting to our own songs. Some guy halfway back promises he and his buddies will move closer if we play the Stones' "Honky Tonk Woman" which we do even though we've never played it before. Later, I give some guy with one leg my guitar to play on our long jamming end of "When I Go." Everybody loved that. Shit, we'll do anything to bridge the gap between us and the audience.

It's good and packed for our second set. In between sets, I move all the tables in front of the stage to along the walls so it's standing room only up front. As we start, I motion for everyone to stand in front of the stage so we can feed off their energy. Works too. A totally different vibe from the first set. Everyone goes apeshit for "The Who Thing" which looks like a keeper. We all think we just killed tonight. Except for George. He tells us a guy said the mix was shitty. Typical George, he lets one random comment ruin the whole night for him. We're all talking about emotionally connecting with the audience and tearing down barriers and George lets success hinge on one negative comment from some random stranger.

After the show, we get invited to a party thrown by a very cool guy named Mark who climbs in the van and rides with us over to his place. He tumbles into the back and a pained look comes over his face. "Guys, no offense, but what *died* in here?"

"Sorry, dude," Dave says handing him some matches. "Light this."

"And where's the windows?" Mark asks. "Don't you guys get claustrophobic back here?"

"It helps to be so wasted you just pass out," George says, already pretty lit.

It's a pretty typical college-pad party. Everyone chips in to buy beer. People are either hanging out in the kitchen or crowded around Mark's record collection taking out their favorites in a game of pull-out-the-coolest-record oneupmanship.

I get into this very deep conversation with a pretty black-haired girl with a nose ring named Christina who calls herself a French-Canadian Socialist. She says she's going to Nicaragua this fall to see for herself what's really going on down there because she's grown distrustful of the mainstream media's slant. It's nice to talk with someone who doesn't smell like the inside of a van.

Man, these Canadians never grow tired. We've been trying to match them drink for drink, but Canadian beer contains about three times the amount of alcohol as American beer, and we're all going to be ready for rehab if we try to keep pace with them. It gets late and the exhaustion and alcohol slow the room down to about 16 rpm. I guess George is still brooding about the gig and whatever else because he gets pretty plastered and starts saying some crazy shit.

"I'm telling you, Raj, just fucking listen," he says weaving a little. "We've *got* to make it happen *now,* motherfucker. I don't fucking know about you, but I wanna be fucking *huge*, a fucking *king*. And we're not gonna fucking do it playing shitholes like the fucking Nash surrounded by a bunch of fucking dirtheads, pimps and whores."

Raj looks up at George and says evenly, "Got it, George. No dirtheads, no pimps for you."

"And no whores," I remind him.

"Wait, no whores? You sure?" Ian pipes in. "What about girls with, say, a morally casual attitude?"

"All right, keep the fucking whores," George says, taking another long swig. "But that's fucking *it*! Now listen, motherfucker. This is *all* shit, I'm telling you. We're supposed to be taking over the goddamn world, and we're not gonna fucking do it stuck out here in the sticks of Canada. We've got to fucking take over and rule, goddamnit. 'Cos if it doesn't start happening, and I mean right fucking *now*, we may as well just go home. And I'll tell you another thing. I'm not sleeping at that shithole again tonight. Got that Raj? When we get back in that fucking van, you just keep driving and don't stop at that sewer pit."

"Got it George," Raj says looking over at me and smiling. "Straight past the Nash and check into the Hilton."

Well, like I said, *sometimes* George's visions of grandeur are endearing. Other times, his whole "we better become huge or forget the whole thing" gets a little grating. We'll see what he remembers tomorrow.

When we get up to leave, Christina turns all sad and pouty wanting to come back with us. She's really pretty and all, but I don't know. Maybe I'm just being loyal to something that's not really there anymore with Mary. I'll admit it: I'm scared of not being attached to someone while we're out here. Being attached to someone grounds me. That's what fucked me up the last six months with Mary and me being on and off — mostly off — and all this new stuff coming at me. For the first time in my life, I got some real outside validation. Caught me completely off guard too. Hell, I think it catches anyone off guard if you never had it before. It's like fear of starvation. You panic and think the first taste is the last you'll ever get.

The night it kind of all changed for us was this gig we did downtown at a place called the 116 Gallery opening for fIREHOSE right before we started recording *Through and Through*. The night we turned the corner and became a player in the L.A. club scene — a night a young band dreams about.

The place is just packed. I'd never taken the stage and seen wall-to-wall people staring up at me. A big unfamiliar crowd can paralyze you. They're impatient for the headliner, standing there with that look that says "O.K., impress us." But if you can deliver in that setting, well, you might be on your way. After we finish our first song, the crowd's reaction is unlike anything we've experienced before. It was actually startling. I look over at George and he has this look like "So, *this* is what it's supposed to be like." In the middle of the next song I glance over at him, and he's just gone — on the road to bliss. Raj, same thing. So I go too. Every insecurity that's ever held us back falls away. At last we have our invitation to that great highway we always thought was off limits.

During Raj's solo on "Look Book," I jump up and grab hold of the ceiling fixtures and climb jungle-gym style until I'm halfway out into the room. I look down at an ocean full of heads swaying and arms reaching up to me. At that moment, I don't know if I want to jump down there and throw my arms around every one of them or start throwing punches. It's hard to explain — it's this primal urge to fuck and kill everyone. And not just who's there. It's the ghosts of who's *not* there, it's who's *supposed* to be there, and the people you're hoping are *gonna* be there one day.

It really wasn't until I was onstage — with this band — that I felt...*necessary*; that I felt *relevant*. Away from the stage, living someone else's dream, I've felt a fake and unable to connect on any meaningful level with anyone. The stage is the only place I feel authentic, outside of maybe Mary when we were getting on. I remember Oliver Goldsmith wrote, "On the stage he was natural, simple, affecting. 'Twas only when he was off he was acting."

We'd had some good gigs before but never in that setting with the stakes so high. Droves of strangers come up to us after the show saying how much they dug us, the sort of people I'd see at big shows around town, the ones I always wished were at our dinky little gigs. The impeccably hip sort that rolled their eyes when I tried to give them one of our crummy flyers.

Then this woman comes up to me and asks me to write out the lyrics to the song I'd introduced as being about Jim Carroll, the poet/author/musician. I really dug his *Basketball Diaries* and wrote a song inspired by it called "In the Country (For Jim Carroll)." All she says is she wants to "show them to someone." A few weeks later she calls Mary introducing herself as Rosemary Carroll, Jim's wife, and says he wants us to open for him when he comes to town. That story got a lot of press and ended up being a pretty big deal.

I walk around the place just soaking it in. It feels great, but I'm sure we're transparent. Like we're the hicks who win the lottery, and we're at our first glitzy affair at the country club. I don't know, maybe I was afraid it was going to be our last taste.

As fIREHOSE begins their set, this girl comes up to me and after some frivolous chitchat, she takes my hand and leads me into a downstairs utility room, closes the door behind us and before I know it she's pressing herself against me. I hear fIREHOSE playing "Chemical Wire" right above us as I fall back against the door. She drops to her knees and unzips me. I look down and her eyes are shut very tightly. She makes loud moaning, humming sounds with her mouth, which sends little waves through me. I try to pull her up so I can kiss her, but she clearly has her mind set on what she wants to do. I try to warn her I'm about to come, but she just carries on. After, she stands up and washes it down with her Corona. We walk back out into the main room again, and before I know it she's disappeared into the crush of the crowd. It was all so surreal. I could almost hear the insinuating narrator's voice say, "Welcome to the party, pal."

Day Eleven
8/7/87

The moment we walked into the playing room at the Nash two nights ago, Raj says right off that the low ceiling might tempt him to pull the old Pete Townshend ram-the-guitar-neck-through-the-ceiling bit. Earlier today, he tells me he's feeling more and more out of control onstage, particularly on our set closer "Look Book." I tell him that's the best thing I've heard him say since we left.

"Bill, I know I've been pretty out of it on this whole tour," he says to me. "I just want you to know that today when you guys went out and I stayed behind, it was because I wanted to work on some of my parts. I know I haven't been holding up my end, and I just want to show you guys — at least onstage — you don't have anything to worry about. Onstage is really the only time I feel free to be, you know, *this*. I'm not going to let anything get in the way of that anymore, OK?"

He wasn't kidding. We close the first set with "Look Book," and he not only rams his guitar neck repeatedly through the ceiling panelings, but then he takes a mic stand to his guitar and creates the trashiest sheet of sound this side of Sonic Youth. Mark, the guy who threw the party last night, is so overcome he starts jumping up and down punching holes in the low ceiling with his fist. It's like an open invitation, I guess, because everyone in the club starts punching holes in the ceiling too. The club can't do anything. It's like a blackout when a crowd realizes there's too much chaos for the police to catch all the looters so everyone just goes apeshit.

We're just going with it digging on the chaos when Caesar, the Nash's crusty old owner, walks right onstage and grabs Raj by the arm and drags him and his 125 pounds off the stage like a rag doll through the club and into the back pool hall.

The three of us are left onstage in shock. The song limps along on autopilot for about 30 seconds before collapsing. Dave finally snaps out of it, throws down his sticks and marches right through the crowd to the back of the club and pushes through the double doors leading to the pool hall.

A college-age rock crowd goes to shows at the Nash, but a tough, older cowboy/trucker crowd hangs out back in the pool hall. Maybe to throw a few beers back after renting a room for an hour, or just to get wasted. When we first checked in, we poked our heads in there but quickly hightailed it outta there because there were some fucking scary-looking individuals lurking around.

When the rest of us catch up with Dave, Caesar's thrown Raj against a wall, and he's ranting to a bunch of cowboy types about how "this little brown fucker" is trying to destroy his place. "Someone call the fuckin' police," Caesar orders. Then one of Caesar's little flunkies realizes they're running a brothel and whispers that calling the cops isn't such a swell idea. It was classic. Caesar pauses to consider that, and then points at all of us and yells, "O.K., we won't call the cops...but you guys are gonna pay!"

Dave had heard enough. He stares everyone down, grabs Raj by the arm and says, "Come on, Raj, no one's gonna touch you. Fuck these guys. We don't have to take any of this shit." The rest of us circle around Raj and Dave marches him right out past the big group of goons back into the playing room. As soon as we all reappear, everyone in the place just starts cheering and begins chanting "Fuck Caesar!"

Raj is now sky high. He carries us through our second set which just rocks non-stop and is driven home with an emphatic encore of "The Who Thing" culminating in Raj throwing his guitar javelin-style across the stage. The crowd just loves it.

Caesar starts barking a bunch of crap at us about holding our pay and more bullshit about calling the cops. Ian calmly walks over to Caesar and tells him that the club is a dump, already trashed, and he can't pin on us the damage everyone else had done.

"Caesar, don't try and fuck with us in front of a crowd. It only makes you look like an even bigger ass than you already are. This club is the only thing that makes you legit, so why don't you just shut the fuck up about calling the cops or we'll just blow the whistle on your whole front here. You're no businessman. You're just a fuckin' pimp." I'm so proud of Ian. He even gives Caesar two light slaps against his cheek Mafioso-style. Caesar starts seething, but knows it's the truth and disappears into the back room and nurses a drink for the rest of the night.

Mark's brother Tom and his roommate Eric are hosting another party tonight. George is too wiped out and just wants to call Deb and catch up on some sleep. We're like Calgary's second sons now. Everyone at the party tells us almost starting a riot at the Nash has elevated us to legendary status. They all pitch in to buy us pizza and enough beer to start a brewery. The pizza is a welcome relief from the PB&Js, and other sordid concoctions we've been creating. Raj got so desperate for something different I caught him making a bologna and jelly sandwich today.

Tonight definitely puts Raj back in the game for the first time since the Seattle show over a week ago. At the party, Ian and Raj fall for a couple of cuties named Melissa and Jennifer. It's so great seeing Raj finally allow himself to take some pride in turning people on. I get into a heavy discussion with Mark and Tom about how Canada has adopted something of an inferiority complex about the U.S. Their take is that it's born out of sharing the U.S.-controlled media's slant on everything night in and night out. Christina is at the party again and we flirt a little, but that's it.

On our way back to the Nash, the sky has the first hint of that yellow-reddish hue you only see just before dawn. We open the sliding door of the van and Ian and I literally spill onto the sidewalk, completely shitfaced.

For some reason, I can't sleep and decide to take a walk. The sun is just rising, and the blinding morning rays feel like daggers in my eyes. I come to a pay phone and stare at it trying to decide what I can say to Mary. I dial and wait through three long rings.

It was late last year that Mary's and my relationship fell apart for the first time, right about the time the band started taking off. Word got back to me that she had an affair and when she finally copped to it, she said I'd smothered her and had become too needy. I feigned understanding it all but my world's been pretty much rocked off its axis ever since.

I guess I *had* become needy. After my grandfather died last year, I'd leave 940 and drive off to see her. I was so desperate for an escape, for a place to hide. Sometimes she wanted to be the one to save me. She reveled in it. Then other times, without so much as a warning, she resented me for leaning so hard and needing her so badly. She told me I needn't be a martyr to get love, but before I came to believe it I'd smothered her and soon her mind and her body were elsewhere.

For a time, I knew what true devotion was. She was all I wanted. No other girl looked attractive to me. Learning she looked elsewhere for affection pushed me into a period of moral bankruptcy that, I guess, is still going on. I've had one affair after another.

Mary's not picking up, and I can't think of a more lonely sound than that long tone from her answering machine. I freeze up, the words sticking to the very back of my throat, and I just hang up. I turn away from the pay phone and head back to the Nash singing the Replacements' "Answering Machine." "How do you say I miss you to an answering machine..." I climb up the fire escape and just sit there looking out at early Saturday morning arrive wondering where she is, what she's doing, who she's with.

* * *

Day Twelve
8/8/87

At around 4 p.m., I finally start to come to. The sound of the Ramones' "Blitzkrieg Bop" on guitar is reverberating from downstairs. I know it can't be Raj. "Strawberry Fields" maybe, but not "Blitzkrieg Bop." I look over and Dave is starting to stir. "Dave, you among the living?" I croak.

"Yeah, barely," he groans.

"Do you hear that? What the fuck is that?" I ask, trying to lift my head which feels like it weighs a ton.

"I don't know," he says, "but it's not helping my hangover any."

"No shit," I say throwing my feet onto the ground and staggering up.

Dave and I lumber out into the hall, and there's Ian and Raj looking disheveled and wondering the same thing.

"Who's playin' me axe?" Raj asks.

"Hey," Dave says suspiciously, "where the fuck is George?"

We all follow the sound downstairs and peek into the darkened club. There's George living out his rock god fantasies, slashing away at Raj's Les Paul, his Marshall blasting louder than it's ever been pushed. We watch just smiling until George executes an ending fit for a Who farewell concert. As we all cheer wildly, George quickly shrinks into that 12-year-old who gets caught trying to start the family car.

Dave reminds us we made plans to meet Mark and Tom for a Calgary favorite, chicken and chips and 60-cent drafts at a place called the St. Louie Hotel this afternoon. A couple former next-door neighbors of Dave's from Falls Church, Virginia live in Calgary and are meeting us there. They've invited us for a home-cooked meal tomorrow night, our last night in town. We try to convince Raj to come, but he says his family told him to try and find some cheap arthritis medicine for his mom. Not sure how he's gonna pay for it. We can barely afford our next meal.

After dinner and several 60-cent drafts, we go back to the hotel and relax before our grand finale at the Nash tonight. We don't get much rest though. Somebody's getting all they can for their hour's worth next door. The paper-thin walls leave little to the imagination. Can't tell if somebody's having the time of their life or if a damn homicide is going down. It finally grows silent so I poke my head out into the hallway but see nothing. I turn to head back into my room when a door flings open and this Amazon-like woman walks out. I can't help staring at her tits barely covered by a tank top. If they were drooping any lower, she'd be kicking them like a couple of soccer balls.

She looks me up and down and then roars, "What in holy hell are you looking at?"

"Oh, you're alive," I deadpan.

"Don't worry about me baby," she says lighting a cigarette. "But you might want to check the pulse of the motherfucker I just worked over."

"Should I tell Caesar to call an ambulance or the morgue?" I say turning to head back inside.

"Hey," she says right before I close the door. "I'm good to go again if you want it baby." I just close the door. Entirely too frightening.

We're all dragging our asses tonight. We're somewhere between being hungover from last night and buzzed from this afternoon's drinking. Unlike the first couple nights here, a good number of people are already in the club waiting on us as showtime nears. The faces are becoming familiar. Something must be working because people keep coming back to check us out. Ian is messing around on George's bass, and I ask him where Dave and George are.

"Dave's in the little boy's room," Ian says, "and he took something to read so he might be a while. And George is on the phone with Deb — again."

Our new friend Tom, back for more, has my guitar and Mark climbs on the drums. Slowly the familiar strains of "Sympathy for the Devil" emerge from this new lineup, and it doesn't sound too bad so I join in. As we hit the "who-who" refrain, I spot Dave walking in through the back with a big smile on his face. He grabs a tambourine and joins along singing backup. George then appears and picks up some maracas and starts shaking them. I pull up some more people from the crowd and pass the guitar around. Soon, more people are onstage than in the audience. The stage is jammed with people, and the show hasn't even started.

We just play on and on tonight. Don't even bother with a break between sets. Sandwiched between our own stuff we do "Born on the Bayou" with more guest guitarists including George now that he's a certified Guitar God, "Fire" by Hendrix, "Sympathy" again and finally finish off with another resounding version of "The Who Thing." During the day, Raj still looks lost and disconnected, but onstage he's playing with as much focus and fury as I've ever seen.

Caesar waddles up to us afterwards and says he's deducting $50 from our fee for the damage. George, who's on the other side of the stage and still on a high from the show, lights into him: "Caesar, goddamn you. Get the fuck over here. If you think for one minute we're paying you shit after what you did to our guitarist...Caesar! Come back here, you little troll!" Caesar cowers away mumbling something over his shoulder about settling it tomorrow morning at checkout time and disappears into the pool hall.

Mark and Tom and the rest of our Calgary friends take us out for one more night on the town. After some barhopping, we end up at an after-hours club called Ga-Ga's on the other side of town. We all sit down at a little table in back with the girl who runs the place and tell her we don't have to be in Edmonton for another two days and wish we had a show to play tomorrow. She tells us we can play Ga-Ga's tomorrow night if we don't mind playing for what we can earn passing around a hat. "Sounds great, everybody cool with that?" Dave asks us all. I look over and George looks like he has to choke down some medicine, and I scowl at him. Raj quickly lightens up and says, "We'll be there. *Anything* but an off day."

* * *

Day Thirteen
8/9/87

George and I go downstairs to settle the score with Caesar who does deduct $50 from our $700 guarantee. Fifty bucks is actually not that bad considering the amount of damage that was done. Plus, we haven't made a dime since I begged that $75 out of the Vancouver booker last Tuesday, some five days ago, and the band's fund is basically tapped. Really, it could have been a lot worse. Caesar could have turned those cowboys loose on Raj and played a quick game of Stomp the Indian.

George is in a bad mood again about the indignity of having to haggle on our own behalf, and it's starting to get on my nerves.

After we pack everything up in the van, we head back upstairs one last time to make sure we haven't forgotten anything. We walk by Dave's room and notice he's taken all the light bulbs out of the sockets and he's pitching them one by one out of his second story window.

"Dave, what are you doing?" Raj asks innocently.

"Just giving the Nash back all the love it gave us," he says mischievously as we hear a light bulb explode on the street below.

Taking Dave's cue, George starts pulling the towel racks off the wall before taking aim at the dumpster in the alley. Ian then makes a knapsack out of a blanket and we throw everything we can in it — water glasses, the doorknob, the Bible, more light bulbs. Dave grabs his morning beer, takes a nice long swig and pours a chaser over the big heap. We haul a mattress out into the hallway and stuff the knapsack under it. We then each take turns making long running approaches down the hallway before pouncing on the big heap and marveling at the array of crunching sounds it makes. Maybe we've developed a complex from playing all that stuff by the Who.

Man, the Nash is the place time forgot. You could set a bomb off here on the second floor and no one would know, and if they did, they'd probably cheer. What a fucking dump.

On the way out, Dave punches a few more holes in the ceiling for good measure, and George and I spell out "Fuck Caesar" with duct tape on the back wall which Ian photographs for historical purposes. Finally, we steal four mic stands and a few patch cords and split. That oughta even the score for fucking with Raj.

When we get to Dave's old neighbor's house, they've fixed us a fabulous chicken curry dinner. Our two hours there sitting at a real table with clean napkins and silverware feel like a return to civilization after living with the scum the past few days.

As we pile back in the van to make soundcheck, two girls call down to us from a second-floor window in the house next door. The cute one with the cowboy hat eating an apple yells, "Hey, are you guys in a band or something? We like guys in bands."

Ian and Dave start walking toward their window. "Come on guys," George calls out. "They're just local yokels and jailbait at that."

After soundcheck Raj splits to call home, and Ian and Dave can't resist going back to try and persuade the two lovelies to come down to the show. They ask me if I want to come, but I say no thanks and go outside to talk with George who's sitting on the lip of a guardrail watching the sunset. He's been moody the last couple days. I take a seat next to him.

"Say George, what's the story?"

"What do you mean?" he asks.

"I don't know. I just want to make sure you're O.K., and we're all moving in the same direction. Just seems like you've been stressing more and more and kind of negative about everything."

"Hmmm, I don't follow."

"Well, all that stuff you said at that party the other night about how we've got to get huge, and if it doesn't happen — like *right now* — we may as well just go home."

A pained expression comes across his face and he says, "Well, I was pretty fucked up."

"Right," I say, "but it wasn't all that different from what you said to me in San Francisco the first day out."

"I won't lie. I *do* wish we were bigger. I *do* wish we had roadies and a kick-ass booking agent and bigger management that would crush any fucker who tries to screw us. And yeah, I wish we could fly Deb in so she could be with us. I won't apologize for being honest about that."

"I'm not expecting you to," I say a little exasperated, "but look where we are George. Slugging it out like the Minutemen and Hüsker Dü did on their first tour. It took them years to start breaking through. You *know* that, and you *know* the deal. It's little by little, day by day."

He pauses and looks out across the parking lot before saying soberly, "Bill, I don't know if I have that kind of time."

"You mean grad school?" I ask easing off. He doesn't show me anything, but I know it's either that or Deb's been at him again about how we should be bigger and further along — but I don't touch that. "I get that George — I *do*. But this is what's here and now. It's not like we have other options. If you're gonna keep stressing because we're not on some kind of fast track, it's going to be this very self-defeatist thing."

"Yeah I know, but come *on*," he turns it back on me. "You want to make it more than anyone."

"Yeah, I do, but for me, the minute I climbed in that van I had everything I ever dreamed. This is all I want."

"Oh *come on*, the fucking Nash? And tonight, playing for tips thrown in a fucking *hat*? I know you Bill. That's not *all* you want," he says staring holes through me. "You *know* we're better than that."

"You might be right, but look around," I say extending my arms outward. "This is all there is right now. And I'm all in for as long as it takes. Are *you*?"

"I am. I mean, I *want* to..." he pauses looking a little exposed. "Believe me, there's a part of me — a *big* part — that envies the rest of you guys. I wish I could just forget school, and forget everything else for that matter, but I *can't*. Don't take this the wrong way, but I've got more than the band. If I could just get some sign that we're really on our way I'd chuck all the rest, believe me, but..." He trails off.

As uncomfortable as I am leaving it at that, I don't really want to push this conversation any more than George probably wants to so we both head back in the club and see Dave skateboarding back and forth on the empty hard concrete floor.

"Any luck with the two lovelies?" I ask Ian.

"George was right," he says. "Jailbait."

Ga-Ga's is a real club, not like the makeshift scene in the basement of the Nash. Good sound system. Cool indie décor. Totally different crowd. All young college-age types, no dirtheads. Nice low ceiling, low stage, people jammed up to the front. More our element. As we watch the place fill up, I can tell it's going to be a good night. I'm in my red long-sleeved shirt, newsboy hat, black jeans. I walk to the mic and say, "Hey, we're Divine Weeks from Los Angeles, but don't hold that against us." A smattering of applause. "Listen, we need some love. We just spent the last few days at The Nash so cut us some slack, will ya?" I motion for people to move closer as Raj hits the intro to "Copper Wire" which has emerged as our full-time set opener. With that, a row of people take a few big steps toward the stage. When Dave and George launch in, I see big smiles appear on the faces of the people up front.

Toward the end of the set, I pass around a hat for contributions. We actually get $47 thrown in there after I turn on our now finely polished plea for kindness.

Mark offers us his floor tonight. He and some of his friends help pack up our gear. I go back in for one last look around to see if we've forgotten anything and overhear the soundman giving Dave a lesson in how to make homemade magic mushrooms. The guy says he can give us some sort of concoction of mixed manure, secure it to the roof of the van, and with some long drives coming up and all the warm weather, we'll have a great supply of fermented shrooms in just a few days. Dave looks intrigued from a strictly scientific point of view but wisely decides it's probably not too keen an idea to be driving through Canada with a mobile mushroom farm on the roof of our van — a van, you might remember, rented by a guy 2,000 miles away, a van whose odometer has been disconnected and which wasn't supposed to be driven outside of California, let alone the U.S.

So Dave does the only sensible thing. He buys some already fermented shrooms instead and he and I pop them on the spot. After we pack up and are about to leave, we start to take off. Dave and I are in the back with George, and before long, I convince Dave that the intense look on Joe Strummer's face in the Clash poster we've taped to the roof is the most frightening thing under the sun. We keep pointing at poor Joe and can't stop either laughing or being completely horrified.

"What in the hell are you two motherfuckers *doing*?" George demands.

"Fucking Joe Strummer, dude," is all Dave can manage to say, and I start laughing my ass off again.

When we get back to Mark's place, I climb in my sleeping bag and put my headphones on. My mind's racing like a semi that's lost its brakes on the way down a windy mountain road. My eyes dart about the tiny bedroom and watch the flashing lights from passing cars dancing across the ceiling. I put on side two of *What's Goin' On* and close my eyes. I'm just starting to relax when I open my eyes and see a cat appear through a tiny window above the door. It jumps down to the floor and approaches. Not sure if I'm hallucinating or not, but I keep watching it until it nestles up next to Ian, who is hopelessly allergic to cats. The cat starts pacing back and forth until finally arching its back and striking that familiar pose of imminent bowel movement. Poor Ian. The cat leaves him a little present not more than six inches from his head. Satisfied, the cat curls up next to Ian and falls asleep.

* * *

Day Fourteen
8/10/87

Predictably, Ian has a horrendous allergy attack. Doesn't smell too good either.

We all agree Calgary Mark is what you might call living proof that kind-hearted folk still roam the planet. Kind of easy to forget in the City of Angels. Before we leave, he asks us to sign a poster from one of our shows in town which he promptly puts up on his wall. He then gives us a few tips on places to stop on the way to Edmonton and assures us we have a place to crash if we come back to Calgary in the fall.

Unlike the scenic drive from Vancouver to Calgary, the drive to Edmonton is like crossing a sheet of glass. Just nothing but flat land. It pours most of the way. Raj is distant again. Must be the phone call home he made this morning. Man, every time you think he's finally on board after a great show, he gets sucked back down again.

George puts on the Flying Burrito Brothers' first record and drives the last leg. As we near the city, we hear a strange hissing sound. The rain stops, but it sounds like we're still traveling on wet surface. While we try to figure out what's going on we realize George has gotten us hopelessly lost.

"You know, this bridge seems a little familiar," George says with genuine curiosity.

After a long pause during which the rest of us exchange incredulous glances, Ian finally says "George, we've passed over this bridge three times already."

"Bullshit," he says with little conviction.

I pat George on the shoulder and say, "Fella, I've got news for you. We're lost."

When we finally find the place an hour later, a club called the Piazza, we get out and discover the pipe that connects the muffler has busted. Not good. We got paid well at the Nash, but Ian tells us to forget we have it because that's earmarked to pay Tom back for renting the van.

"Ian," I say fearfully, "tell us gently how much we've budgeted for mechanical problems."

"Ah, that would be nothing," he says flatly.

"Well," Dave says opening up the back, "we can't sit here and tug our puds over it. We'll deal tomorrow. Let's get our shit in there and take care of what's in front of us."

Arriving in town, unloading our gear and reading the vibe of a room has become very ritualized. Ian heads straight into the club to hook up with whoever's in charge, somebody who can give us answers. When are we really going on? Was there any advance promotion? Is our record in the local stores? Has the college radio station been playing our record? Not to mention, is there any free food and beer to be had?

Dave oversees unloading gear and kicking George in the ass. George has a penchant for disappearing whenever we're loading or unloading. Kind of like the guy who splits for the can when the check arrives. Dave catches George drifting away and bellows, "George, I see what you're doing. You think I don't, but I do. Now get over here and give us a fuckin' hand." George sheepishly slumps back over and grabs a guitar case.

Tonight we're opening for a punk band called Fang from San Francisco. Their singer has a wooden leg. No fancy prosthesis, just a hunk of wood jammed into his midsection. About as high-tech as a pirate marching around a ship on a sawed-off mop handle. The rest of the band is copping a bit of an attitude, but we're too tired and hungover to feel intimidated so we disarm them by just throwing our stuff down and introducing ourselves. After giving us the once-over three times their guitarist asks us how our border crossing went. We tell him it went surprisingly well.

"You're lucky," he says rubbing his backside. "We got a cavity check."

"A cavity check?" Raj asks innocently.

"I don't think he's talking about a trip to the dentist," Ian whispers in Raj's ear.

"Huh?" (Long pause). "Oh." (Growing recognition). Ohhhh. (Hits home).

"Man, that's gotta hurt," George says. "I guess we got lucky."

Just then the booker comes up and welcomes us. We ordain him a king of kings after he places down three large pizzas and three pitchers of beer. Commiserating over free pizza and beer is an unfailing uniting force and soon Fang loosens up.

After I finish stuffing myself, I get up to take a look around the place, and a tall pretty girl with short, dyed blonde hair and a checkered miniskirt is standing in front of me. "Ah, hello," I say.

"Hi, I'm Toni. Heard you guys were from L.A. I thought we should talk."

"We're aiming to destroy that stereotype, actually," I quip.

"How long are you guys in town?" she asks chewing a strand of her hair.

"A couple days," I say. "So what's there to do in these parts?"

She tells me Edmonton has the biggest mall in the world and she can get us in for free tomorrow. "A mall?" I ask, sounding disappointed.

"I know. I know. But trust me, it's worth it," she says. "Hey, I saw an article about you guys and thought I'd check you out. "I write for a local fanzine. Can I get an interview?"

"Sure. Hey, where's that article anyway?" I ask, pleased some sort of promotional push preceded us here.

"There's a copy of it over there, let me get it for you," she says. I watch her prance over to a large stack of giveaway rags in a far corner.

"Here," she says twirling her hair in her fingers. "I thought it turned out cool," obviously intent on waiting for me to read it with her just standing there. I pick up the magazine and notice on the cover that Johnny Marr just left the Smiths. While I skim the article, I realize Toni's thing is to invade your personal space and wait for a reaction. She knows she's gorgeous, and I'm sure she doesn't face rejection too often.

I look around for George to show it to him but everyone's disappeared. "Clearly, I'm going to have to be careful of you," I say playfully.

"Ah, don't worry sweetie," she says, "I just want to have some fun."

"That supposed to make me feel at ease?" I say sitting down again.

Toni does a short and pretty silly interview with me before the rest of the guys return from a walk around the neighborhood.

George sits down and says, "Just nothing here. This town is flat as a 13-year-old's..."

"Don't say it," Raj jumps in.

"I was just going to say a, um..." George pauses.

"Billiard table, George?" Ian swoops in.

"Yes, thank you Ian," George says smiling. "Flat as a billiard table."

Three of Toni's friends show up and join us. Toni, sounding like our publicist, tells them we're a hot band from L.A. George whispers in my ear, "Is Edmonton so dull that even we seem glamorous?"

"Apparently so," I say.

"Oh, then I take back what I said about this town," he beams. "Love those provincials."

While we wait around for showtime, George and I go outside and have another talk. "George, what are we going to do about Raj?" I ask him.

"Oh God," he says rolling his eyes. "Unless Raj is onstage, he's a complete basket case."

"I know," I say, shaking my head. "I've been worried about him the whole trip, and I have to be honest, I really don't know what more I can do. We play a great show, and I think he's finally all in, then the next day I look across the van, and he's sunk into the depths again. I'm getting so tired of trying to hold him up." I pause. "But that's not even the half of it."

"What do you mean?" he asks.

"See, I used to see it all working," I sigh. "You know, all of us sharing everything, the triumphs, the failures — right to the end. We're out here now with it all in our hands, and…I can't get Raj to let go to save my life. *You're* in crisis. And then there's Mary. I don't know what I'm coming home to there." I pause. "I guess I'm scared we're not going to all make it together, and I can't seem to let go of that idea. It's like I've failed."

"Well, I don't know about that," he scowls. "Listen, don't worry about me. I'll be O.K.," he says — probably as convincingly as he can. "As for Raj, fuck. We can't make him see the light. He's got to be the one who sees it for himself. And as far as this idyllic vision of us making it all together, I don't know, Bill. That ended when we kicked Brad out of the band."

"I don't know," I say. "I can't give up on Raj. We've come too far, he and I. I can't imagine not seeing Raj to my left onstage. Maybe I'm too fucked up in the head about Mary to get it, but I'm not going on without Raj. And I sure as hell don't want to go on without you."

He smiles, and we both just sit there together and watch the wind blow riots of color into swirling mini tornados until it looks like big broad paintbrush strokes of maroon, midnight blue and orange. Finally I say, "I've got to make a call."

I walk down the road and after a couple blocks I spot a pay phone. As I get closer to it, I slow down like the phone itself is going to interrogate me. I dial and wait through three long rings until Mary picks up. I ask her if she has a minute. "Actually only a minute," she says, sounding out of breath. "I'm packing to leave for Arrowhead. You know the annual family trip to the lake? Yippee-skippy. So, give me the latest but make it the abbreviated version."

"I don't know if I can do that," I say.

Silence. "Hey, I miss you," I finally say.

"Well, I miss you too," she says, breathing heavily and obviously not stopping her packing.

"I, uh, I need to know if you've given up on me. And us."

More silence before she finally says: "It's not a matter of giving up Bill. It's just...you know, this isn't a good time for this. I mean, I'm out the door here, and there's still so much of the tour

33 Days

147

left, and well, to be honest, I don't know if I *should* believe much from you while you're in the middle of all this."

As much as I know she has every reason to think that way, I hate her for saying it. Jesus. And I fucking hate myself for calling her, for standing here and giving her a free shot to the gut. I don't even know if I want her to tell me she wants to walk along a beach holding hands or tell me how bad she wants to fuck. Maybe I just want her to fire that shot that kills us once and for all. Before I know it, she's downshifted and starts reeling off reminders left and right and telling me to take down so-and-so's number.

This is an all too familiar cycle — one we trade back and forth. My turn to be the pursuer, which gives her back the upper hand. I offer up my beggar's bowl and wait for her to drop something in it. She seizes the upper hand and punishes me for being so vulnerable and needy.

It's Fang's crowd tonight, and they came to hear music that thrashes. We're no punk band, but we've got a punk ethos that comes through loud and clear. We'll go out there to meet a crowd halfway. We've played to punk rock crowds before. The most memorable was an all-day, all-night blowout to close the infamous Cathay de Grande in Hollywood.

You can't be too precious. You're going to get verbally abused, spit at and get some shit thrown at you. You start off with a few rocking songs and then unless you're just so abysmal they don't bother with you at all, they'll start to jump around, shoving and pushing, completely oblivious to what you're doing. At some point they stop shoving and pushing because someone finally clues in the song stopped a minute ago. Someone then shouts, "Come on, play a fuckin' fast one, man." In our twisted little world that means it's time to do a ballad. Naturally, this is met with the touching lament, "What's this mellow shit, man?" All good fun.

We played our guts out tonight, left it all onstage, and though it wasn't our crowd, we made sure they remembered us. Loads of people crowd around us after the show all pretty much saying the same thing: that we were one of the most intense bands they've ever seen. Fuck, we'll take that any day. Everyone asks us when we're coming back.

I mean, it's been such a trip. Even though no one knows us out here, we've been getting these amazing responses. Sometimes you can tell a crowd *wants* it. Like in Seattle. Other nights, like the first show in Calgary, you've got to walk to the precarious end of that tree branch and show everybody you're willing to put out before getting anything back. It's all about earning trust. I mean, it's our first tour. We're nobodies. We can't wait for people to notice how *grand* we are. We've got one hour to hijack someone else's crowd and take them as our own, and we'll do it by any means necessary. We have to. We vowed to from day one.

See, you have to understand something. We really do *believe* we're operating on a totally different plane than other bands. I know it's crazy, and we're completely full of ourselves, but we *do*. We know music can't change the world, but music changed *our* world, and it *could* change theirs. It's not even like we're trying to convince anyone *our* music can change their world. We're just trying to show people we feel reborn doing what we're meant to do. So let your dreams take hold and watch what can happen. Take that idea and pass it along to anyone else you know that's dying out there and too scared to move their feet.

I'll admit, we do walk on some pretty high moral ground, and out here we're learning to wise up, or we'll burn out like Abbie Hoffman. We may be idealists, but we're not fools.

Take "Dry September" or "Bitterness," both of which are about bigotry, something the band collectively decided was important to us from day one. Still, we've got to be careful and not underestimate an audience's intelligence, otherwise you're just bellowing a hollow church hymn that only momentarily raises the spirit and affirms the goal.   Playing "Dry September" or "Bitterness" isn't going to make racists recoil in shame or provide any solution.   It gives *us* an outlet to express our horror over how blasé society feels about it, but ultimately the onus is on us to provide something more substantial than shallow social analysis.

Still, it must be said, when we play "Dry September" and "Bitterness" something inexplicable happens.   It's like this righteousness possesses us.   We sense the stakes are raised, and it's this acknowledgement of honor and duty to take up arms the only way we know how.   That's Raj's history, our core beliefs and our collective brotherhood crystallizing and playing the part of the muse.   If Divine Weeks is known for nothing else but playing like our lives depend on it, that's enough for me.   And *that's* what's palpable.   *That's* what resonates with an audience.   *That's* what earns a trust.   And that's what happened tonight.

As we pack up, Toni bounds up to me and says she loves us and would have put us up for the night but her dad, a cop, would be pissed if she brought home five guys to stay.   The prude.

"Listen," she says moving closer to me.   "Come by the mall tomorrow, I'll get you in.   Trust me, it's worth it."   She kisses me on the cheek and skips away.

Ian found some guy named Spider, who's wearing a Manson shirt (looks like him too), to put us up for the night.   Great.   We're staying at Manson's place tonight.

* * *

Day Fifteen
8/11/87

We arrive an hour late for our interview at the University of Alberta. George's fault. Practically had to airlift him out of bed and into the van. After some on-air bantering, we do our first-ever acoustic version of "Dry September," which I dedicate to the South African miners' strike which just ended. I sing the song right at Raj trying to connect with him.

Radio spot at CJSW, Edmonton. From left: George, DJ, Dave, me and Raj. Photo by Ian Bader

Before we head off to try and get the van fixed, I stop at a pay phone to call a Winnipeg newspaper and plug our upcoming shows there. The interviewer asks me how we got signed to Steve Wynn's label.

Mary and I used to go see the Dream Syndicate's front man Steve Wynn play these acoustic shows around town during the Syndicate's downtime. Eventually we work up enough courage to give him our demo tape. The next time I bump into Steve, he tells me how much he likes our demo, especially a new song called "Bitterness" which he says sounds like a cross between Van Morrison and R.E.M. I invite him to our next show, and he brings his girlfriend Johnette Napolitano, whose band Dream 6 just changed its name to Concrete Blonde and got signed to IRS Records. They both say how much they loved the set. Steve asks me how many songs are ready to be recorded. I say we have tons. I figure he's just curious.

A few weeks later, he calls and asks the band out for some hamburgers and beer at Radion. I figure Steve's just extending a hand to a struggling band. Maybe give some counsel. So, we meet up and crowd into a far corner booth, and while we fail miserably to look cool and unimpressed, he tells us he wants to put out our record on his own Down There label, which he said just got picked up by Restless Records.

* * *

A guy at the radio station recommends a mechanic just down the road so we head over there and boy, does Dave spread our sad story on thick. "Hey, we're just a touring band from L.A., not making any money," he starts in. "Just out here living our dream. Don't even know if we've got the money to get us to the next town. Without that van we're screwed. *Just screwed.* Anything you can do to help us would be fucking great."

"Cal" it says on the name patch of his shirt. Cal's probably in his mid-40s, graying hair poking out the back of his CAT cap, blue jeans with grease stains at the hips and weary old piercing blue-gray eyes. As Dave goes through his spiel, I'm watching Cal's eyes scan the inside of the back of our van with more than the usual casual curiosity we get. Finally he gives an odd sort of smile and says, "Tell you what. Let me take a look. Give me about a half-hour."

We all walk over to the Denny's across the street to eat what we hope isn't our Last Supper. "Do you think it's possible this guy won't give us the royal screw?" George asks warily.

"Not bloody likely," Raj sighs. "Ian, tell us again. Just how much cash do we have in reserve for repairs?"

"Ah, that would be still be — nothing."

When we finish lunch, we shuffle back expecting the worst. "So tell us, Cal," Ian asks with more than a hint of dread. "How bad is it?"

"Follow me, I want to show you something," he says waving us back toward his office. We all look at each other and shrug and file into his very cramped office. The walls are filled with Edmonton Oilers posters and other memorabilia.

"Big Oilers fan, huh?" I ask.

"Oh yeah," he says, reaching into the bottom drawer of his old beat-up desk and pulling out a book which he opens to a stack of photos tucked between the pages. "See this?" he says. "That's my band. I'm the second from the left. 1968. Neil Young just made his first solo record and bands in these parts were popping up everywhere and heading off to L.A. like Neil to try and make it too."

"That a real Gretsch?" Raj asks squinting at the shot.

"Nah, just a crappy copy," he says, "But I lived to play that guitar. Everything else in the world disappeared when I played that thing." He keeps shuffling through the photos but doesn't show us any others.

"So," Ian asks tentatively, "What happened? You guys go down to L.A.?"

He keeps looking through the stack of photos then says, "Never did. Rest of the guys did, but, uh, I stayed here."

"Ever think about what would've happened if you went?" I ask.

"Only every day," he says with a wistful smile.

"Ever find out what happened to the rest of the guys?" Dave asks.

"Mmm, couple of 'em stayed down there, a couple came back. They never made it happen, but…at least they fired their shot, you know?" he says looking at us all.

Silence. We all look at each other. Dave finally asks, "So, what do we owe you?"

"Oh, I just soldered the pipe together. No charge," he says.

We're all blown away. "Seriously?" I finally say.

"Everybody could use a break, eh?" he says extending his hand to us. "And good luck to you."

We've got no gig scheduled tonight so we take Toni up on her offer to check out this so-called biggest mall in the world. She sneaks us in and we soon realize if there's a bigger mall in the world you'd have to show it to us to believe it. This place has submarine rides, a mini zoo, millions of shops, miniature golf, bungee jumping, a batting cage, and the biggest water slide I've ever seen, which we can't resist.

Toni says she has some hash so she, Dave and I head out to the van to get stoned. She climbs in back and gasps. "You guys have *got* to be kidding. What *died* in here!?"

Dave and I are immune and all we can do is shrug. "We get that a lot, actually," Dave says as he does up a makeshift bong out of an empty crushed Coke can using a Divine Weeks button to poke holes for ventilation.

"Nice dual usage of our tour merchandise, Dave," I say, taking a huge hit and about choking to death when I notice Toni sitting Indian-style revealing a garter belt holding up her white lace thigh-high stockings. She catches me looking and says, "You like what you see?"

"I reckon you'd arouse the dead my dear," I say smiling. She smiles back, and there's definitely a white elephant now in the van. I won't lie. She looks amazing, but I don't know.

We're starving but broke so Dave figures why not try and scam some free food. The man's on a roll. While the rest of the guys stroll around a nearby record store, Dave and I shuffle over to a food stand for a look. "Let me handle this," Dave says. Taking a deep breath, he launches into his spiel: "Hey hi, how are ya. Listen, we're new in town, just a band on the road, not making any money, just livin' our dream, and we don't want to get you in any trouble or anything, but we're really hungry, and if you could spare something we'd be eternally grateful."

The lady is so caught off guard she figures either "what the hell" or "shit, I better fork over something because these guys look a little unsteady." All I know is that free hot dog tasted mighty fine and so did the free grape soda. The rest of the guys come back listening to George fretting, "Well, count one more record store without our record in it...hey, how in the hell did you guys get that food?"

"Where there's a will, my friend," Dave says wolfing down the last of his hot dog.

We'd made arrangements to stay tonight with a girl named Chantal who works at the Piazza, and when we call her she tells us a spot just opened up for tonight's show, and if we want it she can get us $50. Hearing this, Raj immediately lights up.

We hurry over there and play a loose and fun set mixing in some of the covers we worked up at the Nash with our originals. During a break while Raj changes a string, Dave goes up front and grabs the mic and does an acapella version of "Cover of the *Rolling Stone*" in a mock southern accent. Later George adds to the levity while Raj changes guitars: "Hey, two ladies are in a park and a flasher flashes 'em. One has a stroke but the other couldn't reach. Hey thanks, we learned that one in Calgary."

After the gig, Toni suggests we all go get something called schooners and pizza at this place called the Rose Bowl close by. A load of folks we meet after the show follows us over there, including a lovely, shy girl named Aileen who takes a liking to Raj.

It's late and we have the place nearly to ourselves. Our big group takes over the large rectangular table in the middle of the sawdust-covered main room adjacent to the bar. Edmonton Oilers and Canadian Budweiser banners cover the walls. The smell of beer-soaked sawdust fills the room, with shitty lighting an aging actress would appreciate. We order some pizza and schooners and Toni tells us the locals call this place the Hosed Bowl because you go there to get hosed. And no wonder. These schooners must hold a gallon of beer.

While we make several schooners disappear, the rest of us keep stealing peeks at Raj and Aileen who look like they're in their own world at a far end of the table. It's so great seeing Raj finally let go and enjoy himself a little.

Ian takes pictures and addresses are exchanged. Toni returns from the restroom and hands me under the table her garter belt and whispers, "Maybe when you come back through town in the fall we can get closer."

What a glorious evening. After two weeks on the road, Raj's daily emotional roller coaster rides, the fucking Nash and that shithead Caesar, chasing that asshole Jonathan for the lousy 20 bucks, we're finally hitting on all cylinders. And it's like we're getting these little signs telling us to keep going. Like the BBQ at Sandy's and Mindy's, and meeting Cal today. See what happens when you don't act on your dreams?

The Rose Bowl, Edmonton. Right before it all blew up. Clockwise from bottom center: Raj, George, Dave, Me, Toni (in cowboy hat), unknown, Aileen.
Photo by Ian Bader

I sit back surveying everyone getting on and think to myself, "Things are so completely coming together for us now."

And then the goddamn sky falls. A fucking anvil drops on our little slice of wonderful.

This bumbling, heavy-set lady, probably in her late 30s, staggers up to Raj and Aileen and just stands there weaving in front of them. She's kinda tall, dark hair just below her shoulders, in blue jeans and a dark blue blouse. Dead eyes. Raj glances up at her, smiles, and then turns back continuing to talk with Aileen.

"Just what do you think you're doing?" the lady spits out.

Bewildered, Raj says, "Just having a good time, eatin' some pizza. What's the story?"

"And what are you doing with him?" she says to Aileen, pointing at Raj. "You know how they are."

"Excuse me? What?" Aileen asks.

"Him," she says still pointing at Raj. "The Arab. They kill us and our children. They're all alike, brown and dirty. What the hell do you think you're doing with him?"

Aileen starts to stand up and says, "You don't know what you're saying. You're drunk and you need to leave."

Raj gets up and stands between Aileen and the woman and says unwavering, "You don't even know me. Who are you to judge me?"

Then this guy with a mustache and a tattered old brown coat over an ugly green T-shirt comes up and tries to calm things down. "Don't pay attention to my wife. She's had a lot to drink." His eyes are just dead too.

"You stay outta this," she scolds him. "You know how they are. He wants to kill us. He's a Paki. A Kadafi lover. They drop bombs on us and our children." She then takes her hand and makes like it's a jet flying and simulates a bomb dropping.

No one else but me had tuned in. I'm just stunned. Everyone else is still carrying on laughing and drinking. However, with the word "Paki," this pall comes over the table and suddenly everything falls deadly silent.

I start to get up. Dave and George rise to their feet. "He ain't a fuckin' Paki," George shouts from across the table. "He's Indian, 'ya stupid cunt."

"Well, whatever the fuck he is, he doesn't belong here," she says menacingly. "He shouldn't be here talking to that girl like he's one of us. That's just the truth."

"Thanks, but I ain't one of you and you ain't one of us," George shoots back as he walks toward her.

"You're just a fucking piece of dog shit," Dave sneers at her as George hocks a huge loogie in her beer.

Raj steps in front of Dave and George and tells them to stop. Then he turns to the woman and says forcefully but still calm, "Do you *know* me? Do you *know* Arabs? I'm not even Arab, but if I was, what does it *matter*?"

"I know what you are," she says. "All of you brown people are the same. You're all disgusting. You come here, you take our homes and our jobs. You all disgust me."

"You're just an ignorant racist," I say moving right in front of her. "Why don't you just put on your white hood and goose-step off a fucking cliff!"

Her husband steps in and says to me, "Don't talk to my wife like that. Now you back off!"

"That's right," the woman seethes. "Don't fuck with us. We'll kill you right now before you can kill us. That's the only way to deal with terrorist scum like you. I hate all of you brownies. *All* of you!"

I feel the bile rise up to my throat and a rage fills me that I've never, and I mean *never*, felt before. "You motherfucking piece of shit," I scream at her. "This man is a hundred times the person you are. I swear to fucking God, you get fucking close to him, and I'll fucking kill you myself!"

"You think I'm the only one who thinks like this?" she says chillingly. "Grow up. Don't act all fucking high and mighty. You want me to bring more down here so you can see and hear for yourself?"

"Go ahead. March 'em all down here," I shout at her. "We'll fucking have 'em all."

"You're just spitting venom, you fucking snake," Dave says to her. "You're nothing but an old...fucking...bigot...bitch."

"You just hate your fucking self so much, don't you?" I rage on. "You can't fucking handle how goddamn decent someone is who doesn't look like you. That's it, isn't it? God, you are such a fucking miserable excuse and a waste of DNA."

Raj shoves me back. "It's not worth it, Bill," he pleads. "She's just a drunk crazy bigot. It's not worth fighting for. Don't lower yourself to her level. Trust me on that."

I don't hear him right then and even if I did, I couldn't have stopped. I move closer, and I'm pointing my finger into her chest when the Rose Bowl's owner races over and puts me in a bear hug and screams, "I want all you guys the hell outta here, or I'm calling the cops!"

"Calling the cops? On us?" I scream as the bartender and a bus boy come over and start shoving us all out the door. "Yeah, let the fucking racist stay," I scream. "Well, fuck you. We'll see you motherfuckers in hell!"

The place is a near riot. Chairs are getting pushed over, things are flying everywhere. We're all getting herded out the door as Raj wiggles free and stands right in front of the woman. He just shakes his head and finally says, "I feel so sorry for you. You're nothing but an ignorant racist. And that's *all* you are."

We all stumble into the parking lot and as the first breath of crisp cold starry night air fills my lungs, I feel my whole body shudder, and I feel deathly cold. Our whole party is wandering around the parking lot looking like we've seen ghosts. Just blown to bits. I look at Raj, and he's turned from this steely grace I saw just a moment ago to this softened sadness. He feels all our eyes on him and looks cornered and ashamed. We look in each other's eyes for just a second and then he turns away and starts toward the van. Like zombies we follow him there to the only thing that feels like home right now.

The scene is utterly absurd. Aileen's passing Raj her address, Toni's trying to say goodbye to me with a crazy sexy smile. The rest of our party is all waving goodbye.

Raj is already in the driver's seat with the motor revving as we start to pile into the van. All he says is he wants to drive straight through to Regina, our next stop. I watch him drop his head and cry very softly for just a second and then he quickly pulls himself out of it. No one says a word. We're numb. Raj takes us back out on the highway, and soon the hum of the motor and the movement of the van lower a curtain on this night.

I lay in back staring into the ceiling of the van with a thousand words to say but my mouth can't move. The silence is deafening, but what the fuck can be said? Gotta put the armor back on. We have another town to get to. That's all we know. All we've got is each other. Our little road trip just turned into something immensely profound and we all know it. Four college Joes waiting for a bus just had their shit turned inside out. But who *are* we now?

After about an hour or so on the road, Raj says to Ian, who's lying next to me in the spot right behind him: "Ian, you're not asleep, are you?"

"No," he says quietly.

I watch Ian reach his hand around the driver's seat and place it on Raj's left arm where it stays for a long time. I just lay there watching, wondering if we're going to make it.

* * *

Day Sixteen
8/12/87

I guess I finally fell asleep because the next thing I remember is it's daylight, and my head is just pounding like a pneumatic drill. Dave's taken over driving and Raj is collapsed in back next to me.

"Where are we?" I ask no one in particular.

"About an hour from Regina," Dave says as the Stones' "Moonlight Mile" plays.

As we forge on east, the sun rises over the roadway in front of us. Ian reminds me we have to do another phone interview with someone from a Winnipeg newspaper this morning, so we stop in a tiny little town in Saskatoon called Claike to call. It's the type of place where the whole town knows someone new just pulled in within a couple minutes. It's a time warp. Looks like nothing from the last 25 years has made it here yet.

I crowd into the phone booth and dial. I look over my shoulder and the rest of the guys have all gathered just outside on some steps leading up to a brick building. We all look like a train wreck. I don't know what to say to this interviewer. After a few typical preliminary questions he innocently asks me how we like Canada so far. I just can't contain myself.

"Up until last night we've found the Canadians the most giving, genuine and decent people we've ever come across." I stop and don't say anything for a minute.

"You there?"

"Yeah, sorry," I say trying to collect myself. "You see, last night was a bad night for Divine Weeks, and I don't know how we're gonna carry on." I go through what happened at the restaurant. The poor guy is stupefied. "The thing about the past is everything is funnier in retrospect, funnier and lighter and cooler.

Maybe years from now we'll see it that way. Just not now. I mean, you can laugh at anything from far enough away. But right now it's in our faces. Smothering us. Right now, we're just gutted. We can't put up any airs. It's just...raw."

The guy tries to steer the interview back to get something he can use, but I finally just say, "Listen, I'm sorry, man. I can't think of anything coy or flip to say right now. When we left a couple weeks ago, we set out to drink in all we could and maybe sell a few records. We grew up instead. I'm really sorry." I hang up and walk in a trance back to the van.

Hanging in balance. Me doing a phone interview the day after Edmonton. From left to right: Me, Raj, George, Dave. Photo by Ian Bader

"How'd it go?" Ian asks me weakly.

"Probably not too well for him. I just spilled my guts and then hung up."

"Let's get out of here," Dave says. "This town gives me the creeps."

We finally roll into Regina in the late morning. We still can't get a straight answer if Regina is pronounced like the girl's name Gina or a girl's, well, you know. Tonight's gig is at a place simply called the Club and after soundcheck the owner, a guy named Trent, treats us to empanadas which are so spicy it sends us one by one into the can to do the Aztec Two-Step.

Ian goes off to do some laundry while the rest of us head back to Trent's house. We're all gamy and a shower and a nap is the order of the day. It's clear Raj doesn't want to talk about anything. Still hasn't said a word since last night. I know he doesn't want our pity, but we're all in this now. We're all stuck hanging in this agonizing state of suspended animation. This is all of ours now.

While Raj takes a shower, I write him a letter.

> *Dear Raj:*
>
> *What just hit us? Wasn't it just last week we were in 10th grade, sitting on the sidelines, two losers watching the parade go by? It's frightening enough leaving home, who invited the real world in? Who decided we needed racists to drive reality into our heads? God, Raj. I know I'll never know what that lady made you feel last night, but I love you for your unfathomable grace. I can't imagine what you're feeling, but I know what it must have stirred up being called Paki like those motherfuckers you told me about back in England. I guess I just want you to know that if you want to go home right now I'll go with you, and that's the damn truth. But I think you know you belong out here — now more than ever. All I know is the van is the only place that feels like home, and thank God*

we have our music to turn to. I hope you know it's there for you, for all of us. 'Cos that's all there is now. Just us. Raj, I can't fully explain what just happened to us all. Only in time will we know. For now, we'll have to withstand today until tomorrow and see what we are then. No, nothing adds up and everything falls short. I'll leave you with a John Lennon quote I've always loved: "To leave me with my words leaves me alone with my own stupidity." What can I say, but I stand by and for you now and even until the end of the world.

Love, Bill

I leave the note on his sleeping bag and wait for him to come out of the shower. When he does, he sits down cross-legged, unfolds the note and reads it. Twice. He keeps his head down. Doesn't look over at me. I then watch him fold up the note, put it in his duffel bag and lay down in his sleeping bag.

I stay in my sleeping bag the rest of the afternoon just staring into the cottage-cheese ceiling trying to make sense of something. Man, we thought when we pulled out of Raj's driveway 16 days ago we were merely joining the procession of Ford Econoline vans out on the highway. We figured we'd just follow the breadcrumbs left by our heroes and things would just, I don't know, work out. I guess each of us has to decide what last night means to us. For me, my cage is pretty rattled. I've never felt capable of homicide until last night. Nothing scared me more than what I felt capable of. It was pure hate for hate, and it's scaring the living shit out of me. All my life, I've been drawn to folks like Martin Luther King, Jr. and Gandhi because I think we attach ourselves to people and ideas that are elusive and in which we are deficient.

I have to ask myself, what was I trying to prove going after that woman? Exactly what *was* my motive? Was I enraged she'd hurt a friend, and I thought I was so omnipotent that I could make the pain go away? Was I pissed she shit on our little troupe just when everything was starting to work out? Was I appalled she disrupted some social sense of order by letting her inhibitions down and speaking her horrible truth? I don't know. Maybe it's just folly and shortsighted to damn that woman. I mean, to damn her *alone*. She wasn't born a racist. What a fucking crapshoot it is for all of us. You're either exposed to it at an impressionable age or you're spared. Was it passed to her from her father? Or was she more prone to it because there was no father around at all to nurture her?

I can't say I understand that or accept it right now as I lay here inside a sleeping bag on a stranger's floor in a foreign country, but something's been pounding on my brain all day like some dripping water torture, and I can't turn it off. I just don't fucking know.

As the afternoon drones on, the rest of the guys have all fallen to sleep, and I'm flipping around the channels when I come across *The Grapes of Wrath*. That great scene is starting where Tom Joad is talking to his Ma. She asks him how she'll know where he is when he sets off, and he says, "I'll be all around in the dark. I'll be everywhere. Wherever you can look. Wherever there's a fight so hungry people can eat, I'll be there. Wherever there's a cop beatin' up a guy, I'll be there. I'll be in the way guys yell when they're mad. I'll be in the way kids laugh when they're hungry and they know supper's ready, and when the people are eatin' the stuff they raise and livin' in the houses they build — I'll be there, too." His Ma says: "I don't understand it, Tom," and Tom says, "Me neither, Ma, but it's just somethin' I've been thinkin' about."

The words soak through my skin and enter my bloodstream, go straight to my heart and then go pumping back through every part of me. It feels like I've just heard a clarion call and there's nothing gray left in this world. It's like everything I ever loved or dreamed or cared about comes down to those very words. This all goes right back to ever since I first heard my mom treated like the black sheep of the family. Ever since Raj first told me about England. Ever since Larry See fucked us over just because he could. Ever since, well, it's like Tom Joad says, "A fella ain't got a soul of his own, just a little piece of a big soul.

The one big soul that belongs to everybody." All I can make sense of is this: Nothing you can have for yourself matters if someone's been trampled over and dehumanized to get it. Nobody's free until everybody's free. I've been saying and believing that my whole life, but when we pulled out of town a couple weeks ago that felt like an albatross, a curse, and I had to let it go. But it's really true.

So fuck it. Let someone better than me turn the other cheek. I've played that out and don't have shit to show for it. I don't know what's gonna happen the rest of the way. The only thing I know is I'll be right next to Raj doing it, and God help me, if another motherfucker comes at Raj again, I'll do it all the same way as last night. All we have is each other, and there's nothing but ourselves worth saving. This tour's something else now. It's about defending honor, living up to our ideals. Everything's changed.

I fall in and out of consciousness the rest of the afternoon. Every so often I raise my head and look over at Raj to see if I can get a read on where his head is, but he's not letting on. It turns to early evening, and I'm half listening to Reagan address the nation about the Iran-Contra affair. George is up now watching it and starts raving as Reagan announces, "Our original initiative got all tangled up in the sale of arms, and the sale of arms got tangled up with the hostages. I let my preoccupation with the hostages intrude into areas where it didn't belong."

* * *

We're not sure what to expect out of tonight's show. Raj still hasn't spoken since last night. During the first few songs it feels like we're standing in molasses and can't find liftoff. Then during "Bitterness" Raj starts playing with as much fury as I've ever seen. Every note, every chord sounds louder, more purposeful, struck deeper. Instinctively, we all turn toward each other — like the way we rehearse to get into a good pocket and seal that intimacy between us. We play that way the rest of the gig.

I think something was freed last night for Raj, and he used tonight to begin again. Toward the end of "Bitterness," I look over at him, and I see something I've never seen before. His eyes fixed on a point somewhere only he can see. His legs spread wide apart as he slashes away at his guitar like he has a machete — lost in some sort of glorious otherworld where bigots never roam. Like he's escaped into the utopian coda of "Bitterness" – "We've found a place where truth is inborn."

Tonight probably wasn't much of a show for the audience, but this may have been the most meaningful show we've ever played. Tonight we played for ourselves, and for us we triumphed. We knew we didn't have it tonight, and by instinct, or maybe because we were scared of everything else, we turned to our music for comfort.

That might have been the first time that's ever happened. I've always over-projected and tried to squeeze something extra out of every performance. I often engage in some sort of hijinx, like climbing atop speaker cabinets, jumping into the audience or handing over my guitar to someone because I worry the music itself isn't enough. Tonight, we didn't have it to give but our music reached down to us and lifted us up and told us not to turn back. It's like our songs went back to where they first were born — in our hearts — and held us up until we could walk again on our own. It's like they gave us back the faith we'd put into them when no one else had faith in them — or us.

Our encore is "Dry September" which I dedicate to Raj. He looks up at me and stares for a moment, then tears into the song like his life depends on it. We all do. Other than that, there's no mention of last night. Words are superfluous. At the end of "Dry September," Raj bangs out the most glorious feedback-laden sprawl of sound on his Les Paul and then he hurls it right at a side brick wall leaving it to blare away. As he walks off the stage, he looks back at the mess he's left and he's got this *look* on his face like "take *that*." It's amazing. We follow him off the stage and when I get to him, I throw my arms around him. "Is my guitar

OK?" he asks, a little embarrassed. "Who the fuck cares," I say and he erupts into his great silent gaping wide-open-mouth laugh.

Afterwards Trent, the club owner, says to us, "I don't know what it was, but you guys were just mesmerizing. I didn't dare leave the room."

After the show we don't split in different directions. We all sit together at a table in back of the club until closing time. Nobody feels much like networking or scamming. I guess we just need to stay close. Finally, Trent puts the last of the chairs on the tables, comes up to us and says, "You guys all right?"

We all half smile. "I think we're gonna be O.K." Ian says. "Right, Raj?" We all look at him.

He pauses then sheepishly says, "Yeah, I think so."

"If you guys are ready, I am," Trent says. "I'm gonna go out for some drinks with some friends: you guys can come with or you can take my keys and go back to my place and make yourself at home." We're spent, so we take his keys and head back to his place. Fucking Canadians. So incredibly trusting. Giving your keys to a rock band you just met?

When we get back to Trent's place, we have the munchies so we raid the cupboards. We all pitch in and cook up a massive spaghetti and garlic bread feast. The pall has lifted. We sit around the kitchen table eating, laughing, sharing stories. Maybe what went down last night was somehow necessary — to our evolution, I mean. Maybe we've been hurtling toward it all along. In some fucked-up way, it gave Raj a platform to seize his moment and speak his truth. And what a damn sight it was to witness. I get this feeling like we're all going to see things a little clearer, look harder and pause a little longer as we make our way over the last 17 days of this tour. I guess we can't bullshit ourselves anymore. It was our decision to leave the safety of our homes and engage with this world. We've got to take the thumb out of our mouths. Sure, it's safe clutching the tree trunk, but the sweetest fruit is at the top of the tallest tree.

* * *

Day Seventeen
8/13/87

It's a longer drive to Winnipeg than we thought. We're running about two hours late. Dave is opening it up pretty good and Raj is up front in the passenger seat singing along to R.E.M. and doing drum fills on the dashboard. He seems in great spirits, like he's turned a corner. Without saying as much, it's obvious the rest of us are relieved as all hell. It's like all that tension, worry and growing resentment about Raj has vanished.

I'm thinking about all that when we get a friggin' flat tire. Dave goes around back and discovers a couple problems. No lug wrench and the tire jack looks like it couldn't lift a Model T. We try the jack but it doesn't even lift the van high enough to remove the tire. To add to the excitement, the van sways violently with each passing truck. Finally, we flag someone down who gets the thing up and done.

By the time we get to Winnipeg, we're several hours late. Winnipeg is the hometown of Dave McKiegan, who co-booked the tour with Mary. McKiegan is a bit of a buffoon but an affable sort, basically harmless with a heavy Canadian drawl (lots of "eh"s and "ham" stuck at the ends of things he says). He meets us in the parking lot and starts telling us to hurry and get our soundman in there to set up the P.A. After a pregnant pause, we all do a double take. "What the fuck did he say?" Dave asks incredulously. "Our own soundman? Set up the P.A.?"

Hearing all this after eight hours in the van, running late all day, the flat tire and all that went down in Edmonton, doesn't warm our hearts. Plus, we don't have our own soundman and none of us are technical wizards.

Dave, Raj and I scope out the joint, a place called the Curtis — a two-story-long rectangular box-shaped hotel on Henderson Highway about ten minutes from downtown Winnipeg. We're playing in the club downstairs which doubles as a sports/titty bar by day. Planted in the middle of the stage is a big silver metal pole presumably for gyrating and such. Dave walks up to the pole and asks me, "Give you any ideas, Bill?"

"Ought to be an interesting show," I say. "If we ever get the friggin' P.A. running."

Raj and I walk over to the soundboard and stare at it with our brows furrowed. "Nice sound system," he finally says.

"Yeah, too nice — for us to figure out, that is," I add.

"Hey," Raj says turning toward me. "I thought you were going to bring that P.A. we used to use in George's basement — you know, for emergencies…like this."

"I would've," I say, "but my mom's fuck-up boyfriend told me they sold it and said the profits went up their noses."

George comes over and shakes his head. He's been in a foul mood all day. "Fucking McKiegan," he says disgustedly. "This is a bunch of shit. We should tell him if he doesn't get this thing up and running we're walking out and playing somewhere else."

Dave, who's taking his turn at getting the P.A. running, slowly gets up and scowls at George. "I've got a better idea. Why don't *you* tell him about all our other offers, and then let us know how that goes. Meanwhile, we'll actually be *doing* something to get the show happening tonight." George slumps away.

After a good hour of knob-twiddling and head-scratching, Raj, Dave and I finally get the monitors working. It's getting late so we just turn the monitors around to face the audience, and that's the extent of the P.A. We play our hearts out, but the sound was so abysmal we're all on a bit of a down after the show.

We've christened McKiegan the "Grand Fuckin' Poobah." After our first set, the fuck starts giving us grief about the sound and that's too much for George. "Listen, goddamn it!" George bellows. "You never told us there'd be no soundman. Or that we'd have to hotwire the fucking P.A. And if *we* hadn't stepped in, you wouldn't have had *any* P.A. tonight. No one, and I mean *no one*, is more pissed off than we are that the sound was for shit. Now keep riding our asses, and I'm not gonna be responsible for what happens next. Now back...the fuck...*off*!"

"Whoah guys," he says backpedaling. "Don't blow a gasket, ham. Lemme turn you guys on to some hash, and we can all cool off, eh?"

We're booked to do two sets a night for three nights here — just like the Nash — minus the threat of crabs. In between sets, Ian and I walk around the place. The rooms are pretty nice, beds with clean sheets, bathrooms and TVs. "After the way we've lived the last couple weeks, I almost feel survivor guilt staying here," Ian says.

After our second set, we get invited by some arty types to go barhopping, but we're too emotionally wrung out from the last couple nights so we take a rain check. Dave and I are roomies this weekend, so we just grab as many beers as we can from the self-serve beer store that sits behind the Curtis and head up to our rooms to wind down. After we finally grow too tired to hold our heads up anymore, we turn out the lights. It's very late. I'm just about asleep when Dave says, "Bill?"

"Hmmmm."

"You think we're cool now?" he asks.

"No. We'll always be wankers, Dave."

"No," he scolds. "I mean Raj and, you know, everything." His voice is soft, unsure. Very unlike Dave.

I think for a minute. "Yeah, I do. I really do."

* * *

Day Eighteen
8/14/87

McKiegan wakes us with a telephone call and Dave and I just smile after glancing at the clock and seeing it's 4 p.m. "Yo ho, ho ho, a rocker's life for me," Dave croaks out.

McKiegan tells us to wake everybody up because we have to get right over to the TV interview he's arranged, and then we jet over to a radio interview. It's our first TV appearance. And the radio spot's at a commercial FM station. Another first for us.

The TV spot went O.K., but I'm not sure anyone saw it. It's some public TV cable station. You probably can only pick it up by hooking up your TV to your toaster. Whatever. We do a very smooth version of "Idiot Child" live.

As McKiegan rushes us off to the radio station, I rest my head against the passenger window and notice in the side mirror dark circles under my eyes. I look like an ad for death. "George," I cry out in my best hoity-toity voice. "I've dark circles under my eyes!"

"Jesus wept," he says sarcastically. "Not a wrinkle too?"

"Hey, you don't exactly look like an oil painting today either," I say.

We've done plenty of college radio interviews but commercial mainstream radio is a different animal altogether. As we walk down the hallway of the radio station, McKiegan says we probably should've come here first because this was scheduled to come off an hour ago. "Then why didn't we?" Ian says shaking his head and sensing something. Before McKiegan can answer, we're inside the DJ booth and things get strange real fast.

"Howard. Howard on the Rock," the DJ says standing up to greet us, revealing he has no pants on. We're about to ask him why he has no pants when he starts cussing at us.

"Who do you guys think you are?" he barks. "This ain't college fuckin' radio, man. This is AOR, fucking commercial rock radio, get it?!" Howard says e-nun-ci-ating each word to show how bloody fucking important his world is.

"I just hate it when I try to help people and they make my show run late," Howard raves on, his face turning a sickly shade of purple-red. "I just hate fucking ingrates and incompetents! I'm telling you guys..."

Out of the corner of my eye, I see George starting to breathe heavily. Oh boy. Here it comes. "All right, just cut it right there, motherfucker!" George explodes. "Just *cut it*! We don't have to listen to this shit. Incompetents? You want fuckin' incompetents, do you? Well, let me bring in the fuckin' Grand Poobah of all incompetents for you...Mr. David Fuckin' McKiegan," George barks, grabbing McKiegan's arm and yanking him into the DJ booth like a rag doll. "*This* is the fuckface who decided we should do a two-bit cable TV spot before bringing us over here. So *this* is the fuckin' guy you need to tear a new asshole for."

It's a beautiful moment. We're not going to be intimidated by anyone anymore. Particularly by some balding washed-up smoothie stuck in the sticks of Canada railing at us in his underwear. Curiously, Howard is cool to us after that and proceeds to direct all his anger toward McKiegan and his flunky staff the rest of our time there.

This Howard is a classic phony, a stereotypical rock jock armed with all the tired old rock-biz lingo. At the commercial break Howard gets on his feet and screams at his flunky assistant, "God fucking damn it Gary! Where's my goddamn coffee cup?!" Gary races in with said missing cup hissing, "Five seconds, five seconds!"

"Gary!" Howard bellows. "What did I tell you about coming into my fuckin' booth, you little...[turning suddenly calm again]:

Howard on the Rock back with you. We've got Divine Weeks from Los Angeles with us. So fellas, how do you like Canada?" Evil Howard magically mutates into Smooth Soothing Howard again.

If you were listening on the radio you probably thought we were huge. Howard plays several songs from *Through and Through* then lets us do "Idiot Child" and "Dry September" live. The guy actually asked some decent questions, and we realize afterwards ol' Howard's just an intimidator. A bully. We called him on his horseshit and he backed off. A good lesson for us.

Live on the air. Photo by Ian Bader

Howard has this poor fool Gary running all over the station getting us sandwiches and drinks and loading us down with every conceivable promotional item: stickers, shirts and hats. Gary then groups us all around ole Howard for a picture. We ham it up and all give a snarky thumbs-up — except Dave, who sneaks a raised middle finger right behind Howard's cue-ball head right when Gary says "Cheese." Man, what a farce.

The two sets tonight are the best of the tour. I sing "Bitterness" right to Raj. We bring "Sympathy" out again, and I pass my guitar to a girl who can't play worth beans and pull onstage a load of people to help sing the background parts. By the song's end, we have a good-sized battalion up with us. And for good measure, I do a little bump and grind on the stripper's pole.

After the show, we follow a big group of people to an after-hours bar called the Blue Note where supposedly Neil Young still hangs out and jams. Raj says he's too tired and stays behind. The rest of us are still vibed from the show so George, Dave, Ian and I go down there, jump onstage and play about seven songs. The place is like a hash house in Amsterdam with folks just openly lighting up. We're all pretty drunk and stoned by the time we play, but it's a gas.

We get back to the hotel close to dawn and realize we have no key so I scale the fire escape and break in through a tiny opening and let everyone in. Dave and I get back to our room and pass out face-first on our beds, still in our clothes.

* * *

Day Nineteen
8/15/87

Roscoe P. Coltrane was at it again this morning. Dave's alter ego sweet-talked a waitress downstairs into a free meal after we miss the free Continental breakfast. Sorry I missed the performance, but I was comatose. I can imagine it, though. "...Yeah hey, how are ya? Listen, we've been on the road for almost three weeks, 10 hours in the van at a time, and we just wanted one good meal...couldn't you bend the rules this one time?"

George and I wander over to the sports/titty bar to have a look. Here we are 22, and we've never seen a stripper show. As we take a seat at the bar, a girl far too young and attractive for this sort of thing is running through her routine, hanging and grinding on the shiny silver bar, barely balanced on some clear platform heels. "Taking notes, Bill?" George remarks. "Now *that's* how to work the pole."

We've been without anything for three weeks, and as we gawk at her tracing circles around her nipples with her long fingernails, George remarks dryly, "Well, *this* is distracting, isn't it?" She finishes up, and we both watch her put on a robe and take a seat next to what appears to be her seething boyfriend who's staring into his morning beer. She nestles up to him and then begins to cry on his very cold shoulder. George and I look at each other, and after realizing we're now both decidedly *not* turned on, George says, "OK, now I feel like dirt." Right.

The Curtis blew up an article from one of the interviews we did from the road and posted it on the wall near the entrance. I'm embarrassed the paper cropped out the rest of the guys from the picture. I'm feeling claustrophobic so I decide to take a walk. I don't like staying here. I feel more at home asking from the stage if we can sleep on someone's floor. Plus, you get stagnant playing the same place three nights in a row.

It's late afternoon and my long shadow follows me as I walk along Henderson Highway, past a McDonald's, a Sobeys and a Shell station. I come to a little park with benches circling a big fountain. I take a seat and catch up on my journal. It feels good to be alone for a spell. Then I decide to write my friend Joy a letter.

After my grandfather died last year and Mary and I started having problems, I turned to a new group of friends who lived out in the San Gabriel Valley. Melody, Joy, her sister Holly, her boyfriend Larry, Melody's sister Lisa and her boyfriend Doug and Susan Rosa. It was easy to open up. I had no history with them and they didn't know anyone in my circle. We'd all talk for hours on Joy's floor listening to music until we were practically comatose.

I've come to rely on Melody as a sounding board and for helping me focus all my disparate ideas on music, politics, religion. She's a real straight-shooter who doesn't let me get away with anything. Joy's kind of like a spiritual counterpart. Patient, a good listener, and completely invests in everything you share with her. Although I've only known Joy since last year I get this feeling like I've always known her. Like there's parts of her that don't photograph.

After I finish the letter, I raise my head and realize it's turned completely dark. I get up and all the blood races to my head. I'm not sure why, but I suddenly feel out of sorts being away from the rest of the guys. I start to walk back to the hotel but soon find myself picking up the pace, and I get this sort of irrational fear like I'm being followed. I don't feel right again until I spot the guys all congregated around a table near the bar.

"Hey, where've you been?" Ian asks me.

"Down the road. I took a walk," I say breathing heavily.

"Nice of you to join us," Ian cracks. "We go on in ten minutes. Hey, what's with you?"

"I don't know," I say. "All of a sudden I realized I was over 2,000 miles from home and needed to see you guys."

Ian looks cockeyed at me for a second and then seems to get it. "Well, take a few minutes, and I'll go make sure the guitars are in tune."

It's Saturday night, and the Curtis is packed. Tonight's shows are even better than last night's. The highlight again is a glorious, building version of "Bitterness." I sing the repeating coda, "We've found a place where truth is inborn," right at Raj with my arm around him. I turn toward the soundboard, and there's Ian raising his arms toasting us. Great moment.

Me and Raj in Winnipeg doing "Bitterness." Photo by Ian Bader

Late in the set, a pretty blonde yells up at us, "I love your drummer."

"We love him too, and you can't have him," I say playfully.

"All right!" Dave calls out. "Give the drummer some."

The plan is for us all to go over to McKiegan's place to settle the score money-wise and plan out the last half of the tour. As I head back up to my room to change into a dry shirt, a short jet-black-haired girl gets into the elevator with me. As the elevator begins to rise, I can feel the holes she's staring into me.

"You guys were really amazing," she says in a tiny shy voice. "You were possessing me."

"Wow, that's…something," I say cautiously.

"I saw the article in the paper," she says leaning in against me. "I really liked what you said."

I look closer at her. Not sure what, but something's going on there. She finally says, "I came tonight to give you my soul."

"It's pretty crowded inside as it is," I say trying to turn this thing elsewhere.

"Well, there's enough room for you inside of me," she says.

I look down at her heaving breasts revealed nicely by a low-cut halter top. Uh-oh, I think to myself. The elevator doors mercifully open, and I begin to walk toward my room as she matches me stride for stride. When we reach the door I stop.

"Is this your room?" she asks moving between me and the door. "You can have me, you know."

I don't like how vulnerable and lonely I feel. In a flash, I picture both the agony and the ecstasy, and finally say, "I don't think it's such a good idea." I turn the key and open the door to find Dave and the pretty blonde who called out to him during the show. They look like they're getting friendly. "Sorry guys. Enjoy," I say grabbing a dry shirt and splitting.

I quickly head back to the elevator and the girl follows me. I turn to her and say, "Look, God knows it would be fun to roll around for a while, but we're all heading over to our promoter's house to settle some business and...listen, you don't really want to do this." She looks unfazed and continues to follow me as I decide to take the stairs to the ground floor.

I find Ian, George and Raj leaning against the bar looking deep in conversation. "I found Goldilocks in my bed," I say to them.

"Huh?" George says downing the rest of his drink.

"Dave is entertaining a young lass and will apparently not be joining us," I announce.

"That young stallion," Ian beams. "I would have hated to report back home that no one on this tour got lucky."

"Who's your friend, Bill?" George asks.

"We gotta get out of here," I say. "This girl says she wants to give me her soul."

"Get outta town," he says peeking over my shoulder to get a better look.

We all head out to the parking lot, and as we reach the van Ian says, "You know, they were taking bets over who would go through the most condoms on this tour."

"Bullshit. Who?" I ask as we tumble into the van leaving the sad mystery girl behind.

"Conrad, Russ, Greg..." Ian says.

"All guys? How sad," I say, looking back at the girl waving meekly as we drive off.

"She didn't look too shabby, Bill," George says looking in the rear-view mirror.

"Nah," I say. "I finally have my eyes fixed ahead, and I don't want to fuck it up."

On the way over, Ian tells us he heard when McKiegan booked the punk band the Exploited's tour of Canada, they got so pissed at him they totaled his car.

"This of course begs the question, why would anyone loan their car to the Exploited?" George asks.

"You think that's something," Ian goes on. "I heard he screwed Rank and File out of some cash so they broke his arm."

"Say what you want about that buffoon McKiegan," George says, "but he has a fine-looking girlfriend."

"Hey," Ian says. "If the Exploited totaled his car and Rank and File busted his arm, maybe Divine Weeks should fuck his girlfriend."

"Fabulous plan, Ian," I say, "but we all know no matter how cool we'd like to think we are, we could never pull it off. We'd probably just become her best friend. You know: 'Oh, you guys are *so* sweet. I'm *so* glad we're friends.'"

"Sounds about right," Ian sighs.

After we settle up with McKiegan, he gets blithering drunk and stoned and turns into a gushing bore droning on about said pretty girlfriend who just dumped him this afternoon. "It's a real pisser, eh ham?" he says before passing out. Yeah, shocking, eh ham?

* * *

Day Twenty
8/16/87

I crashed on George's and Ian's floor last night. Woke up with a bottle full of cotton in my mouth. I got roped into the unenviable task of rousing Dave and prying him away from Goldilocks this morning. When Dave rejoins us, he's already got the tour armor back on. He gets us all organized and quickly packed up. Then right before we leave, he retreats across the parking lot to say goodbye to her. We all watch as he holds her hand and kisses her pouty mouth goodbye.

As Dave settles into the driver's seat and pulls the van out of the parking lot, George breaks the silence. "That was very touching, Dave. Very gallant."

"No breakfast...but a proper and sincere farewell," Ian razzes him.

Dave's not talking. I think he's a little embarrassed it happened.

We all look like a collective train wreck as we hit the American border. Crossing into Canada was a breeze, but getting back in the U.S. is a major hassle. We were sure the cavity check Fang warned us about was coming. It never did, but it was a real pain in the ass anyway. These border agents are on monstrous power trips. And why? Simply because they can get away with it. You're stuck there at their mercy until they see fit to let you through. We were there for hours. They open up the van and go through what seemed like every frickin' inch of it. We all stand there helplessly watching this guy open Dave's toolbox and take out every lug wrench, placing them methodically in four neat rows on the asphalt. He then stares at each row like it's emitting the great hidden truths of the universe.

Meanwhile, another agent pulls out Dave's bag and starts poring over his journal. As he flips through it, he stops to take notes. Probably on the part where Dave wrote how to make magic mushrooms. I don't know if this is all bullshit to prompt us to crack and confess to the killing of Jimmy Hoffa or just what. Basically all it did was fucking bore us to tears. When it's finally over, I ask one of them if it was as good for him as it was for us. He frowns so I decide to shut the fuck up before he tells me to bend over and say "Ahhhh."

Returning to the U.S., it feels like we're starting a second tour. Up to Edmonton and that whole hangover and aftermath was like a tour in itself. God knows it was a mindfuck. Beyond anything we could have anticipated. Now it feels like we've conquered something, and like nothing could possibly faze us.

We've done 17 shows the last 11 nights plus the one without Raj at the after-hours club. We haven't had a day off since the first night in Calgary ten days ago, and there's no open date until after Chicago two days from now. The pace is unlike anything we've ever faced before, and we're a little worn down, but we've finally become the well-oiled machine I always hoped we'd be. As we drive through the Dakotas, we make a vow between us: to dig down   deep   and   stay   hungry.

Tonight's gig is in Minneapolis, home of three big influences, the Replacements, Hüsker Dü and Soul Asylum — bands responsible for us and a lot of other bands existing. But we're a little bummed. We were supposed to play the 7th Street Entry of the infamous First Avenue opening for the Meat Puppets, but lost out to some local group at the last minute. Ian called the booker, Steve McClellan, and promised we'd play extra early for just a half-hour for free, to no avail.

When we pull into town, we press our faces against the glass window of the Uptown Bar where we're playing, but it's closed for another hour. So George and I decide to explore the area. We go along 26th Street until we come to Lyndale Avenue and see a hip-looking record store and decide to check it out. Oar Folk Record Store says the sign. We step inside and see a fellow sitting on the counter reading a *Flipside*. We introduce ourselves. Terry's his name. An affable fellow with soft eyes. "Where you guys playin'? The Cabooze or Goofy's?"

"Place called the Uptown Bar," George says. "Any good?"

"Yeah, way cool, but it's acoustic only on Sundays."

"McKiegan!" George cries out. "Fucker never told us it'd be acoustic!"

"That ought to be real interesting," I say, conjuring up what life onstage might feel like after doing the only two songs we've ever done acoustically.

"We were supposed to open for the Meat Puppets at the 7th Street Entry, but we got bumped," George says.

"Local politics, no doubt," Terry says with a shrug.

Terry tells us that Oar Folk is like a rock 'n' roll town square. He regales us with old stories about the Replacements, Hüsker Dü, Soul Asylum, the Suburbs and the Suicide Commandos killing time roaming the used bins or just stopping in to shoot the shit. Man, if we can just get to that level like the Replacements, that's all I want. Just pull up to the club, climb out of our van and know two or three hundred people are ready to get it from us, then move on to the next town and do it all over again.

As we leave Terry calls out, "Hey, say hello to Anita over at the Uptown Bar. She's Tommy and Bob Stinson's mom. She's tended bar over there for years."

When we get back, Ian greets us with a sour look on his face.

"Where in the hell have you guys been?" Ian asks a tiny bit annoyed.

"At this really cool record store," I say. "Dude who worked there was telling us all these cool local stories." I pause and can tell Ian has something stuck in the back of his throat he doesn't want to tell us. "Ian, spit it out. What's the hassle?" I ask.

"Well, it's acoustic-only tonight and…there's no soundcheck."

"Oh, the guy at the record store broke it to us," George chimes in calmly. "Yeah, it's true. We're fucked."

As we walk in, a sign on the door reads: "The Uptown Bar, Hangout for the Replacements." George says sarcastically, "I'm sure Paul Westerberg *loves* this."

"Well, we better do a quick rehearsal or it'll be "Idiot Child" and "Dry September" and then some horrible space jam for an hour," Dave says leading us out to our van. He jumps on top of the roof and starts banging away on his bongos. "Come on everybody, let's do this."

Raj straps on his acoustic guitar and George grabs some maracas and a tambourine, and we join Dave on the roof and start running through all our stuff as if we're playing electric. People start drifting over to the van and staring up at us like we're doing the Beatles' rooftop concert. Dave hams it up in an old circus ringmaster voice, "That's right folks, if you like what you see and hear then catch us in just a few minutes at the fabulous Uptown Bar. Just step this way." We figure it beats the hell out of walking up and down the street wearing a sandwich board over our shoulders. Ian says we should just do the gig out here under the stars.

We get so carried away we almost miss the gig. The bartender comes out to the parking lot, spots us and the group crowded around our van. "Hey guys, you're on! Get in here will ya!"

We march in with our loyal troupe following us, grab some beers and hustle up onstage which is literally the proverbial hole in the wall. I step to the mic and say, "I hope you all enjoyed Divine Weeks' rooftop show. Sorry we didn't get to do 'Get Back,' but I hope we passed the audition."

We make it through about seven songs until the cook of the joint staggers drunk onstage and won't leave. I figure either be an asshole rock star or go with it. I hand him a guitar that's not plugged in, and he happily plays it for the rest of the set.

We earn a whopping $50 for the night. After my usual plea from the stage for some kindness, three University of Minnesota girls offer us their floor. We thank them by forking over our free drink tickets and promise to do their dishes. We all stay up late into the night drinking and listening to the Blue Hippos' record, heralded as the next big local band. I'm not convinced. When I finally climb into my sleeping bag, I think to myself how good it feels to be back playing in a smoky club and sleeping on a floor again.

* * *

Day Twenty-One
8/17/87

The three girls who take us in share an old two-story Victorian house in the university district. It's Karen, Jack and a shy English girl we never get the name of. Karen does most of the talking. Totally accommodating, sweet and nurturing. However, she creates quite the distraction bouncing around this morning in just a Sonic Youth T-shirt clearly revealing what lovely breasts she has. Her big sweater and pea coat hadn't shown what lovely assets she possessed last night.

I watch from across the very cramped kitchen as Ian pours himself a second cup of coffee. I can see Ian's smile freeze as Karen presses against him as she reaches for some sugar just above him. "'Scuzie," she chirps as Ian babbles, "Homana-homana-homana…ah, take your time dear."

We make good on our promise to clean up the kitchen after breakfast and then all stand like dorks holding our coffee cups as Karen beams at us, "Gosh, you guys are *so* nice."

"It's nice being nice…ah…to the nice," Ian manages to say with a big dumb smile.

When Karen leaves the room, George scowls at Ian. "It's *nice*…being *nice*…to the *nice*? Very smooth, Ian."

"Hey, I didn't exactly hear you speak with the tongue of Socrates," Ian hisses back. "Christ, she's standing there with tits out to here. Gimme a fucking break already."

We exchange phone numbers and Karen assures us that we have a place to stay when we return in the fall. Off to Chicago now.

We're still driving around without a spare tire, but everyone we talk to is trying to charge upwards of $150 for a new one. "So Ian, what you're telling us is we don't have money to spare…for a spare," George says to the groans of one and all. "It's no fair. You guys know all my material."

Ian says he has a friend in Chicago and we can crash at his place. Also says we can find a decent priced used tire in Chicago. "If we make it," Raj chimes in. "Let's not wait too long. We've got a tire jack that couldn't raise a Matchbox car."

As we make our way through the Illinois flatlands, I decide to write my mom a letter as the Stooges' *Fun House* blares over the stereo. It's her birthday in two days, and I want to share the dream I had last night that's been on my mind all day. I'm climbing up this hill, I get to the top, and there's my mom. I don't know if it's heaven or what, but I say to her, "I wish I could have taken away all those demons that haunted you." She turns to me, smiles and says, "Sweetheart, it was never your job. Now go and be free." Then she grabs my hands and twirls me around like I'm four again. Round and round and round until it feels like the force will pop my arms out of their sockets. Then she lets go, and I go soaring through the air. Just a pure blissful infinite flight into the blue and beyond. I wake up feeling weightless. Renewed. Free. Really amazing dream.

The heat is brutal as we hit Chicago. Remarkable, considering just four days ago torrential rains hit here causing the worst flooding in the city's history.

Dave is driving. George in the passenger seat. "Hate to tell you guys," Dave grimly announces. "The motor's been running hot for a while. Gonna have to turn on the heater to take some heat off the motor."

Ian, Raj and I are in back and within minutes we're suffocating. Ian opens the sliding door as we roll along, but it's like a hair dryer blowing in our faces. All three of us in back volunteer to drive, but Dave's not falling for it: "Thanks, but I know what you poor fuckers are trying to do. I ain't getting' back there."

It's a sleepy Monday night, and we're booked at a tiny little blues club called Gaspar's. While we set up, the booker tells us McKiegan never sent anything to him to help promote the show. "Fucking McKiegan!" George bellows to the heavens. As showtime nears, only a couple people are in the audience which puts George in a foul mood. He's starting to really bum us out grousing what a waste it is if so few are here. Dave's not hearing any of it: "George, get off your fucking high horse, strap on your bass and just get up there and look pretty."

Twelve people end up showing tonight and we make a whopping $18 for our efforts. We close the set with "Sympathy..." and make sure every one of those 12 people either play guitar, bass, drums or sing a part of the song. At one point I realize everyone is onstage and no one is left in the audience so I jump offstage and sit in a chair about halfway back and clap along. The rest of the guys catch on and join me at a table. We sit and watch all 12 audience members carry the song without us. Before the song completely falls apart we jump back up there, grab back our instruments and bring the song home. It's like a small private party, and the audience is really into us. They give us an encore and we kill an emphatic version of "The Who Thing" climaxed by Raj heaving his guitar high up in the air and letting it nosedive on the stage. Raj then stands for a moment and marvels at the beautiful desultory sounds escaping from his amplifier before slumping off the stage. It's a fucking wonder that guitar hasn't fallen apart yet.

After the culture shock and chaos of the first three weeks, we're finally totally focused on the task at hand. But I won't lie: It's hard on nights like tonight. We put out for those 12 people, and ever since Vancouver we've made good on our vow to give everything we can to the people who *do* come and not punish them because there's not some huge crowd worshipping us. We just keep telling ourselves, we gotta stay hungry. Well, except for George, who keeps bitching about no one being here tonight until an over-excitable guy comes bounding up to us as we're loading up and says, "You guys were one of the greatest bands I've ever seen."

"Oh thanks, man," George says, suddenly happy as he watches the rest of us load up our gear.

"I'm Tulsa Dave. You guys coming through Tulsa?" he asks.

"Not this tour, but maybe in the fall," Ian says shoving the last of our gear into the back of the van before adding, "Don't worry, George, we don't need any help."

"Do you want to?" Tulsa Dave asks. "If you can squeeze it in, I can get you into the happening place in town."

We all look at each other. "Shit," Ian says, "we've got a big gap between Kansas City and Dallas next week. If you don't mind, why don't you make a call and see what you can come up with, and I'll take your number and call you in a few days."

"Dude, it's done," he says excitedly. "Don't worry. It'll be killer. I promise. *Call* me."

After 12 straight days of shows my voice is shot. I'm croaking now, my speaking voice barely audible. I was going to just turn in but decide to see if I can catch Mary. I haven't spoken to her since she left for Lake Arrowhead a week ago. As the phone rings I hold my breath. She answers quietly, and I know I've woken her. Hearing her voice, soft and unguarded, pulls at my heartstrings. I tell her I miss her, and she says I sound awful. My heart sinks. I want her to tell me I sound sweet and hoarse and full of longing. She asks if we can talk tomorrow because she's wiped out from driving back from Arrowhead and needs to get some rest. I've been shrieking my guts out for 12 straight nights and bouncing along in the back of a goddamn van, and she can't talk because she's too wiped out from a 90-minute drive from Lake Arrowhead? I just tell her to go back to sleep and hang up.

* * *

Day Twenty-Two
8/18/87

We haven't done laundry since Calgary, and I'm worried my pants are going to run away from me the next time I try to put them on. So other than laundry, we just veg all day at Ian's friend Jim's place. It feels like we're about ten and home sick from school watching *I Dream of Jeannie* and *Get Smart* reruns.

It's our first day off in 13 days, and Raj and I are officially losing it. This afternoon, we're in our sleeping bags and Jim's little black dog stands over us with this sincere and curious stare. We both look at the dog then at each other. "What's the story, dude?" Raj finally asks the dog. Little guy cocks his head and furrows his brows, and this is suddenly the funniest fucking thing we've ever seen so Raj asks him again, "What's the haps, dude?" Same reaction. We can't stop laughing.

Dave, puzzled, raises his head and asks, "Who in the fuck do you two idiots think you're talking to?"

Raj can barely get the words out, "This dude right here" pointing at the little dog. "Can't seem to figure out what the little fella is trying to say," and we both bust up for another five minutes. Just one of those beyond-wasted moments where you're so delirious you can't stop laughing, and you don't even know why.

In the late afternoon we get hungry and manage to work up a nice head of steam raiding the cupboards just when Jim comes back and catches us with our hands literally in the cookie jar.

If it wasn't for a radio interview at Northwestern U. tonight we might never have moved beyond the kitchen. On the way we found a used tire at this tire graveyard. Still had to cough up $60. Then we got an expensive education on Illinois toll roads. One wrong turn and you're screwed. Our quaint half-hour drive to Northwestern turned into an expensive hour and a half as we went back and forth taking one wrong entrance after another. Cha-ching.

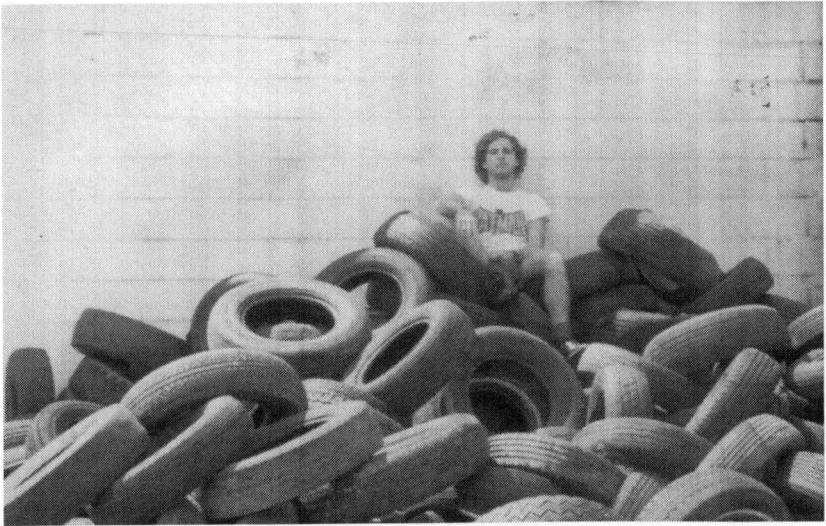

Ian at the tire graveyard, Chicago. Photo by Dave Smerdzinski

When we get to the radio station, we waste no time launching in and have the DJ in stitches with tales of our stay at a brothel, the interview with Howard on the Rock with no pants and our weekend with the yuppies. After we do "Idiot Child" live, we hold a quiz to give away a few of our records. Some folks hear us and dig us enough to drop by the station to watch. So, we bring them in to help us sing along. Unfortunately, we have no gig tonight to beg people to come to, and that's a drag.

Driving back, Dave remarks, "I can't believe we'll be home in ten days" which does kind of shock us all. It's like we've finally found our groove and could go on for months like this.

Ian tells us Mary firmed up a welcome-home gig at Club Lingerie the first Friday after we return.

"How many days is that after we get back?" George asks.

"A week," Ian says. "Oh, and the big *L.A. Weekly* article is coming out a day before the Lingerie show."

"Fuck, a week?" George stews. "I wish we could just cruise back into town, climb out of the van and get right onstage and blow away every single motherfucker who ever said we were shit."

"Let's just make sure we rehearse plenty in that time," I say. "I don't want get all fat and happy and lose what we've built out here."

Dave's art shot of me. Photo by Dave Smerdzinski

* * *

Day Twenty-Three
8/19/87

It's my mom's birthday today and three years ago to the day we played our first gig. I call her this morning just before we head off for Iowa City. I can tell she's been drinking. I'm still thinking about what that crazy lady in Vancouver said.

As usual I can't get in a word, and she floods me with an array or irreverent thoughts and observations. Just when I'm about to cut her off and tell her enough, she says: "B., now don't ever forget, it's not about the having and getting, it's about the being and becoming." I write that out and tape it to the ceiling of the van next to all the flyers, tour mottos and in-jokes we've been sticking up there. That's my mom with the last-second save that always keeps our relationship alive. Beautiful heartbreak amidst sublime flights of fancy.

I put in a mix tape on my Walkman as we near the Iowa border. Simon & Garfunkel's "The Boxer" comes on and my mind drifts back to when it was just my mom and me.

After Larry threw us out, my mom had her first breakdown that I know of, and she had to go away for a while. After she found her balance again, she and I moved into a little apartment in Santa Monica. Seemed like we never had any money. Lived paycheck to paycheck. I mean, why there was no money still baffles me considering what Larry supposedly had, but whatever. It was chaotic and unstable, but it really was the best time we had together.

She got a job delivering newspapers and collecting the change from the racks for the *Evening Outlook*, a small Santa Monica newspaper. She called it a shit job, but she never accepted that was all she was. Always called herself an artist and a writer. I discovered my creative muse while we lived in that apartment. I'd watch my mom furiously write on the fly, in between meals and on the go. She'd pour her latest poem or a one-liner on scraps of crumpled napkins or on backs of envelopes. I do that now. She always told me, "Be ready to receive. You never know when God will gift you."

Mom in our old apartment, always writing. Photo by Bill See

We were not so much mother and son: I was her 12-year-old roommate. For better or worse, I learned a hell of a lot about survival and resiliency. I saw up close, real soon, what was out there, good and bad. I paid for that in some respects, and it alienated me from a lot of my peers. I quickly outgrew friends because I was dealing with the real world by age 11. I stopped hanging out with Clark Barry, the first friend I ever really had, because we couldn't relate on the same level anymore. He was still watching cartoons, and I'm watching household budgets. I guess once you get a taste of *Night Gallery* you don't go back to Bugs Bunny.

I've always wondered what would have happened if my mom and I could've hung in there — just the two of us. I have very warm memories of her bringing home burgers and Suzy Q's from the

Sweet Sixteen café and us sitting down on the floor at her Lazy Susan table talking and laughing for hours. Us against the world.

Unfortunately, it all became too much and she broke down again. She'd been acting erratically for awhile, getting more manic. She invited this guy to stay at the apartment for free. I guess they were intimate or maybe he was bringing in drugs. He had some bullshit story about waiting on some big settlement from a lawsuit he had against Pan Am Airlines and promised to pay my mom all the back rent then. Of course he milked us and then stole a bunch of our shit and split. Just one of many times my mom got taken by boyfriends or shady acquaintances.

Right after that she finally lost it. She went on a binge, and my Aunt Nancy and I finally tracked her down and put her away in the psych ward at UCLA Medical Center for a while, and I went back to live at 940.

*   *   *

What a peaceful, simple existence it is out here in the Iowa flatlands. Could be 1925 for all we know. I get my camera out, and I'm about to take a shot when I notice three phallic shapes appear over the horizon with smoke escaping from each. Yup, that's a nuclear power plant, all right. What a nice picture shot to hell.

Before reaching Iowa City, I jot down some ideas for a new song I'm calling "Preachin' to the Choir." As I lay in back, going in and out of consciousness, I pick up fragments of conversation and radio excerpts, writing down a few lines before falling back to sleep. Been writing a lot like that on this trip. Dave was talking about growing up in Falls Church, Virginia just outside of D.C. That gave me the first line of the song. Later I come to hearing George telling Ian about Tibetan prayer wheels. Then later, I hear a radio report on evangelist Jim Bakker's sex scandal that's been raging this summer.

From the streets of Falls Church to Heritage
He's preachin', preachin' to the choir.
In the name forsaken money'll save his life
He's preachin', preachin' to the choir.
The man he's got the word spread like a forest fire
He's preachin', preachin' to the choir.
He spins the prayer wheel, like he spins a lie
He's preachin', preachin' to the choir.

We have an interview at the Iowa State radio station. We get to be guest DJs. We walk in and promptly take over the station, spinning about half our album including George trying out a little scratching on "In the Country." I have to hand it to George at these radio interviews. Not only is he charismatic and totally comfortable on the radio from all the DJ'ing he's done, but he comes in without his bass, sucks it up and just shakes a tambourine with all his heart and soul getting completely lost in the music. Man, I sure hope he can come to grips with everything hanging over him about grad. school and Deb. I can't imagine going on without him.

We play Jane's Addiction's demo, some Leaving Trains, Minutemen, Hüsker Dü, Meat Puppets and the Jam. Then we do a pretty unconvincing portrayal of Orson Welles' *War of the Worlds* before giving away tickets to tonight's show. We finish up with live acoustic versions of "Idiot Child" and "Sympathy for the Devil," recruiting several of the people who are pressing themselves up against the glass window to watch us.

Tonight's gig is at a place called Gabe's Oasis. The booker tells us that in the day the adjoining bar to the club is frequented by plenty of dirthead truckers, and a few wander over to watch us during our soundcheck.

"You guys know any Skynyrd?" I *swear* one of them asks.

"Nah, how 'bout Aerosmith?" George asks, starting the bass intro to "Sweet Emotion." Dave falls in, and I sing the first verse, but Aerosmith never made it to Raj's bedroom, and it falls apart.

After we finish our soundcheck, the soundman tells us we're louder than even Hüsker Dü when they came through town, which brings a huge smile to all our faces.

A mental ward is adjacent to the club and a couple of the friendly loons come up to us as we're screwing around outside the van. While I sit along a fence and strum Raj's acoustic guitar one of them says, "Hey Mr. Tambourine Man, play a song for me." I do my best to remember the verse about the "magic swirling ship" while another nut starts doing a little shimmy dance. Loons…they just seem to be drawn to me.

Vicki, the music director for the radio station, invites us to dinner at her place. Dave, Gabe's Oasis' soundman, whispers to us that Vicki has a bit of a reputation for having trysts with guys in bands that come through town. No overtures were ever made toward us so I guess we don't get her motor percolating.

Gabe's Oasis has these low girder-like beams overhead that extend from the stage all the way to the back of the club. During Raj's very long feedback-drenched solo on "Look Book," I throw the mic over my shoulder, leap up on the girders and climb my way all the way to the middle of the club and start swinging back and forth. Raj, knowing he has time to stretch it out, takes the microphone stand to his guitar and creates a glorious noise. As I swing back and forth, I sing "Would You Like to Swing on a Star?" and Raj tries to echo the melody back to me on guitar. Later, in the middle of "Dry September," I hold up my guitar case where I'd put the "Fight Racism" sticker Lisa from Portland gave me. This brings a big cheer and equally big smile from Raj who just killed tonight. Great gig.

A bunch of people crowd around the stage after the show offering us a floor to sleep on and wanting to know more about us. We talk long after closing with folks who just seem starved for something. It's pretty humbling feeling like we might actually be bringing a little of that to them. I've gone to so many shows in L.A. and after the band finishes up they sit on the lip of the stage and talk into the night with a big group of us. No rock-star escapes out the back door or any of that shit. I know we're just a little band, but we're just trying to be like that too and never change.

When the last of the people finally head home, we pack up. Every day the equipment seems a little heavier. We're really fighting the fatigue now. Maybe next tour we can afford a roadie. For now, we just gotta stay hungry.

The soundman stole a bunch of beer from the bar and sticks it in Dave's trap case. We decide he's the safest bet for a place to stay tonight so we follow him back to his apartment which is walking distance from the club. Hell, everything seems to be walking distance in Iowa City.

We all sit around talking and drinking into the wee hours while the Minutemen's *Double Nickels on the Dime* plays over and over. George sits in a rocking chair in a state of semi-consciousness holding a beer on his knee most of the night. Every five minutes or so we shout at him, "Right, George?" and he partially comes to, chortling away, then leans forward like the dude on the Pirates of the Caribbean ride only to fall back in his chair and pass out again.

* * *

Day Twenty-Four
8/20/87

Poor George tossed his cakes last night. "I don't know what happened," he says surprisingly baffled. "Must have been something I ate."

"Couldn't have been the ten beers, could it, George?" Ian asks trying to sound equally baffled.

"It's just odd," George says slowly. "Seems like we've been downing about ten beers every night without a problem."

"It's a matter of attrition, George," Ian says shrugging his shoulders, "and you, my friend, are starting to lose the battle."

George and me. Not morning people. Photo by Ian Bader

I didn't even make it to my sleeping bag. Passed out on the floor with my head tipped over at a right angle against the sofa. Woke up with the mother of all neckaches. My neck feels like it did the morning after I first saw the Ramones and bobbed my head for the entire show.

Ian's been on the phone all morning trying to fill our four-day hole at the end of the tour. As I nurse a cup of coffee, I listen to Ian strike out on both Lawrence and Wichita, Kansas. He then chases a lead on Lincoln, Nebraska, but the only opening they have is three days after our last scheduled gig in Dallas which would add backtracking about a thousand miles. We don't have the money for that.

Ian finally gets hold of Tulsa Dave, the over-excitable guy we met in Chicago. To our surprise, he's already lined up the gig and was just waiting to hear back from us.

"Guys, we've got Tulsa firm for Wednesday the 26th," Ian says sounding relieved.

"Thank Christ," I say. "So that means we've just got Sunday, Monday and Tuesday off?"

"Well," Ian tells us, "if we want to go back to St. Louis again after Kansas City, we have an offer to do a live in-store appearance at a record store on Monday."

Dave emerges from the shower and grabs a cup of coffee, then starts poking around the cupboards until he finds some cinnamon rolls. "Dave!" Ian hisses. "You can't just help yourself to those."

"Listen, I'm sorry," he says in between bites, "but if I don't line my stomach with something I'm gonna puke blood."

Speaking of which, George is looking green. Dave looks over at him and says, "George, you look awful. If you're gonna throw up again do it toward Bill, will ya."

Just then Vicki, the music director we had dinner with last night, comes out of the bedroom wearing only a large Butthole Surfers T-shirt. She takes a couple steps out of the bedroom and quickly realizes she has a lot of eyes on her.

"Hi, again," she says meekly.

"Hiii-ie," goes the chorus back at her.

"Looks like the rumor *was* bullshit," Ian whispers to me. "She doesn't target the bands. It's the *soundmen*."

"Come on, let's get going," I say. "Somebody get a spatula and scrape George off the couch."

It's Columbia tonight. Naturally, on the way to our interview at the University of Missouri radio station, the van starts running hot again and we have to put on the freaking heater. It's literally like a mobile sauna. Thank God we're all immune to the smell now. It's probably pretty rancid in here.

We manage to get hopelessly lost again so we stop at this café to call and get directions. "I'll call," I say, climbing out of the van. The sun has long set, but it's still oppressively hot.

I walk in the place — your basic Midwestern college hangout — and dial the number for the station. I glance over the menu on the wall and remember how starving I am. As I wait for someone to answer, I fixate on the posted special of the day. Buffalo burgers? As I picture Indians throwing spears at herds of buffaloes, I start humming along to a very familiar-sounding song that's blaring through the place. "Jesus Christ, that's *us*!" I scream. "That's me singing, that's my band...th, th, th, that's us," I babble looking all around at all the blank stares. Everyone in the cruddy little place has these looks like "Big shit for the fruit" and goes back to their business.

I race back to the van like I just met Santa Claus. "What a trip," I say to everyone. "I just heard 'In the Country' on the radio in that place."

"Get outta town," George says amazed, quickly flipping the radio tuner to the left just in time to hear the last strains of "In the Country." The DJ comes on to say, "That was Divine Weeks, who'll be in-studio guests any time now to promote their gig at the Blue Note tonight."

When we finally make it to the station we start right in. At this point, the DJ only needs to ask one question, and we're off.

"Hey, Divine Weeks here," I begin. "We're from L.A., new in town. Listen, you don't want to wake up tomorrow and realize all you did the night before was stay home and watch *Dynasty* now do you? Now, listen carefully. You're getting ver-ry sleepy…imagine a shiny gold watch on a long chain swinging back and forth before your eyes."

"That's right," Dave takes over. "Just let go now and come with us. You…are coming…to the Blue Note tonight…to be saved by rock and roll. Divine Weeks is coming to lift you from your sad little life…and we're gonna take you higher," he says as we both break into the Sly Stone song.

The DJ looks like he's not sure if we're funny, colossally arrogant or just completely nuts. Whatever, we don't really care what anyone thinks anymore.

We're headlining again tonight so the stage is ours for as long as we want. I'm wearing my Divine Weeks shirt and my hair tied up with Mary's long blue paisley bandana. I step to the mic and motion for everyone to move closer. "Hey, come close enough, and you might wind up on stage. Hey, Raj give me some," and he begins the ringing intro to "Copper Wire" and off we go.

We're putting out but nothing's coming back, and after about five songs we start to get a little frustrated. Maybe it's the heat, but the place is just Deadsville, so we decide to have some fun. We do as many fractured covers we can think of.

The Blue Note, Columbia, Missouri.   Photo by Ian Bader

I pass my guitar around and whisper to whoever has it what the chord changes are. It's a little cheap, but everyone seems to come around and appreciate we're trying to break down the barriers. We get about half the club onstage for "Sympathy," and it's a party so we just let the ending rave-up go on and on with everyone just singing along, shaking tambourines or maracas. The song mutates into "Mona" then "Not Fade Away" then "Summertime Blues" then back to "Sympathy for the Devil." Must have been a 25-five minute version. When I reclaim my guitar, it has only three strings left, and there's a big splatter of blood across the pick guard.

For an encore, we pull everything back into focus and close with our lullaby-like "Wide Eyed." It's not a show we'd want to do every night, but we've reconciled that for a first tour, our prime focus is just making sure people remember us. Lay a foundation. By any means necessary. Then when we come back in the fall we can really seal the deal. Considering how dead it was when we went on, we're pretty pleased with ourselves because by the end people were into us. After the show, the theme continues. Loads of people are buying us drinks and asking us when we'll be back. Good sign.

Weird thing happened, though. While I'm packing up, a pretty girl comes up to me and offers me — as in, *only me* — a place to stay. "Sorry, I go nowhere without the fellas," I say. "Package deal and all."

She asks if I'm sure and I nod. "Hmmm, too bad," she says, sucking hard on the straw to her drink. I take a long look at her, and it occurs to me she might be on something. I'm not sure if it's the sexual lasers she's shooting or something more chemical.

"Let me at least buy you a drink," she says turning toward the bar. "What's your poison?"

"Whatever you're drinking, thanks," I say. "What's that, a vodka and...?"

"Cranberry," she says smiling.

I'm still packing up gear, and when I turn back around, she's holding two Cape Cods. "Last chance," she says. "I've got a nice big bed." I confess: Ten thousand blazing images bounce off the sides of my head and drop to my loins before I say thanks, but no thanks. I ask her to hold my drink for a second so I can run some gear out to the van. I get back and she's gone. Left the drink on a nearby table on a napkin with a lipstick kiss. Oh well. I throw back the drink and head over where Ian is chatting up a pretty brunette named Melissa, the barmaid at the club.

Melissa tells us she's hosting a party at her place tonight and to come on over. By the time we make it over there, I start to feel real strange. Not drunk, just...off.

I grab a beer, sit on a throw rug in the living room and pick up an acoustic guitar that's leaning against a wall. After a few minutes, George tells me I'm strumming a guitar with no strings. I look over at him and tiny trails appear like little comet tails.

George is debating Shakespeare with the DJ who interviewed us earlier at the radio station. "George," I whisper, "I think someone dosed me."

"Huh? With what?" he asks.

"I don't know, acid, ecstasy, shrooms, *something*," I say.

"Was it someone here?" he says looking around.

"No, no," I say. "I think it was a chick I gave the brush-off to at the club."

"How do you know?" he asks quietly.

"I'm telling you, George, I'm *tripping*. Just trust me. But listen. Don't say anything to anyone about it."

"O.K., O.K., I'm cool," he says.

An uneventful half-hour passes with me just sitting tight trying to ride it out. Then I have to pee. As I carefully navigate myself toward the bathroom, a guy comes up to me and asks if I can get him some acid too. Thanks, George.

Someone gets the bright idea if I drink to excess, I'll dull the trip. All that does is make me slow, tired and stupid. It's so fucking hot and my senses are so super exaggerated that I end up sticking my head in the refrigerator to cool off. Pure exhaustion, sleep deprivation and too many substances finally knock me out so completely the trip is left to carry on merrily in my unconsciousness.

* * *

Day Twenty-Five
8/21/87

I rub the sleep out of my eyes to the sight of a girl asleep on the couch right above where George and I finally passed out on the floor. She's draped across the couch with her long creamy legs spread ever so slightly across the arm of the sofa. I think I'm still in some sort of hallucinatory dream state. I look over at George who's starting to wake up.

"George," I ask. "What the hell did I miss last night?"

"If something happened I missed it too," George says, now staring at Sleeping Beauty. "How are you, anyway? You still think you were dosed last night?"

"Well, if I wasn't," I say pulling on my jeans, "that was the freakiest night I've had in a long time."

Just then the girl comes to, smiles at us and pulls her shirt down, and retreats to a back room.

As I wander around the house trying to remember where the bathroom is, I notice a bedroom door ajar, peek inside and see two naked bodies heaped on a sheetless mattress in the middle of the room. The girl white as a ghost, the guy black as coal.

Carson, the guy who shares the house with Melissa, treats us to breakfast. We gladly accept the free grub. We're almost tapped again. Over breakfast, Ian gives us an accounting of the U.S. portion of the tour. We made $50 in Minneapolis, $18 in Chicago and $75 in both Iowa City and Columbia. That's a whopping $218 earned in the U.S. the last five days. Almost half that was eaten up on gas. Plus, we had to buy that friggin' tire in Chicago. We're only getting about nine miles to the gallon with all the equipment weighing us down. With a 20-gallon tank that's roughly 180 miles covered per tank. We're paying almost a dollar a gallon on average so that's around $20 a tank. Since getting back to the U.S., we've traveled about 1,000 miles so far.

That's about five gas tanks full or $100 spent just on gas. So, we're in the red for the U.S. part of the tour.

If it wasn't for the $650 we made in Calgary and $500 in Winnipeg, we'd be fucked. Ian keeps telling us to forget that money because we need almost all of it for gas to get us home and to pay off the van. Plus, we've already started pinching from that so we've got to be careful.

It's hotter than hell driving across Missouri. Just oppressive, heavy, miserable heat. Like you could just reach out and grab a handful of it. Within minutes of my shower this morning I'm sweating and irritable.

Dave's driving all the way today, so it's Zeppelin on the tape deck. It doesn't take long before the van is a rumbling mobile sweatshop. About halfway to St. Louis the motor starts overheating again and Dave grimly announces, "Sorry, guys, but we've gotta turn on the heater again." It's stifling in back so we open the sliding door of the van again.

We pull into town, an area called Delmar Loop by Washington University, and meet up with Lynn, the promoter. Lynn's a dream. A promoter who actually promotes. What a freaking concept. She greets us at the club, a place called Cicero's. She had posters made up and everywhere we go, we see them. She also has care packages sent from home and copies of previews she's managed to get in the local papers for us to see.

Lynn's a short, round spark plug. She's got a big booming voice and wiry yellow-brown hair. The portrait of perpetual forward motion, always jawing and full of ideas. Seen this before. Middle-aged, single woman trying to fill a void in her life, and guys in bands are more than happy to be nurtured or even babied, having uprooted their lives to live out of a van for months at a time. She's kind of like a den mother. We're not complaining. We'll take the TLC.

Before we know it, Lynn has our next several hours accounted for. "You guys unload your gear and get set up for soundcheck. Now, we can't do the soundcheck yet. Just leave your stuff set up. Don't worry, I've told Gary."

"Gary?" Ian manages to squeeze in between Lynn's breaths.

"Gary? He's the soundman. He gives you a problem, his balls are mine. Now listen, we've gotta get to the cable TV shoot I've set up over at Euclid Records. It'll be great. Mojo Nixon just did a spot with Country Dick Montana wrestling in a hotel room. It was an absolute scream! Now come on, let me hitch a ride with you and I'll give you the skinny."

On the ride over, Lynn tells us she's been looking forward to our arrival for weeks. We all just kind of look at each other like, "Who? *Us*?" Man, last Monday in Chicago it felt like the club would've preferred serving the three drunks weaving against the bar all night than deal with us.

We pull up to Euclid Records and Lynn introduces us to the owner Joe and the manager Tony, two very affable fellows. They have us sign our record and immediately hang it up in between signed copies of records by the True Believers and the Mekons. A first for us.

The cable show guys then arrive with all their gear and set us up outside on this tree stump, a sort of indie town square hangout with about a dozen punks sitting around it. Lynn immediately steps in and gives the cable guys a spiel like she's our manager. "Listen, make these boys look good, they're gonna be huge, and you can say you were there at the beginning." If you hadn't guessed, Lynn is our new goddess.

After we tell some stories and do a brief interview, we play "Idiot Child" acoustic. Raj loves it, playing right out on the street and connecting with folks up close. Really cool people. All kind of starving for something. I totally get that, and I take down all their names and promise to put as many of them on our guest list as I can. After the cable guys shoot what they need, they keep the cameras rolling, and we do "Sympathy For The Devil" and everyone there helps us with the "woo-woos". We open a guitar case for contributions, and we make a few bucks. Hey, we'll take it.

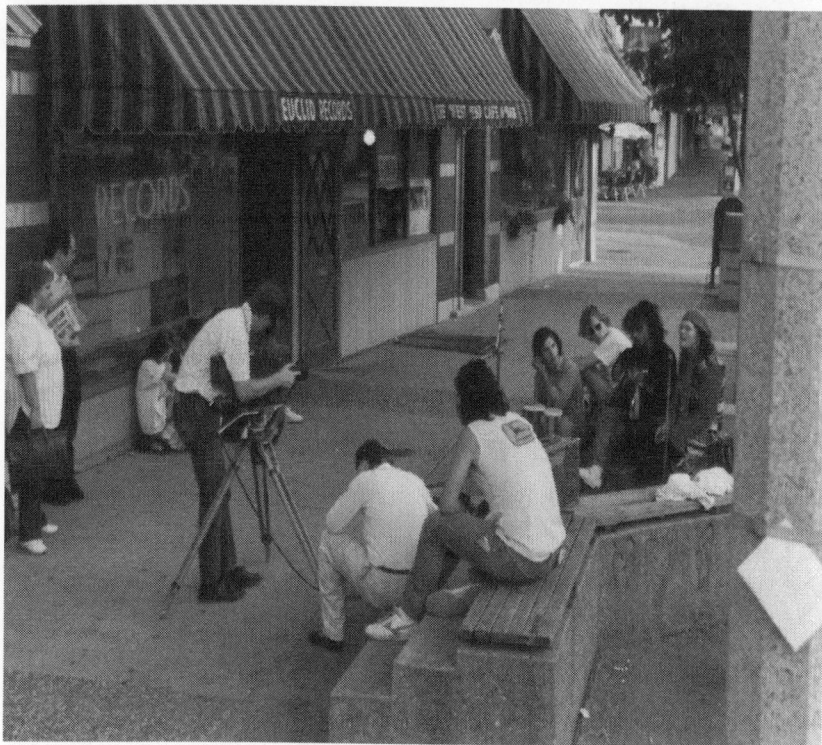

Cable TV spot in front of Euclid Records, St. Louis. Lynn, the promoter, far left.
Photo by Ian Bader

When we get back to Cicero's, Lynn has pitchers of beer and two giant pizzas out for us. Lynn says she gave Mary her address, who then passed it along to Deborah and Raj's folks whose letters arrived just today. Raj, who's coming down with a cold, is very touched and disappears after soundcheck to read their letter and call them. Mary sent me a letter too, but I decide to read it later. I fold it up and let it burn a hole in my pocket.

Deborah sent George a long letter along with two Jane's Addiction live tapes. Before the show, George and I go out to the van to listen to one. He's stressing again how we have to step it up or Jane's is going to crush the whole town, us included. I don't know, Jane's may have a bigger buzz right now, but they're still home and don't even have a record out yet.

Cicero's is in the basement of a pizza restaurant on street level. You go down these stairs leading to the back of the club which has this low ceiling with huge heaters and air conditioning ducts hanging from it. Dank inside, smoke everywhere, shitty lighting. No monitors, just two big speakers on each side of the stage that we've turned inward toward us so we can hear ourselves. No stage. You're eye-level with people standing right up to you. Our kind of place.

While we wait to go on, I lean against the bar watching the opening band just stand there expecting to be adored. I walk over to where Dave is pacing back and forth and looking annoyed. We're not real good waiting to go on.

"Why don't these fuckers just get the hell off our stage?" Dave asks with his usual nervous before-show swagger.

"I don't know," I say massaging his neck. "Why don't we avoid the Christmas rush and despise them now."

On and on they play, definitely wearing out their welcome. "Fuckers," Dave says finishing off his drink. "I guess no one told them you never know when I might kill someone. Hey, aren't you hotter than fuck?" he says looking at me in my serape over my long-sleeved red shirt, newsboy hat and black pants.

"Aren't you cold?" I say pointing at his shorts and tank top I know will be ditched after the first song.

It's a sizable crowd that keeps getting bigger as we set up. Right before we go on, four people come up and say they were at last night's show in Columbia and dug us so much they want a second helping. People driving close to 100 miles to see us again? What a turn-on. So, I empty my pockets of my free drink tickets and give them all to them. "Hey, you guys," I call out. "Give these folks your drink tickets. You won't believe it. They saw us last night in Columbia and drove all the way here to see us again tonight." They promise to cheer like maniacs. And they do.

When we're finally ready, the place is nearly filled. You can tell it's going to be a good night. Dave comes up to me from behind his kit and whispers in my ear, "You know we're going to fucking murder these people, right?" I try and hold my stupid smile as I step to the mic and say, "We're Divine Weeks from Los Angeles, but don't hold that against us. Hey, if you thought it was gonna be just another night at Cicero's, think again. You can sit on your hands for now, but if you're still like that in a half-hour we're gonna come out there and get you."

Raj rips into "Copper Wire." The song soars into rare air and we race out to meet it there. You can always tell before you hit the first chorus of that first song if you're on your way. I don't know what it is, but tonight the spirit is in the house, and we're gonna lift the goddamn roof or die trying. We drive "Copper" home, and I ask, "So, can we stay?" Our new posse yells "yes," but the crowd is still cautious, uncommitted. We don't care. We're not going to be denied.

I dedicate "I'm Gonna Fall" to Lynn. "Hey, we've been dealing with a lot of assholes on this tour so it's a real pleasure to meet up with someone like Lynn. If any of you guys are in bands or the rest of you who go to shows, you're lucky to have her around. She works her ass off." She blows me a kiss and we roll on.

We go through the new song "Animal Move Real Slow," which is really coming together now, and then "All These People Come and Go." With each song, Raj keeps turning his amp up more and more because Dave is playing harder and harder. I detect a little more from the crowd after each song so I keep pleading with them, trying to break down the barrier and force contact.

We start "Sympathy for the Devil," and I start in again over the building intro. "I don't know if you've been going to too many arena shows or what, but look, this ain't no rock concert. No security guards. You want to get up here and be part of this. Come on up. No one's gonna stop you." Our Columbia posse comes up first, grabbing tambourines and maracas, and then when we hit the "who-who"s at the end of the song, I just keep grabbing people and bringing them up to sing. The stage is just wall-to-wall people screaming along. I go to the back of the stage and sing along with Dave and Ian who's climbed onstage too. I let anyone who wants to take center stage. I'm arm in arm with Ian toasting each other with bottles of beer. It's a celebration.

We have the crowd now. I whisper to Raj to start "Dry September." It's a bit risky going heavy after the celebratory mood we just created, but I know we have a great version in us. "You guys keeping track of the coal miners' strike in South Africa? It all starts with one heart. And you watch, Mandela will be freed before the year is over." I drop in a snippet of Special AKA's "Free Nelson Mandela" in the middle of the song and then in the primal scream section, as it's become known, I release every demon left inside me. When the song ends, I get the feeling we've definitely rattled a few cages. What a 12 minutes we've just had from the carnival of "Sympathy" to the exorcism of "Dry September."

We bring the set home with visceral versions of "Soapbox" and "Look Book" punctuated by Raj ramming his guitar into the low ceiling. Pete Townshend would be proud. Our posse from Columbia leads the cheers for an encore, and we oblige with a walloping version of "The Who Thing." As I walk offstage I shout "Take that" and jump into Dave's arms. "We *did* fucking murder them, didn't we?" I say. "Fuckers never stood a chance," he says, pouring his beer on my head. Raj comes up and we stare hard at each other until little smiles appear on both our dopey faces and we embrace.

Then Lynn rushes up to me and says we have to keep playing or the owner might not pay us or her. I don't know if it's bullshit or what, but we figure it's a no-lose situation. So we go back on and play another hour pulling out covers we've never even tried like Creedence's "Fortunate Son" and then "Born on the Bayou" for the first time since Calgary. We even try "Reach You," one of the very first songs we wrote, which Dave lifts to the heavens even though he's never played it before.

Cicero's, St. Louis, breaking down the barriers. Photo by Dan Barnett

Lynn grabs the microphone after our final encore and says, "Listen, I want you to know that Divine Weeks was contracted to play for 90 minutes. They played for over two hours. Anything over 90 minutes, they played because they *wanted* to. Go and buy their record. I promise I will bring them back in the fall." Everyone just cheers and yells for more.

Raj and I stand there arm in arm, leaning against each other, a couple of proud saps. "Can you believe this?" he asks beaming.

"Raj, we're doing it," I say turning toward him and resting my forehead against his. "Just like we said up on Mulholland. It's coming to life, Raj. Us against the world, and fuck them, they've got no shot. We're fucking Divine Weeks."

Raj lets out one of his great open-mouthed laughs, and I can't help but start laughing along with him. It's just pure uncontrollable joy.

"Raj, you know what? I could die happy right now."

He looks at me and blinks. He finally says softly, "Me too. But let's not. We've got a lot more to give, mate."

George then bounds over and plants a big kiss on both Raj's and my lips. We must have been really good tonight for George to let down his cool like that.

We fight through the crowd to the bar where we're mobbed by a throng of people who want to buy us drinks. Everyone has the same question: "When are you guys coming back?"

A guy from *Jet Lag* fanzine says we were the best show that's come through town since Sonic Youth last year. We do a little interview and they take some photos around the bar.

Ian tells me Cicero's owner dug us so much he threw in an extra $75 over and above our $200 guarantee. He also lets us and several new friends we just met stay after closing and celebrate. Dave takes over as guest bartender, pulling pints for everyone for another hour.

Ian also tells me his new friend, a very cute girl he met named Gina, offered to let us crash at her place tonight. I recognize her. She's one of many who came onstage during "Sympathy" to sing along.

When we start to finally come down, Ian pulls me aside. He puts his arm around me and says, "Well, you guys really pulled it off tonight."

"Ian, I knew it was ours the moment Raj tore into 'Copper Wire.'"

"Listen," Ian says pausing and putting both his hands on my shoulders to make sure I really hear him. "Tonight it hit me sometime during the set how proud I was to be a part of this. And how grateful I am that you guys made me *feel* so much a part of it. It's amazing seeing you guys seize your moment. It's really opened my eyes. I don't know what to say but...it's inspiring."

"Shit, Ian, thank you. I mean, we would have been left for dead somewhere in Canada if it wasn't for you. And everyone in this band feels the same."

"Thanks, Bill." We share a real hug that lasts for a full minute. When we release I open my eyes and catch a glimpse of Gina sitting on a barstool, not sure what to make of us.

Gina rides with us back to her place, a huge house with what seems like a mile-long driveway. We roll out all extremely drunk except Raj, our perpetual designated driver. "You guys have to chill out," Gina hisses. "My folks will shit if they find out I've brought five guys in a band back here to stay."

"What? You didn't tell us we had to fly under the radar!" Ian says much too loud. A chorus of "shhhhh!" cuts him off.

"We're gonna stay in my basement, they'll never know," she assures us.

Gina and Ian are getting along. Getting very cozy. Very cool.

We all end up playing with all the old toys in the basement like Lincoln Logs and Tinker Toys and talking and drinking until dawn. If we could have, we would've made tonight last forever.

* * *

Day Twenty-Six
8/22/87

After Gina's folks leave to do some Saturday morning errands, she lets us all take showers, and while I'm drying off I overhear Ian telling everyone if it wasn't for the close sleeping quarters he and Gina would have interfaced last night. "Well," George offers, "you *can* honestly say you did *sleep* with her."

After some coffee, we set off along I-70 toward tonight's gig in Kansas City. We're playing with labelmates of ours, this amazing band called the Flaming Lips. I can't wait to meet them.

We stop for some lunch in the middle of the flats of Missouri. It's an all-you-can-eat super salad-bar joint. Dave goes in alone, buys one plate, eats until he's full, signals to us through the big window, and then one by one each of us discreetly enters and eats on that one plate. Fortunately, the salad bar narc never gets hip.

Afterwards, we congregate in a big booth in back and George again broaches the subject of Deborah coming along for our fall tour. Again, he points out that since Ian can't commit, we need someone to step in. "I know she's a girl, and it's a valid concern whether or not she could pull her weight," he reasons. "I also know you guys are worried about whether or not we could all feel at ease, but honestly, you guys know Deb. Tell me, if there's one girl who can outdrink, outbelch, outfart us all, isn't it Deborah?"

When George first brought this up in Vancouver, the band was against it, and we're against it now. Nothing's changed. If anything, the band is more resolute than ever. Dave, the straight-shooter that he is, says flat out he doesn't want Deborah to come. Period. Raj, always reluctant to take up swords with George, is silent.

"Listen," Ian pipes in, "I'd love to sign up for another tour, but you guys have shown me you gotta go out and live your dream. It's time I go live mine. If my opinion is worth anything, and with all due respect George, I just don't think there'd be that same dynamic that's made this tour not only function so well but made it so special."

"George," I finally say. "You're putting us in a very difficult position. I think you know deep down that putting a relationship into the middle of all this — even someone as adaptable as Deborah — would present a lot of challenges we don't need on top of everything else."

George finally gives up and appears to accept the consensus of the band. I'm sure Deborah kept haranguing him, and he felt obligated to ask on her behalf.

Dave takes over driving, and as we near Kansas City, I finally read Mary's letter. She wrote it on the dock in Arrowhead. It's classic Mary — at turns witty, pithy, guarded and non-committal. Not exactly a love letter. I fold the letter back up and stare into everything we've stuck to the ceiling of the van. It feels like the band, the dream, it's bigger than Mary and I now, and it's out of our control now. Something we've so totally invested in, and there's nothing equally nourishing we can give to each other to compete with it.

The hum of the engine has me in that half-sleep state where nothing really gets all the way into your head — you just float, barely recognizing the little sound bites going off around you. The radio's on. Bad Midwestern FM radio station playing sappy old shit. "On and On" by Stephen Bishop, fucking "Feelings" by Morris Albert. Why doesn't someone turn it off? Before I know it, Cyndi Lauper's latest hit "True Colors" comes on, and I'm *crying* for fuck's sake. I don't even know why. I'm just so tired. Vulnerable, I guess. I'm trying to hide the tears, and I look across at Raj who's face to face with me, and there's tears running down *his* face. We both wipe our faces and give each other a half-smile and a shake of the head. Weird.

Up front, I'm only half listening to George going off. He's spent the last hour dissecting the Jane's Addiction tapes Deborah sent. "Fuck," he says after a particular moment on the tape. "Just *listen*   to   that."

"I hear, I hear," Dave says, becoming increasingly annoyed.

I look across at Raj again, and he rolls his eyes and shakes his head as George goes on sounding more and more bummed. "Christ, Jane's is just so huge and gaining all this momentum."

"Well, shit, George, at least we're out here slugging it out," Dave counters. "At least we're in the trenches. Every time I've mentioned Jane's out here at radio stations or clubs or whatever, no one's even heard of 'em. Myself, I like our chances."

"I know, but fuck..."

"Fuck nothing!" Dave finally explodes. "We're not Jane's fucking Addiction, George. We're Divine fucking Weeks out here doing the best we can, not back in L.A. safe and warm. Sorry we're not getting written up in 'L.A.-Dee-Da' every week."

"I don't want to be in Jane's *fucking* Addiction," George barks back. "I want to be in Divine *fucking* Weeks, thank you very much. I just want to keep reaching, Dave. I want to keep challenging ourselves. I want to sound big and bold and explosive. I want to fucking crush people."

"I don't know about you, George, but I've never been prouder than last night," Raj says quietly. "I don't care about Jane's or the Beatles or anyone anymore. I just want to be Divine Weeks. Isn't that enough?"

"I never said I wasn't proud of what we're doing, Raj," George shoots back. "I *am*. I just want to keep growing. I don't want to get static and staid. I want to..."

"One of the first things I dug about you guys," Ian interrupts, "was you didn't look and sound like every other band. You weren't cool or hip, and you didn't give a shit. I loved that. Don't overthink things and don't get all fucking self-conscious.

And start acting like you've done something. Because you *have*. Trust the response you've gotten out here. It counts for something."

The van turns quiet as we close in on Kansas City, and now I'm thinking about last night's show and about what George was saying. Truth is I share his feelings about us needing to keep reaching and challenging ourselves. But Ian's right too. We've got to be careful not to be so self-conscious that we short-circuit our own natural evolution.

Back home, the idea of success can be an oasis because your world is so small. It's cool the *L.A. Times* named us one of the best bands in L.A., and that our shows are now regularly a pick of the week and all that, but going on the road has really shown us how insulated a world that is, how relative that sort of success is. Out here, being almost completely unknown, the world seems so massive. When I told Raj I could die happy last night, maybe it was that old fear of success talking or some sort of acknowledgement of the true distance we still have to go. Or, maybe deep down, I never really believed we'd even get this far. I don't know. Maybe I've just never come to grips with what my idea of success even is. It's easy to give George a hard time about wanting to be huge, but maybe I'm the one who's full of shit for not knowing what making it even means to me.

Thing is, I never really got hung up on superstardom and all the materialistic shit that comes with it. I soured on all that when my mom and I were with Larry and money and entitlement ruled the day.

All I know is I've never been happier than when I first sat in the driver's seat of this van. Never felt more free than waking up on Lisa from Portland's floor. Never felt more sure of what we were doing than after that BBQ with the yuppies. And I never felt closer to people in my life than onstage in Regina when everything else in this universe disappeared, and it was just the four of us and our music.

I just want...*this*, and I want to do it with *these* people in *this* van. All we've got is each other and this music. I've never been that good at paying myself first, but standing up for this band and who's in it, that's different. That's righteous. I'll lay down my fucking life for that. I don't know what that means as far as defining success. I just know this van feels like home and I finally know I'm where I'm supposed to be.

We're playing a place called Elijio's Cantina tonight. By the time we unload our gear, the Flaming Lips are already soundchecking. It's like a show in itself. They're doing what seems like a serious version of the Cult's new single "Love Removal Machine," with a ton of dry ice going off reducing visibility in the club to a few inches. The Flaming Lips just put out an amazing freaky debut record on Restless Records. Great guys too. Their singer, guitarist and head visionary is this guy Wayne Coyne. He and I talk after soundcheck over 50-cent tacos. Wayne has some far-out ideas about what can and can't be accomplished touring in a tiny van. While we're talking I keep looking around for George so he can get in on some of this, but Ian says he's off calling Deborah again. I exchange addresses with Wayne so we can try and hook up again for some shows in the fall.

The place is packed when we go on. The stage is low so you're basically playing face to face with people jammed right up to the front. Just the way we like it. We deliver again tonight and get two encores. Over the last week, we've really hit our stride. We're a very confident band right now. At the start of the tour, we figured if we gave enough of ourselves we might have a shot to connect. Now, we *expect* to turn a roomful of strangers into converts because now we're that good. We've totally transformed.

After the show, a ton of people come up to us saying they saw us on *120 Minutes* and have been counting the days for our arrival. It's so otherworldly to hear that. Tonight was a really strong show, but we couldn't quite whip everyone into the frenzy we managed last night even though we were every bit as on.

While the Flaming Lips roar on behind thick gobs of dry ice, I tell Ian about this in a tiny booth in the back of the club. He thinks for a moment then says, "You know it's self-defeating to expect the type of magic that went down last night every night. Frankly, had St. Louis never happened, tonight's gig would have been considered one of the great successes of the trip."

"I know, Ian," I shout over the Lips, "but after last night, it's hard to make those kinds of allowances. You just get insatiable and keep expecting more."

"Yeah, I know," Ian jumps in, "but just stay true to what you guys are about, and when you come back in the fall you'll really start making some inroads. Remember, trust is earned city by city, person by person."

"I know, you're right," I say pausing. "Listen, Ian, you sure I can't talk you into hitching up for another tour in the fall? I mean, if it was only down to coordinating dates and yapping at crooked promoters it wouldn't be that big a deal. But man, Ian, you've helped make this trip into so much more."

"Believe me, it's tempting. And thank you by the way," he says looking away. "And in a way, it would be comforting to go out again with you guys. I know what George is going through facing a decision on grad school. Shit, not having to think about that or actually getting a real job sounds all right by me." He pauses again and squints through the smoke before a wistful smile appears. "You guys aren't the only ones who've had an awakening out here. Seeing you guys try to swallow the whole world and finally live your dream is like some big booming voice in my head asking, 'Now what are *you* gonna do with *your* freaking life?'"

George returns from talking to Deborah and plops down hard on the seat next to me. He looks morose. I ask him what's wrong, and he pulls me aside.

"Listen, I don't know how to tell you this, but what would you say if I suggested blowing off Tulsa and Dallas and heading straight home?"

"*What*?" I say completely stunned.

"It's just... my head's all jammed up right now about grad school, and the band, and I know I put on this air like nothing bothers me, but it's just, Deb's going through a really tough time right now, and it's hard not being there for her. I guess I didn't realize what an effect the distance was going to have."

"But George, we'll be home in less than a week," I say. "We've finally got all the drama behind us, and we're hitting on all cylinders now."

"I know," he sighs. "It's just...I'm starting to question this whole idea of chasing the dream if the price is going to be this high."

"But George," I pause. "I'm...speechless."

He raises his eyebrows and shrugs. I think for a second, then lean over and tell Ian to rustle up the rest of the guys for a band meeting. When everyone regroups, we go upstairs where we can hear each other. As the rest of the guys slide into a booth I think about the road we've traveled so far.

Raj? God, after that first day out when he and I walked around San Francisco, he looked like a soldier after his first day in combat. And it didn't get any better anytime soon. Constantly being pulled back by the guilt and all those cultural expectations. Then when all that shit went down in Edmonton, I meant what I wrote him. If he'd told me that he couldn't go on, I'd have gone home with him. But ever since then, we've become this impenetrable, fearless, unrelenting gang.

Ian? Well, he basically sees the tour like he did back at Al's Bar in L.A. when we toasted the great unknown. He's got an adventurer's mindset — this steadfast belief that near-death experiences make you feel more alive. I've seen him freaked out a little out here, but it's like the idea of missing something because he blinked or looked away is completely unacceptable to him.

Dave? The guy's a rock. Just steps into whatever role is necessary. He relishes holding it all together and nothing fazes him. Hell, he lived on an abandoned balcony for a time. Lived out of his car. He's not going to flinch if things get a little challenging.

"Guys," George begins. "I guess I'm too tired to put on any airs." He bows his head and lets out a long loud sigh. "The thing is, Deborah is going through a really tough time now, and not being there for her is taking its toll. I've been doing a lot of thinking about, well, a lot of things. Like how long it's going to take to make it on the road we're on. About this big decision I have to make about grad school. And the thing is, for me, making it won't mean anything if losing Deb is the price. And believe me, I'm as surprised as anyone to hear myself say it, but what would you guys say if I suggested blowing off Tulsa and Dallas and heading home now?"

We all sit back and look around at each other's shocked expressions.

Then a beautiful thing happens.

"Am I hearing right?" Dave asks incredulously. "I mean, I can't *believe* this. You guys made me believe what we're doing is something special and different from other bands, and now you want to pack it in? What the fuck *is* this?"

George looks down and Dave goes on.

"George, who *says* the price you have to pay is losing Deborah? Who *makes* these rules, George? Stop being so fucking self-centered and realize this is all of ours, not just yours. Did Raj ask us to pack it in after Edmonton? Jesus fucking Christ, George, if we turn back now the price you'll pay will be a hell of a lot greater than anything you can imagine. Maybe not today, or in a week, or a month, but you bail now, and one day you'll hate Deborah for it, and she'll hate you for blaming her."

Dave pauses for a minute and looks at all of us. "Look how *much* we've been through already. Look how *far* we've come. We've lived ten lives' worth out here. You can't blow off Tulsa and Dallas. How about honoring the fucking *commitments*? Not just to the clubs and whoever's pushed the shows, but how about honoring the commitment to *ourselves* to walk it like we talk it? If we don't keep fighting until the last hour of the last day, we're gonna hate ourselves forever."

We all shoot looks at each other, then set our stares back on George. He looks around at all of us then finally says quietly, "You're right, Dave. I can't stand how right you are, but yeah, we've got to finish this thing off."

* * *

Day Twenty-Seven
8/23/87

Day off today. This girl named Donna who worked the door last night offered us her floor. The soundman followed us back to Donna's place and then disappeared into her bedroom. We were so drained we just threw down our sleeping bags on her living room floor, crawled in and quickly became unconscious. This morning we realized the guy got lucky with Donna.

We're starting to get a real complex. "What the fuck is going on here," Ian shakes his head. "The myth is shattered. It's the goddamn soundmen who get all the pussy on tour."

Being in the middle of a postmortem of a one-night stand makes for an interesting morning. Romeo slithers out just as we're rolling up our sleeping bags. Donna comes out and asks where he is, and we have to break it to her that he left no sweet note for her.

George has been quiet and distant all morning. Maybe he's embarrassed. At least I hope that's all it is.

We feel bad for Donna so we let her tag along to breakfast at a Denny's down the road. However, before our meal even arrives she proceeds to lose any sympathy after sharing a story which she said was *absolutely hilarious* — several times — about how a friend of hers paid a little black kid two bucks to act like a monkey all day. We just sit there in silence while she chuckles for a few moments until she realizes she's doing a solo act.

I finally break the silence. "Sorry, but it's a touchy subject for us."

Donna's rail-thin with dirty blonde hair and a cute upturned nose. She talks a pretty good game, name-dropping and posturing as well as anyone can who lives in Kansas City. She's probably about 21. Acts about 14. Uses that overwhelmed little girl persona to her advantage. Not going to work with us though.

After breakfast, Donna shows us around Kansas City. Dave asks her where a good place is to have a drink. "Missouri doesn't permit the sale of alcohol on Sundays," she says.

We scowl. "Don't worry, take that road up there and head east," she says.

"Don't tell me," George says. "Moonshine from Jethro's distillery?"

"No, silly," Donna giggles. "We're going across state line into Kansas. They sell booze on Sundays."

"Heathens," George says in mock disgust.

We have no real gig until Tuesday in Tulsa, with only the in-store appearance at Euclid Records back in St. Louis tomorrow, so we pick up some libations, rent a couple movies and head back to Donna's place. We overhear her on the phone saying, "Yeah, cruise on by, there's this cool band from L.A. crashing at my place."

"Boy, are they going to be disappointed," Raj whispers to me.

While *Kentucky Fried Movie* drones on, George splits to call Deborah. After a while, I realize he's been gone for ages. I get worried and go out looking for him. I walk endlessly around the neighborhood. Every damn apartment building looks exactly the same. I finally manage to find my way back and hear uproarious laughter coming from our van which just reeks of pot. I poke my head in through the passenger window, and there's Ian and Dave getting very stoned with Zeppelin blasting from the tape deck. Ian takes a huge hit from Dave's makeshift Coke-can bong and starts shaking his head back and forth wildly from side to side as "Whole Lotta Love" blares on.

"Ian, what in all fuck *are* you doing?" I ask.

Still shaking his head wildly he says, "I can't help it. You hear this song and your head just starts doing this."

"Have fun," I say smiling before starting up the stairs to Donna's apartment building. George is just walking up the block.

"Where the hell have you been?" I call out.

"Not gonna believe this," he says disgustedly. "It took me forever to find a pay phone, and then I kind of forgot where we were staying. All these damn apartment buildings look the same."

"I believe it. I got worried and went out looking for you, and about got lost too."

By the time Donna's friends finally arrive, we're all in our sleeping bags on the floor looking like we're hibernating in little cocoons. I feel bad and am a little embarrassed. They're in a local band and want to rap about what it's like to tour and put records out. Raj and I do our best to rally and not come off like burnouts, but we can barely lift our heads.

* * *

Day Twenty-Eight
8/24/87

We've had our share of Kansas City so we head back along I-70 to our new favorite town, St. Louis, for our in-store appearance at Euclid Records this afternoon.

I drive all the way today with George up front playing navigator. Hendrix on the tape deck. He's quiet, distant, very unlike George.

"George, talk to me," I finally say. "Don't let whatever it is fester."

He sighs heavily then says, "I guess I'm a little embarrassed asking to go home early. I mean, *look* at me. I hardly recognize myself. We're supposed to be living out our rock and roll dreams, and I'm a wreck."

"But who are you trying to impress?" I ask pointedly. "So...George Edmondson is not the cocksure, carefree rock god he thought he was, so what?"

"When we left, I thought I had it all figured out," he says looking out at the Missouri countryside. "Just total commitment, no looking back. I just wasn't prepared for the distance and that helpless feeling of not being there for Deb." He shifts in his seat and goes on. "No one ever missed me like Deb has. No one's ever told me how much they need me before. It's really made me take a look at where I am with my life, Bill."

We pause to listen to the intro to "Voodoo Chile (Slight Return)." "I love that part," I say.

"Me too, but hey," he says, turning the tape deck down. "Remember that story about Bruce Springsteen when he was still struggling to make it, and he bumps into an old band member who'd left to have a family. Bruce asks him if he's still playing music, and the guy says he's still trying to make it. Bruce looks over at the guy's wife and infant child and says..."

"'Well, you're never gonna make it with them.'" I interrupt, finishing the line. "Sure, you told me that story right after we first started the band."

"I always thought those were words to live by," he says shaking his head. "Now...I don't know. I don't want to wake up one day and realize all I've had were moments stolen between shows and no one to go home to. No one to share the triumphs and the heartaches with. I don't want to end up like you and Mary..."

"Hmmm, touché," I say feeling like I just stepped on some broken glass.

"Hey, I'm sorry," he says. "I just meant...I never knew you guys were disintegrating in direct proportion to the band taking off. And I gotta tell you, ever since you told me that back at the campsite it's been haunting me. I don't want that to happen to me and Deb."

"I get what you're saying," I say, looking off and thinking about that for a minute. "Anyway, it's different," I continue. "You and Deb aren't like me and Mary. Plus, what did Dave say the other night? Who *says* it can't all work? I mean, it's probably too late for me and Mary, but not for you guys. At least you know where home is and have someone to go home to. The only thing that feels like home for me is this van. I don't want to, but I've got to face this next part of my life alone. That's something I've never done before, George. And believe me, it scares the living shit out of me. Honestly, if I had my druthers we'd just keep going and never come home."

"It's just, I never saw any of this coming." He gives me that wistful smile of his.

"You're not supposed to see it coming, George," I smile back at him.

It's early afternoon when we blow back into St. Louis. We have a little time to kill before our in-store appearance at Euclid Records so we head down to walk alongside the Mississippi River. We take some shots in front of one of those classic Mississippi riverboats. Then as we walk further along the river, the Gateway Arch comes into view. The Gateway Arch was one of my grandfather's favorite architectural structures. He adored its simplicity. I feel something trigger inside and the long arm of neglected grieving starts pulling at me. I drift from the rest of the guys and walk straight toward the Arch.

"Bill?" I hear Ian call from behind, but I keep walking.

I climb the steep grass hill leading up to the Arch. When I get directly under it, I lie down on the grass and stare up at its massive underbelly. You can take an elevator to the top, but I have absolutely no money for it. Without warning a rush of sadness overcomes me. I have no time to brace myself for it.

In the little over a year since my grandfather died, I haven't allowed myself to even approach that place in my mind that stores last Memorial Day weekend.

I'd returned from a show of ours at Safari Sam's in Huntington Beach late on a Friday night. It was a good show, and I flop down on my bed replaying the gig in my mind when the phone rings. It's my Uncle Brian calling from the hospital saying my grandfather had a massive heart attack, and it doesn't look like he's going to make it.

As I drive to St. John's Hospital, it never occurs to me he might die. He'd had two heart attacks before, quadruple bypass surgery, and I don't remember a time when he wasn't regularly popping nitroglycerin tablets. Still, the thought of this God-like figure dying was completely unfathomable.

My mom and I return from making a visit to the chapel when the doctor comes out and tells us he's about to die. My grandmother wants to see him once more. I take her by the hand, and we go in to see him. I start getting a haunting, sick feeling inside remembering what I said to him the night before. We argued about something so fucking unimportant, and I stormed out shouting, "You've lived your life, now just let me live mine." What a dumbshit thing to say, and now I'm gonna have to fucking live with it.

We enter his room and his skin is pasty blue-white like the color of nonfat milk. My grandmother rests her head on his chest and says she loves him. She looks half gone herself. I lean over and beg him not to leave. He raises his eyebrows and tries to motion to me, but he can't lift his hand.

We rejoin the rest of the family in the waiting room. My mom is nervously talking to me, but I hear nothing. Then the doctor comes out and says he's gone. Just like that.

In the weeks following his death, people around town come up to me just wanting to tell me how much they admired him. They speak of him in these mythical terms which kind of freezes his legacy so I don't dare dig through the rubble.

I turn over onto my stomach, cup my hands over my eyes and bury my head in the grass. Slowly, up from the deep recesses, a picture comes into focus. Something I haven't revisited ever. Just that first time through and then I quickly buried it.

My grandmother would start drinking when it got dark. At first she's funny, dancing an Irish jig or singing a song. Then she gets nastier. She starts in about how she could have had any guy in town but settled on my grandfather instead. "I had dreams," she says. "Big dreams and big plans, but I gave it up for this life." So it went. "I give and give and give. And what do I get back?! Nothin'," she spits out.

My grandfather takes it for a while by burying himself in a book. She keeps at him until he finally tells her to shut her mouth or he'll shut it for her. "You gonna hit me?" she mocks him.

Finally he grabs her by the arm and drags her into their bedroom and through the door you hear her say mockingly, "You won't fuck me anymore so why don't you just hit me?" You hear some scuffling and some more screaming, the type you never want to hear. Then finally it stops and a long time passes before my grandfather reemerges with this look like: "Don't even fucking ask me." So you don't. It's not until the next afternoon that my grandmother finally comes out of the bedroom. No one says a word about it. Poof, it's gone. Never happened.

Man, no wonder I lived in the fantasy. No wonder I constructed imaginary stairways that led to sunlight.

And my grandfather? All those books he had going at once, the long drives he took, leaving at the crack of dawn every morning for work that didn't start for hours. He was trying to escape the insanity too. It was retirement that killed him. He had no escape hatch anymore.

I wipe my eyes with the sleeve of my John Fogerty Pendleton shirt, turn back over and sit up. I've been trying to hold everything together this whole tour…Mary, Raj, George. I guess I hit the wall today.

It's turned to late afternoon, and I follow the long, lanky shadow I cast as I walk back down the big grass slope. I spot the rest of the guys sitting alongside the Mississippi. Ian gets up and comes toward me. "You all right, Bill?" he asks.

"Yeah, it was my turn for a nervous breakdown."

"Come on, we're skipping rocks across the Mississippi," Ian says tossing one to me. "Wanna throw a few?"

A crowd of about 20 people are browsing the aisles of Euclid Records when we arrive. We recognize some familiar faces from Cicero's the other night. Gina, which brings a smile to Ian's face. Lynn. Joe, the owner, has pizza and beer waiting for us.

We're not getting paid for this appearance so it's debatable if backtracking to St. Louis for a second trip is worth it on a financial level, but these people put out for us, and it's important to seal relationships and give something back.

I'm so spacey and spent from this afternoon, I have a hard time getting animated to any degree while we play. For the first time on this tour, I don't feel like playing, and I'm kind of glad we're not doing a full-blown show tonight.

We meet a girl named Katie who tells us she works at a café around the corner and says she'll treat us to some potato skins and a round of drinks. We'll take it. We've been dipping into the money saved to pay off the van so we're really pinching pennies now. As Katie sets down our drinks, she tells us our show at Cicero's the other night was the best to come through town since the Meat Puppets played at Mississippi Nights earlier this year. That prompts us all to make dramatic mock proposals to her, on bended knees no less.

Ian tells us Lynn put us all on her guest list at Cicero's tonight, and if we make enough noise for the band she's booked she'll keep sending rounds over to us. So we kidnap Katie and head back to Cicero's. Ian spots Gina at a table with some friends and waves us over. Ian gives everyone the scoop on Lynn's proposal, and we all get very drunk in the process. Lynn's band must have thought they hit the rock-star lotto. We singlehandedly got them three encores.

Gina sneaks us back in to her folks' basement again. We raid her old toy cabinet again and play Chutes and Ladders before finally collapsing. A perfect regressive ending to a very heavy day.

* * *

Day Twenty-Nine
8/25/87

Before leaving Gina's, we call the promoter in Tulsa. Guy sounds a little creepy, but he offers us free lodging tonight even though we won't be playing until tomorrow. We'll take it.

Raj drives all the way today. We listen to the advance tape of R.E.M.'s new record Conrad gave us. There's a song on there that's kind of a rip-off of the Minutemen's "Stories." "Shameless," I say, adding, "What a coincidence the Minutemen opened for R.E.M. last tour." Now George and Ian are arguing about whether it's outright theft, or flattery.

I lay in back alternating between reading Jim Carroll's latest, *Forced Entries*, which is not as good as *Basketball Diaries*, and trying to write some lyrics. I've got that phrase "stay hungry" on my brain — our tour mantra since we crossed the border last week. Didn't get very far, just: "By God, I know one thing, I know hunger like it knows me. As soon as you make the break, they'll fucking break you right in two."

Dave pulling into town.   Photo by Ian Bader

God, Oklahoma is so non-descript — flat and dirt-brown. What's this state have against the color green? Hasn't anyone around here ever heard of planting a fucking tree or some foliage? When we pull into Tulsa, we're greeted by the promoter, this cat named Habib, who shows us to the one room we'll all share. Habib is an oily, smooth-talking New York transplant who brags that he, alone, is going to bring some East Coast cool to this sleepy town. As I'm unrolling my sleeping bag, George is talking to him across the room. Poor George looks nauseous listening to his horseshit. "This club is ved-dee, ved-dee happening. I've brought the best of New York hip to Tulsa." Blah, blah, blah. Just a load of manure. Type of guy who pisses down your back and tells you it's raining.

This motel is one for the fucking books too. Don't want to sound ungrateful, but this building should be condemned. There's literally a hole in the floor of the second floor hallway leading to our room where you can actually see all the way through to the ground floor. Inside our room, there's a fist-sized hole in the wall and someone wrote in Magic Marker: "Glory Hole — Enter At Own Risk." I'm scared to look out the window. I get the feeling there'll be a wrecking ball headed straight between my eyes.

We all hold off on the booze tonight. I remember Falling James of the Leaving Trains telling me after one of those grueling SST tours that at some point you can't drink any more beer. You just get full. That is, until the next night when you can't come down, and your head won't turn off.

* * *

Day Thirty
8/26/87

I showered with cold rust-colored water slowly trickling out of the shower head this morning. Actually this afternoon. Haven't seen a lot of mornings lately with the late hours we've been keeping.

I hear Ian rustling about and ask if he wants to go grab some coffee or something.

"Sure," he says getting up. "I can't stare at this ceiling anymore."

"Hey, you guys want to go grab something?" Ian asks to a collective groan.

George and Dave want to catch up on some sleep. Raj is still battling a cold and wants to vegetate. So Ian and I wander around the neighborhood which looks totally deserted. "Ian, is a tornado coming and no one told us?"

"Don't even kid about that," Ian warns. "This is prime tornado country."

We finally find a diner that's open, but we can only afford one lousy breakfast between us. As we drink cup after cup of coffee Ian writes some postcards and I catch up on my journal until it's time for soundcheck.

I'm not going to say soundchecks are exciting. After all, how many times can you stomach hearing a soundman say in a voice suggesting he'd died ten years ago, "All right boys, give me the kick drum now..." Boom. Boom. "All right now, give me the snare." Crack. Crack.

To combat this, we try to be a little creative in between the endless tweaking and microphone adjustments. Maybe work up a cover version of a song, rearrange our own stuff, try out transitions between songs or tweak the set list. And, if we get lucky like we did today, write a new song. As the soundman rakes his hand across his throat to bum-rush us off the stage, George starts slapping out a quasi-funky riff and Dave counters with a tribal beat on his floor tom. Raj falls in with some sonic bass-heavy riffing, and I try out the new lyrics.

By God, I know one thing, I know hunger like it knows me
As soon as you make the break, they'll fucking break you
right in two.
Mother, I still need holding, you've seen me in all my
glory.
I shrink into myself just to start the next morning...
I stay hungry...I stay hungry

George and Raj working out "Stay Hungry" in Tulsa. Photo by Ian Bader

Tulsa Dave, who'd scored us the gig, shows up after soundcheck and invites us back to his place for dinner. Nice enough fellow but a bit of a swinger and a schmoozer. We help him cook up a spaghetti dinner, and then he sits us all down in his living room to show off his quadraphonic sound system he's been raving about.

The guy champions himself an electrical wizard of sorts, and I have to give him his due. His stereo is wild. He hooked up a panning device to his stereo receiver and by using a remote he can spin the sound around at varying intervals into the four speakers mounted in the four corners of his living room. He gets us all stoned (sans Raj) and puts on the *White Album*. Tulsa Dave has a big dumb grin on his face as he jimmies the remote and pans the song in all different directions until it seems like the guitars are colliding off the bass lines in some stoned-out parallel universe.

I ride back to the club with Tulsa Dave. On the way, the biggest damn electrical storm I've ever seen erupts. Huge, vicious bolts nose-dive into the ground off in the distance straight ahead of us. He calmly explains, "When it nose-dives like that, it means two bolts just collided somewhere up above and then it's 'look out below.'"

"Um, we don't get a lot of that in L.A.," I say nervously looking down at a garter wrapped around his gearshift. "What's this supposed to mean?" I ask.

"It means I got laid," he says sounding suddenly macho, which I hate.

"Ask a stupid question, right?"

"Hey, you guys been gettin' a lot of pussy or what?" he asks hopefully.

"Hate to disappoint, but we've found the guys who get the most action on our tours are the soundmen."

"Say what?"

"Never mind," I say sighing. "It's a long pathetic story."

When we get back to the club, the opening band is flailing about looking entirely too precious for anyone's good. Kind of a

Talking Heads rip-off. Not a good idea unless you've got David Byrne's genes.

This club looks like some sort of time-warped discotheque. Brass spiral staircases lead up from the dance floor to a three-level stage illuminated by mirror balls and rotating lights. Looks like the set from *Dance Fever* or something. Not to mention a big brass stripper's pole coming down from the ceiling into center stage — the second stripper pole of the tour.

I look around the place and spot Habib looking entirely too impressed with himself trying to scam on two girls who look underage. I try to duck out, but he spots me out of the corner of his eye. "Beeel, Beeel" he calls out motioning for me to come over. "Shit," I say to Raj who's just saddled up next to me. "If I hear any more of that guy's horse manure, I'm not gonna be any good for the show. I'm gonna split for a while."

I'm feeling pretty good so I decide to see if I can catch Mary. I dial and wait through three rings. "Fuck," I say hearing the answering machine pick up.

Then, "Hello? I'm here. Hello?"

"Hello from a discotheque in Tulsa," I say.

"Christ, what did Ian get you guys into?" she asks.

"It's all right. Maybe we'll cover 'Life During Wartime.'"

"This ain't no party. This ain't no disco? That one?"

"Right," I say. Long pause. "Hey, I miss you, honey."

"I…miss you too," she says quickly in that forced chirpy non-committal way she has.

Another long pause. "Listen, I want to begin again with you. When we get back, I want to start over."

She doesn't say anything. I'm picturing her hold the phone out and that *look* on her face, and I start to feel panicky. Without warning, it starts just pissing down rain, and I can't stop myself. My lips start moving, and I'm saying things I have no business saying. "I know you said you shouldn't trust anything I say with all these miles between us, but by the time I get back it's gonna be too late. Listen, I want to go away with you when we get back. Maybe go up to Santa Barbara or something. You think we can do that?"

"I don't think it's that simple," she says. "I mean, that would be nice. I guess," she adds.

"I know I asked you to save me," I say, "and maybe that was wrong, but I think maybe you liked being asked to."

"I don't think you ever really wanted to be saved," she says, her discomfort obvious. "Because deep down, Bill, I think you're scared if you ever let anybody save you, you'd somehow cease being."

I feel myself slipping backwards to that horrible, vulnerable, desperate feeling I get whenever she seizes the upper hand, and I play the pursuer.

"Listen," I say, now very softly. "I want us to get a little place and move in together. I can't go back to 940. Too much has changed. Come on, honey, please, think about it. Couldn't we just..."

"Please stop," she interjects, sounding both annoyed and hurt. "Could you please just finish the tour, get home safe, and then we can talk on level ground with some sense of proportion. I'm begging you now. *Please stop.*"

Everything's turned black in my head. I hear her ask me to stop, but I don't because I never do and because I never fucking knew how.

"I don't know when it started," I say, wiping the raindrops rolling down my forehead through my eyebrows and into my eyes, "but at some point, the band, the dream, this thing we've invested *everything* in became bigger than us and started filling all those holes we grew up with. I know it must feel like this thing is filling all those holes better than we ever could together, but think about it. Do you *really* think that's true? Honey, please tell me you don't really think that."

"Just *stop it*," she interrupts me angrily. "What gives you the authority to decide — with the safety of thousands of miles between us — that you've got it all figured out now? Forgive me if I sound skeptical and I'm not swept up in your romantic mea culpa, but am I supposed to just forget the last six months and how we've treated each other? And do you *really* want me to tell you what's filling the holes now?"

"No," I say quietly. "I don't."

She knows she got me so she takes her foot off the accelerator. "Just go and do a good show tonight," she says starting her victory lap. "You'll be back soon and we'll talk. And don't forget to tell Ian to call ahead to the Dallas promoter. Susan's her name. Are you going to remember that? Susan in Dallas, call her and tell her when you'll be in because she's setting up an interview before the show."

She's giving me her last-minute laundry list and summation at a hundred miles an hour. Gone.

The rain lets up, but now I'm soaked to the skin. I grab a dry shirt from the van, my long-sleeved red shirt, and pull my serape over it. My hair's all wet so I put my newsboy hat on backwards and head back in the club. Everyone's all ready to start. Ian looks relieved to see me but knows better than to sound panicked. He can tell I'm not all there. "Hey, what's with you?" he asks.

"I just talked to Mary, that's all."

"New band rule. No talking to girlfriends right before shows," he says.

"Oh Ian," I shake my head, "if Mary was just a girlfriend, you think I'd be this fucked-up?"

When I went outside to call Mary the place was practically empty. Now it's actually filling up quite a bit. I walk to the lip of the stage and look out at the crowd, and under my breath I thank God I have this band. I'd be utterly lost without it. I look over at Raj to my left and then at George to my right. Dave motions he's ready. I step to the mic and say, "Hello Studio 54, you guys ready to hear a little K.C. and the Sunshine Band?" I hear a few catcalls go off. "Donna Summer?" I smile and say, "Me neither. Hey, Raj. Lift us up."

The show takes on the theme of so many of our shows on this tour. Cautious crowd waiting to be impressed. We say "fair enough" and walk out to the end of the tree limb to show we'll take the risks. Sure enough, after a few songs, and the alcohol has a chance to sink in, people start to come with us on our mad trip through the heart.

About midway through the set, I start pulling people up on the upper-level stage above where we're playing and do my best to bust a few disco moves. I motion for them to follow suit. Quite a few actually stay up there for the rest of the show just dancing away. I give a guy my guitar to play the long jamming end to "When I Go," and he's amazing, riffing like Neil Young. Afterwards I announce, "Hey, this guy needs a band. Hands up, who can sing? Any drummers? Anyone play bass? I want to get this guy a band." After the show, I see three guys sharing drinks with the guy at a table looking deep in conversation. I wonder if a little band is hatching. That would be so cool.

* * *

Day Thirty-One
8/27/87

I can't help but project what lays ahead as I slowly come to this morning. Dallas tonight is it, a 25-hour drive straight home and then what? Man, how can I go back to 940 and that whole dynamic after all this?

And did I really ask Mary to move in with me last night? Wasn't I just telling George I'm going to have to go it alone this next little while?

And Divine Weeks? Is there a ceiling to this big sky-dome we're dreaming under, or can we poke a hole right through and blast into sweet oblivion?

Ian turns over and sees I'm awake. "Well, this is it," he says.

"Unreal isn't it?" I say. "I can't believe I'll be back to that shit job in a few days."

"So, are you really dropping out of school?" Ian asks.

"Yep," I say sitting up. "Never been more sure of anything in my life."

"Well, that's huge, Bill. This tour..." he says shaking his head. "You've got every reason to believe now."

"You know what really clinched it?" I say rubbing the sleepy seeds from my eyes. "That stupid barbecque at Mindy's and Sandy's. That whole scene is like a microcosm of everything we're fighting against. It just completely justifies everything we're doing. It's not even like we're making a choice to go counterculture. It's like...it's a moral imperative now. The consequences are too dire to do anything but."

"Yeah, they were scaring me, and they're *family*," he chuckles. "And speaking of scaring, I've got to go and talk to that fucking

Habib about getting the $50 he didn't pay us from last night. I've got a feeling he's gonna get slippery."

"Well, that shouldn't be a stretch for that oily little troll," I say pulling on my jeans.

"Just tell him to pony up or we'll leave this shithole like we left the Nash," Dave croaks from under a heap of blankets.

Habib ends up giving us $30 but buys us all a huge breakfast. Fair enough.

Before we leave we call Susan, the Dallas promoter. She gives us directions to a 7-11 where she'll meet us near downtown. The four-hour drive to Dallas is quiet. We're all pretty trashed. I drive the whole way while everyone else sleeps. I keep myself awake listening to a best of the Clash tape all the way through almost three times.

When we pull up, Susan's waiting out front smoking a cigarette and holding a Super Big Gulp. She climbs in the passenger seat and rides with us to the radio interview she's set up across town. Susan's got shoulder-length wavy bright orange dyed hair, and she's wearing an oversized green army jacket with the anarchy symbol written in black Magic Marker over a Joy Division T-shirt. Knee-high black Docs. Very heavy Goth-like eyeliner.

On the way over, she gives us an unsolicited scoop on her life story. She'd done the L.A. circuit, hung out with the wrong crowd, got hooked on junk and moved to Texas to detox. She just got out of a halfway house last month and although all her counselors advised her to stay away from the music business she just "had to be involved...*somehow*" so she started booking this club.

"They say it's a 97% failure rate for junkies," she says shrugging. "But who's to say I'm not in that 3%? Plus, I was just a recreational user and things just got a little out of hand."

"Yeah well, you know what they say," I offer. "If God has something better he's saving it for himself."

Our interview is at a pirate radio station located at the top of a rickety old rundown three-story Victorian house. As we climb the staircase, we stare into a tiny room on the second level that appears to be housing nine or ten black kids of varying ages. Straddling the doorway is, I assume, the mother, who has this look on her face that seems to say "Don't fuck with me because I've forgotten more shit that's been done to me than you white boys combined will ever know."

Susan tells us a guy named Miller runs the station: "He's a little over the top, but he cares about bands."

Miller greets us on the third-floor landing and leads us in. "Cool, you brought some instruments. Gonna do a few songs?" he asks blinking rapidly.

"Yeah, we get tired of hearing ourselves talk. Is it cool we do a few songs live?" Raj asks.

"Yeah, 'course, 'course," he chirps. We quickly notice that Miller has an annoying habit of moving his jaw about in a circular motion and grinding his teeth.

Ian whispers to me, "I think our friend Miller's a speed freak."

Miller plays three songs off our record, and after we make our now customary on-air plea for people to come down to the show, we do our street-corner treatment of "Idiot Child" then a somber "Dry September" live. While we play it, the hardened black mother and three of her little girls clinging to her hip come up and peek in to watch. I look into the black pools of the mother's eyes as the song hits the staccato section, and I make sure not to look away. Raj catches on and starts playing so hard he breaks two strings, then becomes so caught up that he hacks at the other strings until two more break.

Miller comes back on the air and tells us the song sounds scary.

"Great music *should* scare you," George says. "Should scare the living crap out of you."

As we head back down the stairs, I say hello to the mother. She doesn't say a word, just stares holes through me.

When we pull up to the club, we unload our gear and can't help notice the entire place just reeks of piss. Not that that's unusual, but give this place its due. This joint stinks of piss more than any other place we've been, and that's saying something.

After we soundcheck the new song, "Stay Hungry," George heads off to call Deb, and Ian tries to hunt down some strings for Raj. The rest of us go out front and suss out the area. Two clubs sit adjacent to each other on the main drag of this part of town called Deep Ellum, a sort of hip warehouse district just east of downtown Dallas. Dave, Raj and I stand out front watching people walk down the street poking their heads into each club, waiting to be enticed. It dawns on us that these folks are up for grabs, and if we wait inside like rock stars for our coveted wangers to get sucked, we'll end up playing to empty chairs and another soundman no more than rumored to be alive. So we start chatting people up as they walk by. "Hey," I say to a couple of girls slowly strolling past the club. "You know, this place right here is where it's all gonna happen tonight."

The taller of the two is cute as a button and doesn't let on for a minute that we're anything but shit. Whatever. At this point it's about not letting one moment pass without maximum effort. I go on. "Hey listen, we're new in town. Divine Weeks — from L.A. Come on, you might end up onstage shaking a tambourine or singing backup for us."

The two huddle and then start giggling before they head across the street toward the other club.

"Good grief," Raj says disgustedly.

I watch the two girls walk slowly through the doorway of the club across the street. The cute one looks back just before disappearing inside. "They'll be back," I say before starting in on another group headed our way.

We probably did more promotion out front than Susan did all week, and it paid off. A good-sized crowd cozied up to the stage by showtime, and I recognize quite a few of the faces from outside.

It's the last night of the tour and right before we go on, we huddle together like a football team and vow to leave it all onstage. We've been operating on such a primal level lately. It's like we're being fueled by that beautiful intangible element I've always dreamt of. Something's definitely carrying us along now. That's all I ever wanted. To find myself lost out there trekking across terrain no compass can navigate, struggling to lay claim to that indefinite quality to call our own. In the last month, for the first time in my life, I've been able to reconcile that disconnection I've always felt from society and not be alienated by it. I think we finally know this is what we *are* — and maybe that's not much, but whatever it is, it's *everything* to us, and I'm starting to believe we might actually be able to take the river all the way to the sea.

After Edmonton, the stakes got raised. When we climb onstage now, it's like what I was saying to Ian earlier today. It's like everything is on the line. It's a moral imperative. We've only got an hour up there, and if we don't use every means necessary, a little bit of ourselves that we'll never get back will die away. Nothing is as distasteful and unacceptable as coming offstage knowing we could have given more.

We've been kidding Raj all tour that it wouldn't be a Divine Weeks show unless he inadvertently unplugged his guitar cord at least once. We'd be gathering momentum and then he'd do a Pete Townshend leap and disconnect himself, leaving the rest of us hanging. It's like your mom walking in on you masturbating.

The "blue ball special" we call it. Instant flaccidity. Ian had seen enough, so while he was at the music store, he got a remote so Raj can roam about unencumbered. And man, the fucker ran with it. Literally. Raj spent more time tonight on the tabletops and bar tops than onstage. Poor Raj almost killed himself leaping from one part of the bar to another, hit a wet spot and about went ass over teakettle.

Oh yeah, remember that girl? Cute as a button? Midway through the show, I look down and there she is with her friend we saw outside. I kneel down at the lip of the stage while the band blares away and motion for her to come closer. She doesn't at first, then budges a little. Then closer still. "I knew you'd be back," I say, grabbing her by the arm and pulling her up onstage. I give her a tambourine which she proceeds to shake wildly out of time until she starts smiling and getting into it. Then a big jughead jumps onstage and screams into the microphone, "I want some pussy!" and grabs her by the arm and yanks her back into the crowd.

The crowd is wild tonight. Lots of pushing and shoving. Some slam dancing. Raj gets so caught up, he jumps down into the throng and some meathead blindsides him with a body slam that sends Raj and his scrawny frame sprawling across the floor like a running back rocked out of bounds by a bruising linebacker. George and Dave don't notice what happened, and they keep the song going. I jump down to check on Raj, who did a face-plant into a side booth. I pull him up, and he's laughing and asks me, "Didn't happen to get the number of the truck that hit me, did you?"

After our encore, Dave kicks over his drum set and Raj throws his Les Paul high in the air and lets it crash-land on the stage where he leaves it and walks off. A din of feedback blares until the soundman races up on stage and flounders about for several minutes unsuccessfully trying to kill the sound.

I climb offstage and go right up to Dave. "Hey, thanks for making sure we finished this thing off right," I say with a big stupid smile on my face.

"No fucking charge, man," he says. "No fucking charge. Hey, is there a way to just keep going? You know, just not come back?"

"I know what you mean," I say. "The van's our real home now."

Susan invites us back to her place to shower before our long trek home. Ian emerges with a big cake to celebrate the end of the tour which we end up shoving into each other's faces.

I can't believe how lucky we are to have found Ian. He knew the time out here was something we'd never have again. He knew we'd never see through these eyes again. It was Ian who handed George a copy of *Huckleberry Finn* when we were in St. Louis and told him to sit beside the Mississippi and read it. It was Ian that made sure pictures were taken at every crucial moment. It was Ian who made certain those signposts stuck alongside the highway were acknowledged. He pointed at them and said to us, "Would you guys just *look* at what you've done!" He's been priceless.

* * *

Day Thirty-Two
8/28/87

Twenty-five hours to L.A. and God only knows what then. Raj takes the first shift driving while George and I escape inside two sets of headphones plugged into my Walkman in back. Kind of like sharing a malt.

As we drive in the blackness of the night through endless west Texas, I am quite literally dreading going home. I'm terrified of going back to that toxic place and losing everything I found out here.

I drift in and out of consciousness being woken from time to time by bumps in the road and a stop to pee and get gas. I take over driving near the New Mexico border and get us to Albuquerque, where we stop to eat. "Only about 800 miles to go," Dave says over breakfast. "Be home about 3 a.m."

After we eat, Ian takes over the wheel, and I climb in back again and return to my dream state until I hear Ian cry out, "Fuck, we drive all this way and in the last leg I get nailed!" Nabbed for speeding — our first ticket the whole tour. George calms Ian down by getting him very stoned under the little teepee we've erected with a bedsheet held up by a broomstick in the back so the smoke won't bother Raj. "What's this, a peace pipe?" Ian asks, exhaling.

Dave assumes the wheel for the last leg somewhere in the Arizona desert. I finish up the lyrics to "Stay Hungry" as I stare through a tiny opening through two amps and out the back window. There's an even bigger lightning storm than we saw in Tulsa. Huge lightning bolts look like leafless tree branches in winter, filling the desert sky. I fret for a while that our van is a rolling metal lightning magnet, and pull my newsboy hat down over my ears like it'll somehow help protect me. Not sure when, but at some point I fall into a very deep sleep.

* * *

Day Thirty-Three
8/29/87

I wake up to Dave singing "Hollywood" at the top of his lungs. I shoot up and look around and realize we're on the Hollywood Freeway just two exits from Santa Monica Boulevard, Dave's exit. Sure enough, just as Dave predicted, it's almost 3 a.m. early Saturday morning.

The rest of the guys quickly come to. "We're home?" Raj says with astonishment.

"Yeah, buddy, 25 hours straight to L.A." Dave says. "And I am feelin' fine."

I look out the back window at the skyscrapers downtown and then at the near-empty freeway ahead of us. As we pull off the freeway, L.A. feels different. Like maybe it holds a little less history over me. Like maybe some space was cleared for us while we were gone.

Dave turns the van onto Tamarind, and slowly rolls down his street. It's silent in the van. As he pulls into his driveway and shuts off the motor, I feel a little pang in my gut. I stand outside sort of unconsciously helping Dave unload his things. We all take turns hugging Dave goodbye. Damn, we'll see him in a couple days for rehearsals and then the homecoming gig at Club Lingerie Friday. There'll be more gigs in town, then a fall tour. Still, letting go of the first of our little troupe is like releasing a lifeline. Something precious will cease being, and we all know it.

We all watch Dave go up his walkway, turn the key and open his door. When we realize he's not going to turn around again, we climb back in the van, Raj taking the driver's seat. Slowly, he pulls away from the curb and heads back up Tamarind toward Sunset Boulevard. It's early Saturday morning and Hollywood is about as quiet as it ever gets. It's eerily silent in this little van we've called home for the last month, but I know the little gears are grinding hard in everybody's head.

George wants to be dropped off at Deborah's. We all help him unload his gear, and after he says goodbye to everyone, he throws his duffel bag over his shoulder. I walk a few steps with him away from the rest and we stop. "George, what is there to say?"

"Nothing that would sound halfway intelligent," he says.

"I know," I say managing a smile. "But listen."

"Lay it on me or I'm gonna crash right here on the sidewalk," he says.

"Even though all these great things started happening for us this year, I just went sideways. Fucking around, boozing, drugging. Just totally morally bankrupt."

"It wasn't as bad as you think Bill," he says shifting his duffel bag over his other shoulder.

"Trust me, it was," I say looking down. "But listen. That day we spent in Regina, the night after Edmonton, I really didn't know if we were going to make it. I knew the band's fate hung in the balance when we stepped onstage that night. And I'm telling you, when we made it through that show and realized Raj was all in, everything crystallized. Our little tour became something more. It wasn't just about playing music anymore. It was about restoring ideals. And *honor*. I know it sounds crazy, but suddenly I felt righteous and, I don't know…virtuous again. Like when that girl in Winnipeg came on to me with that whole giving me her soul trip, it's like, I became monogamous again even though I was facing disintegration with Mary. Must have been something in the air out there. I became full of wonder again. It was redemption."

"Well, I'll say this," he sighs taking off his glasses to rub his eyes. "It stripped away my defenses. What can I say? I guess I'm just as needy and insecure as everyone else. I'm definitely coming home a different person."

"But it won't mean shit if we can't bring home what we found out there and make it part of our lives."

"Well, I don't know about that," he says, pausing. "What each of us brings back is down to us alone. The evidence will be in each of us and each of us will be the verdict. For me, it's time to see if it all really *can* work — like Dave said. And listen, I'm sorry for pussing out and asking to go home. I'm all in, Bill. I'm not gonna let you guys go and make it without me. Count me in. So…what about you?"

"I asked Mary to move in with me," I say shaking my head. "Crazy, huh? She told me it was just the distance talking. Which it *was*. And that's why it's so crucial to bring back what we found out there. I'm scared to go back to that house."

"Be who you need to be, Bill," he says, assuredly. "But make the motive be you. Whatever happens, I'm here for you while you walk through it."

"Same here, brother. And hey, glad you're still with us. There's no   Divine   Weeks   without   you."

He gives me one last wave as he starts up the stairs to Deborah's place. I watch Deborah open the door and jump into his arms, and I smile and keep watching them hold each other. Nice. The hum of the van's motor is like a nagging "come *on*…" so I lift myself back in the passenger seat and rest my head against the side window as we pull away.

The sun's still not up. Raj drives us north up Lincoln Boulevard and slows as we approach his place. He looks in then says he doesn't want to barge in pre-dawn, so we head back to my place. Ian promised to help me return the van tomorrow, er, today, that is, so he's crashing at my place too.

Of all things, fucking "Can't Find My Way Back Home" by Blind Faith comes on the radio as we near ol' 940. Raj slowly pulls the van up the steep asphalt driveway, and the sound of the old chassis creaking wakes up one of our many dogs. Soon a symphony of howling fills the neighborhood.

"So much for a quiet return," Raj says, stopping just short of the garage door and yanking hard on the parking brake. As he shuts off the engine, we all exhale and look at each other. After a pregnant pause, we all break up laughing.

My mom comes out to greet us and gives us all hugs. Raj and Ian are out on their feet, so she sets up some pillows and blankets on the couch, and they crash almost immediately. I'm wasted, but too wired to shut it down. I go out front and take a seat on an old beat-up wicker chair and put my feet up on a brick planter. My mom brings me some orange spice tea and takes a seat next to me, and we watch the sunrise greet a gorgeous late summer morning.

"You remember when I used to get earaches when I was a kid?" I ask, taking a sip of tea.

"Sure, of course," she says dragging hard on her cigarette.

"Nothing would soothe the pain," I continue. "You'd bundle me up in a blanket in your old VW bug, and we'd drive up the coast."

"Yeah," she coos. "And we loved when it rained..."

"Yeah," I jump back in. "And if it wasn't raining, you'd turn on the windshield wipers and put on the window squirter or whatever that thing is called, and we'd pretend it was."

"Oh God, I used to drive us up the coast and put on *Aftermath* by the Stones and before long we were just singing and laughing and your earache would be gone."

We both smile and sit in a comfy silence.

"Good times, huh?" I say.

"You seem happy, B. What happened out there?" she asks.

"God. What can I say? I guess for the first time ever, I chose me. I gave myself the gift of...opportunity." I lean forward and place my hands on my knees and lower my voice to a near whisper. "And you know what's out there mom? Everything you could ever want. It all felt so palpable...like I could reach right out and seize it as mine forever." I look right at her, and I know she knows just what I mean. I feel like I'm an escapee coming back to share what it's like out there.

"Mom?" I ask tentatively. "Do you think you could do that too? You know...give yourself the gift and...you know, choose you?"

She doesn't say anything for a very long time. I watch her take puff after puff from her cigarette. Finally, "You mean with a clear conscience?" she asks. "I...I don't know if I know how."

Man, this fucking house. We were taught a completely backwards way of living. It wasn't even living. It was just coping. Ever reactively, backpedaling and always on your heels. Don't make anyone else sad by showing them you have dreams that are still alive. It's like this self imposed prison you keep yourself in because you can't rid yourself of the guilt imposed on you.

We sit back in our chairs and watch people collect their morning paper, walk their dogs, water their lawns. Finally I ask, "Everything that's pure and good always gets poisoned here doesn't it?"

My mom just looks away, nods and puts out her cigarette and lights another. God, I fucking hate what this place does.

I'm starting to crash from exhaustion, but I pull myself up and call Tom Hasse to assure him the van is still in one piece and make plans to return it a little later.

"Damn," Tom says sarcastically. "I had a big story concocted for the rental company."

I feel kind of numb. Out of place. Feels like we should all still be together, packing up and moving on to the next town. I don't want to give up that van. It's home.

Ian emerges from the shower. "Where's the radio interview today, Ian?" I ask him.

"Sorry. Ugly reality beckons," he says.

After reconnecting the odometer, Ian and I pull the love seats out and throw them back in my garage. We then take a hose to the van's insides. Little shards of our journey wash down the driveway. Faded-out flyers, badly folded maps of various states, pens, a melted Hendrix cassette that's been sitting on the dash, Toni's garter belt.

Tom shows up in a cloud of smoke peering out his little stoned eye slits. Ian and Raj climb in the van, and I follow them all in my car.

It's a lazy breezy Saturday and as we make our way along Sunset through Beverly Hills, I listen to the tops of the swaying palm trees knocking against each other. We cut down Doheny, turn onto Santa Monica Boulevard and into Boys Town to the Dollar Rent-A-Car.

We all stand at the counter utterly convinced they don't believe for one minute that this van only went just over the allotted 500 miles in the last 33 days. To our amazement, the little fellow at the counter just quickly processes the paperwork and calls a porter to take the van around back and out of our sight forever.

We thank Tom for everything, then watch him get back in his car, lean over and take a huge hit off his pipe. He mightily exhales, gives us a "hang loose" sign and peels away with AC/DC blasting away on his stereo.

"Gotta love it," Raj says shaking his head as Ian pumps the devil's horns in the air to "Highway to Hell."

After we help Ian with all his stuff, he takes a seat on the hood of my car.

"I just can't fucking believe you dropped into our lives, Ian," I say squinting at the morning sunlight coming through his hair. "Where were you all this time?"

"Just waiting for a good enough offer," he chuckles.

"Gonna be there for the show Friday?" Raj asks him.

"You kidding? I'll be there. I gotta make sure you guys don't go and ruin everything by coming back and sucking."

"Hey," I say clumsily. "I don't know what to say but thank you, you know?"

"What's that saying?" Ian asks smiling. "True friends are hard to find, difficult to leave and impossible to forget."

I drive Raj back to his place in silence but for Pete Townshend's *Empty Glass* on the tape deck. The Strip looks like crap on a Saturday morning, remnants of Friday night partying at the Whisky, the Roxy, Gazzarri's and the Rainbow. When we get to his place, I help move his guitars, his Marshall and his duffel bag to his door stoop, then we both walk back to my car. We stand in front of each other and both start shaking our heads.

"Hey, I told you I'd get you back in one piece," I finally say.

"You call this one piece?" he says before erupting into one of his wonderful open-mouth laughs. I start laughing too, and we keep laughing until we don't even know what we're laughing about.

"It'll never be the same again, will it?" he asks.

"God, I hope not," I say. "Why do you think we went in the first place?"

"I guess you're right," he says pausing. "You guys don't realize how close I came to not coming. Even after we left, I almost turned around and went home about a hundred times. I just couldn't let go."

"Raj, I know," I say putting my hand on his shoulder. "Scared to give yourself the gift. I know. I was too — my whole life."

"I didn't tell you about that dinner I had to go to with that family friend in Vancouver. It was like an interrogation. My family told me they talked to the guy after, and he told them I was just a loser with long hair, taking drugs, wasting my life, and couldn't understand why they let me go. I felt so rejected by my family."

"Well, it's like what I told you in Seattle," I say. "At some point, you just gotta say 'it's either them or me.' That's what I did. I had to, or I was gonna to die."

"Hey," he says, "I never thanked you for having my back in Edmonton. All you guys. No one ever stood up for me before. I've had bottles thrown at me, a noose tied around my neck, had my life threatened — just completely dehumanized. And no one *ever* stood up for me. Thanks, mate."

"Brothers," I say resting my forehead against his. "Always."

As I drive off, I feel a pull and instinctively turn back one last time. There's Raj frozen on his lawn not daring to move until I've disappeared.

And now Mary. When I close in on her place, I can't find a pay phone that works so I drive down Montana until I find one at the liquor store at 26th Street. I feel my insides tighten when I hear her voice.

"Hey there," I say cautiously. "I'm ah...I'm home."

"Where are you?" she asks.

"Close, real close."

"Oh, then come over," she says, her voice not revealing much though I was listening damn hard for it to tell me something, anything.

I walk down her long driveway. That same driveway I first saw her rise up from that night we all went to see R.E.M. almost exactly three years ago to the day. I reach the back door that leads to the kitchen, pause and take a breath before turning the doorknob. I hear her dog Molly bark, and I hear her footsteps coming through the dining room. I stop and see her appear and our eyes meet. I feel like less than change for a nickel, unkempt and a mess. She looks beautiful in just her gray drop-waist dress, her hair up, barefoot. I prayed something poetic and sweet would land on my tongue, but it doesn't. Mostly, I just want her to tell me she has a place for us to collapse together, some place soft and warm. Put the storm windows up behind us and fall into a glorious cycle of lovemaking and sleep.

I close in to kiss her, but she puts a stop sign up and turns her head away. I guess I'd hoped that when she saw me after 33 days somehow our burden would be lifted, that we could get beyond this push/pull thing we've been doing the last year, but I guess it's all just folly.

* * *

Homecoming
9/4/87

Tonight's our first ever headlining gig in town. For the first time the big, tall, thin Club Lingerie ad in the *L.A. Weekly* that I've stared at for years has our name on top in big bold letters. Under it, it says "Back from their first National Tour."

I park my car up Wilcox and when I turn the corner, people are lined up along the wall of the Lingerie well down Sunset Boulevard. It's amazing. It's just like all those big shows I went to here. Inside the place is packed. It's like dropping in on a reccurring dream I've had a million times. Totally otherworldly.

At the Lingerie, the backstage area is at the rear of the club. As you make your way to the stage, you walk right through the crowd like a boxer making his way to the ring, bumping and jostling with the weight of the crowd closing in. Familiar faces and strangers are slapping us on the back, wishing us luck. This girl leans in and says, "Hey, look!" showing me the sleeve to her jean jacket which she's sewn a heart onto — just like the lyric to "Bitterness" ("...so sew a heart on the side of your sleeve..."). Mark Sanderson, the only friend from high school who's always been supportive, leans in and says, "Hey Bill, did you hear? It's a sellout. Congratulations! You guys are *doing* it. You're *really* doing it."

We climb onstage, and I look to my left at Raj who's standing ready with his eyes fixed on something no one else can see. Like he did in Regina right after Edmonton. Good sign. I look to my right at George who's chatting with Russ Bates at the lip of the stage, heartily laughing away over something. Dave is busily adjusting his hi-hat and nervously moving his drum stool two inches forward and then two inches back to the same spot it was before. He finally looks up and says he's ready. "Time to destroy, Billy," he says. "Fuckers don't have a chance."

I step to the mic and say, "Well, we're back." A little cheer goes up. "We had to go away and grow up. And God help us, we'll never be the same again. Hey Raj, lift us up." The show goes by in a blur. After "Copper Wire," a different kind of cheer erupts — one reserved for bands that have fans who follow its every move, not the polite obligatory applause you hear at club gigs. During the show, people call out for songs. The voices are unfamiliar not like back in the day when you recognize every voice and hear every clink of a glass.

Me at Club Lingerie. Photo by Shannon Smerdzinski

I remember a huge, building version of "Bitterness" that I dedicate to Raj. I remember Raj tried to say something at the start of "Dry September" about Edmonton and then I practically pass out screaming my guts out during the crescendo of the song. George dedicates "On a Soapbox" to the lying sacks of shit that covered up the Iran-Contra scandal. And I remember freezing for a moment when Mary flashes me "I love you" in sign language during "Stay Hungry." Other than that, the show is a blur.

We finish up with a torrid version of "Look Book" and a giant cheer goes up as we walk back through the crowd with people shouting "more" at us. For an encore, Dave leads everyone through "Cover of the *Rolling Stone*" a capella and everyone sings along like an English soccer crowd. We then tear through the "The Who Thing" and just like that, it's over.

After the show, Raj pulls at me and says, "I kept looking down and saw people like Mark and Conrad and Laura — people who've been there every step the last three years — and they're looking up at us with this look like: 'It's all yours, it's O.K. to take it,' you know? You know what that did for me?" he asks, his voice cracking. I look hard at him. "Bill, I felt free. Free to just freaking be," he says resting his forehead against mine. We just stay like that staring into each other's eyes.

I head upstairs and join the big group of well-wishers, and it occurs to me that a lot of folks came tonight because they're proud to have been a part of something that's evolved, in part, because of them. They've invested in us the past three years and so tonight they dragged people to the show like it was *theirs*.

I see my friends Joy and Melody, and I'm embarrassed by all the people surrounding me so I wiggle away and the three of us come together and hug like we all just triumphed.

"Oh Bill," Melody says looking straight into my eyes. "The floors and the walls were just reverberating with this intangible power and essence. Everyone knew you guys were going to make it." She then turns to Joy and says, "I guess we'll get to find out what it's like to be friends with rock stars."

Mary finally makes it upstairs. She brought some movie director who's scouting bands for a party scene of a film he's doing. I don't think he dug us.

"I'm beat," Mary says. "We're all splitting. Did you see what I flashed you during 'Stay Hungry'?"

"I did. There was a little light that shined on you right then so I could see it."

She smiles and tells me we were good. It's loud and too many people are crowding around. "O.K., I'm heading out," she says above the din. "Are you coming or basking?"

"Um, I'm gonna hang out for a bit," I say.

"You can come back to my place later, if you want," she says. I smile, and she turns to go without waiting for a response. I watch her walk down the stairs until she disappears through the exit. Whatever.

As the place slowly empties out, I sense tonight's an end of sorts and the thought of leaving this place, this night, well, it scares me. Tomorrow…well, tomorrow we'll have to dream up new dreams and maybe go without the comfort of our innocence, without our "just happy to be here" safety net. We're *somebody* now. Not much, but we *are* somebody or some *thing* beyond ourselves now. And this town, it gets impatient and expects you to keep on that ever perpetual upward trajectory or it moves on to something else fast.

Finally, Joy and Conrad are the only familiar faces left. Conrad suggests we go grab a bite at Ben Frank's.

Just then George and Deborah climb upstairs to say goodnight. They're holding hands, looking blissful. "Well, we're splitting," George says. I notice Deborah holding George extra tight.

"I thought you two already left," I say.

"We were making out in a dark corner," Deborah says smiling.

"You guys want to go to Ben Frank's with us?" I ask.

"Nah, we're spent," George says weaving a little.

"Well, O.K. then. Goodnight, you two," I say with a wee smile. I watch them both walk down the steps, past the bar and into the street looking like they've found each other's missing halves.

I take a seat with Conrad and Joy, and we watch the bartenders and waitresses close up the place. Hundreds of scenes dance through my head fighting for my attention until I finally hit on one from about two years ago, the day George and I danced like little kids in the street.

The band had been playing around for just a year or so. We couldn't score much better than late weekday gigs around town. No weekends yet. We'd literally beg our friends and families to shows. If we were lucky, we'd get ten people.

It's a Thursday and, like always, I head down to get an *L.A. Weekly*, an *L.A. Reader* and a *BAM* at the 7-11. Thursdays are a special day in L.A. for people who play in bands or go to clubs. If you're a band with an upcoming gig you grab those three rags, go straight to the club listings and the "Picks of the Week." One, to make sure you haven't been unceremoniously dumped off the bill. And two, to see if Scott Morrow of the *Weekly,* Chris Morris of the *Reader* or Cary Darling of *BAM* wrote a little description elevating you from an anonymous name to a band to watch. It was instant credibility.

So, I pick up the *L.A. Weekly* and flip to the listings. And there it is. Scott Morrow wrote that we were "…an aggressive, exciting upcoming band to watch out for." I have to do a double take, three times over. It's not much, but to get *anything* other than just our stupid band name listed was huge.

George was working a shit temping job in Westwood so I call him and say I have something vital to show him and he *has* to meet me downstairs right away. I race over. When I spot him, I practically skip up to him. I hand him the *Weekly* and point madly at the listing. He just stares for a moment and then his eyes widen. Then he drops to one knee right there on the sidewalk pumping his fist as if he'd just hit it big in a game of craps. *"Right...fucking...on,"* he says slowly and defiantly. *"Christ All-Fucking-Mighty. At last!"*

We start hugging and jumping up and down. It's the first moment of unprompted, unsolicited success. We're so overcome with joy and relief we let our cool down and allow ourselves a pure moment of satisfaction.

"Bill?" I turn back to Conrad and Joy.

"Sorry, you guys ready to split?" I ask.

Climbing into Joy's car, I think about George and Deborah sharing the triumph of this glorious night. I think about Mary's invitation. It doesn't head me back toward her place, though. I don't really want to answer why I don't go. I'm just glad there's still a couple people left who don't want to face the end of this night — who want to carry on a little while longer...squeeze the last bits out and just, well, anything other than pull the curtain down on this night.

* * *

epilogue.1

Divine Weeks would go on more tours, make more records and keep fighting the good fight until calling it quits in 1992. When we got back in the fall of 1987, we never stopped to realize we were standing where few bands like us get. We didn't realize how infinitesimal and fleeting that window of opportunity is. I guess we figured you just keep ascending, you never give ground and just keep getting more.

For all the consternation Jane's Addiction caused, I ended up turning down a chance to join them. Jane's was readying its Warner Brothers major-label debut when they had a huge falling out over publishing. I was visiting them at El Dorado Studios one night when Eric Avery and Dave Navarro pulled me aside and asked me to be their singer. They said Rick Rubin would sign any incarnation that included the three of them without Perry Farrell. I was flattered but declined as I was convinced Divine Weeks would make it.

Mary and I finally fell apart for good Easter weekend '88 up in the Bay Area. We got into a big fight after a show in Berkeley. She didn't think we played well, and I thought we did. I asked her to show me someone who agreed with her and a minute later she returned with a pretty redhead named Kelly.

Kelly was a little older than I. She was real. No bullshit. She saw things in black and white. I was tired of the vicious cycle with Mary, and I had to get out of 940.

I moved in with Kelly shortly after our summer tour in '88 and within two years we were married. A few years later we had a daughter we named Maeve. My little love light. God love her, she thinks she's going to marry a prince and live in a castle.

I remained enmeshed in 940 long after I moved out. Every time the phone rang, I'd get the chills sure it was my mom calling and running on adrenaline too potent to bottle. I'd run at the drop of a hat back to that place thinking it was my job to rescue her from her latest mess. When I left my mom behind, maybe I didn't feel worthy of a family and a household of my own. Maybe I couldn't shake that old survivor guilt. Maybe I was just looking for someone else to save me. I don't know. Kelly and I ultimately didn't make it.

George became the college professor he was born to be. I heard he just got tenure at Dartmouth, and he's a real rock star of the classroom. He and Deborah didn't last. George married a friend of mine named Dawn. Raj married that girl Kimberlie who made me that Divine Weeks shirt. They have a son named Devan. Raj and Kym are the physically and emotionally demonstrative parents Raj's weren't and, not coincidentally, Dev is the most joyful and loving little kid you'll ever know. Dave got together with this great girl named Shannon he met at one of our shows. They're happily married and living in Orange County now. Ian's a high school teacher up north with a wife and beautiful kids.

Mary ended up marrying Steve Hochman, the *L.A. Times* music critic and early ally of Divine Weeks. After being estranged for years, I ran into her at a party, and we made peace. I then saw her at some Al-Anon meetings, and we became friends again. But sadly, after a long 12-year battle, Mary finally succumbed to breast cancer early last year.

* * *

epilogue.2

Before he moved back East, Divine Weeks reunited for one show as a send-off to George. Right before we go onstage, Raj and I duck into a little room backstage, just the two of us. We rest our foreheads against each other like always, look into each other's eyes and make a vow to play with fury and joy and leave it all onstage. It's a glorious night before a packed house, and we blow up the past for good. Sadly though, George comes away from it feeling the evening fell short for him.

After George moved, he cut off L.A. and everyone attached to it. A few years ago, he sent me an email: "That whole time, the band, the dream. It's just too powerful. I won't lie. I wanted to make it as much as anyone. I never had your hang ups about deserving it – I expected to make it. But I guess I'm not like you. I never enjoyed the journey…the little moments of relative success that you're supposed to acknowledge that affirm the goal. It was never good enough for me. Everything always fell short. I know that's not good. I finally had to drive a stake through the heart of rock and roll – I wouldn't have survived otherwise."

I haven't heard from him since.

* * *

epilogue.3

I've got this indelible memory that stays with me. Maeve is six and wants me to read her the Dr. Seuss book, *One Fish Two Fish Red Fish Blue Fish*. She loves this one page with this classic Dr. Seuss creature, all yellow, hair coming out every direction, and he's screaming all crazy. "The Screaming Guy," she calls him. When I get to that page she screams then dummies up. I say, "Was that *you*?" She erupts in laughter: "No, it was the *screaming* guy!"

She's restless so I sit with her in the darkness. She tells me a girl *made* her feel bad at school. I remind her that no one can *make* you feel inferior without your consent. That's a little heady for her to process so I tell her to remember she's the boss of her feelings. She gets that. Maybe if someone had instilled that in my grandmother when that fucker Jascha Heifetz told her that her violin would make for good kindling, a lot of us might have lived better lives.

Finally Maeve is quiet and still, and I get up thinking she's fallen to sleep.

"Daddy," she says in a tiny voice. "Do I make you happy?"

"Of course, sweetheart."

"And um, will you always love me, Daddy, even when I marry my prince?"

"Of course, little sweetie," I say. "But why do you ask?"

I can hear her little eyelashes flapping in the dark and then she says, "Because when I marry my prince I'll live in a castle, and you always said castles are far away..."

"That's right..." I trail off.

"Well, I just want you to be happy Daddy, when I'm gone."

"Sweetheart," I say. "You don't need to ever worry about me. Nothing could make me happier than knowing you feel free to be whatever you're meant to be."

I stay with her and stroke her long beautiful blonde hair until she sighs deeply, signaling she's fallen into deep-sea dreams. So many nights through the years I've held her, singing to her as she's fought off sleep. And while I've sat with her, I've often looked back on that time we all chased a dream — about what it took to get in that van and what it took to make it out.

See, when I thought the dream died, I thought I died too. You know, like I *had* to die because the dream *was* me, and I *was* the dream. I kept telling myself that Divine Weeks just wasn't good enough to make it, that I wasn't good enough to deserve it. Like always, it was just easier that way.

Over the years, I've spent a lot of time trying to reconcile the past and find some kind of peace, but really, it's been here all along. Little by little, day by day, being in the trenches with Maeve, helping nurture her dreams, making sure she feels free to be whoever she's meant to be. And by showing her I'm not defined by a shit job, but by the light I shine every time I pull out my guitar.

It's the same for Raj who mans up every day at a crap job and finds the same kind of solace in his son Dev, who he plays guitar for all the time. Maeve and Dev are older now and have grown up knowing that music is their dads' own private stairway to the stars. And maybe their light shines, in some small part, because Raj and I are still shining ours.

See, for Raj and me, it was never really about a career. It was about deliverance, redemption and transcendence. Aspiring to be artists in the purest sense. Like my mom said, "It's not about the having and getting, it's about the being and becoming...we're artists, wounded birds...descending, ascending...always chasing the muse."

George did what he had to do, and I couldn't be happier for him. But I'm not like George. I'm not gonna drive a stake through the heart of rock and roll and kill it and everyone attached to it. I can't. That would kill me. I live to make music. Even if it only ends up in a shoe box in the back of my closet, I'll be making music until my last breath. It's like what Salinger said when they asked him why he gave up writing and, astonished, he said, "What do you mean? I write every day."

A little while ago, I came across that list of ten targets I wrote out for the band after our first rehearsal in George's basement.

1. Get a gig at a Hollywood club.
2. For the *L.A. Weekly*'s Scott Morrow to preview us in the club listings.
3. Be a pick of the week in the *L.A. Weekly*.
4. Have a feature story in the *L.A. Weekly*.
5. Get a write-up in the *L.A. Times*.
6. Do a live appearance on KXLU.
7. Get a record contract.
8. Go on tour.
9. Have MTV play our video.
10. Sell out Club Lingerie.

I hadn't seen that list for years, and it blew me away. I mean, we reached every one of those goals, and when that sunk in, I finally stopped beating myself up. We stayed true to our ideals and never licked a boot to become stars. We wore our hearts on our sleeves and played like our lives depended on it every night. We stood at our crossroads and didn't turn back. We fired our shot. You see, success is something you have to define for yourself. You can't buy into anyone else's idea of it. Only your own.

It's late now. I've kissed my girlfriend Cindy goodnight. The house is quiet. It's just me. Me and my guitar. Back to the start. Where it all began. I'm sitting in an endless trail of cables encircling and intertwining in every direction around me. I'm inside my headphones where I'll be for the next several hours. I come here armed with the belief that something great is always imminent. That's my mom's muse running through me, just like always. And if I don't connect tonight, no matter, for I'll be here again tomorrow and the night after that in an infinite continuum. Always chasing the muse.

* * *

Bill See has released five solo records. He lives with his daughter Maeve and his girlfriend Cindy and her two children, Emma and Alex, in Los Angeles. This is his first book.

Visit the *33 Days* official website at: www.33daysthebook.com for photos, videos and free MP3 downloads of Divine Weeks' music.

Become a fan of *33 Days* on Facebook.

Check out Divine Weeks on www.youtube.com

33 Days is available on amazon.com, barnesandnoble.com, lulu.com and can be ordered from any bookstore via ISBN 978-0-557-75881-4.

email: billsee@dslextreme.com

Made in the USA
Lexington, KY
13 May 2014